THE ACCIDENTAL EDITOR

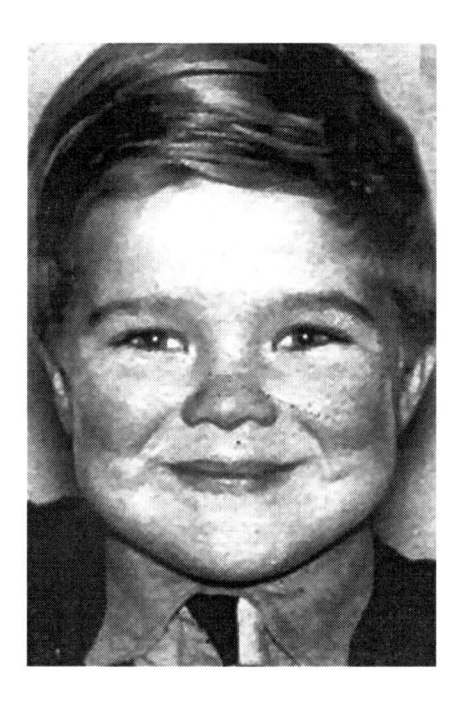

*How a boy who only ever wanted to go to sea
ended up running a provincial daily newspaper*

RICHARD HARRIS

AuthorHouse™ UK Ltd.
500 Avebury Boulevard
Central Milton Keynes, MK9 2BE
www.authorhouse.co.uk
Phone: 08001974150

© 2011 Richard Harris. All rights reserved.

No part of this book may be reproduced, stored in a retrieval system, or transmitted by any means without the written permission of the author.

First published by AuthorHouse 10/25/2011

ISBN: 978-1-4567-8817-9 (sc)

This book is printed on acid-free paper.

The views expressed in this work are solely those of the author and do not necessarily reflect the views of the publisher, and the publisher hereby disclaims any responsibility for them.

For my grandchildren

So that one day
they might
know me better

'No man goes further
than he who
knows not
where he is going'

– OLIVER CROMWELL

PROLOGUE

HE DIDN'T BOTHER to get up as I entered the room. He just lolled there, slouched in a leather armchair, an untidy tangle of arms and legs and bedraggled hair. Such was my introduction to Alvin Lee, guitarist and brains behind the cult rock group Ten Years After who, though largely forgotten now, were then enjoying a cult popularity out of all proportion to their one hit record.

At that time, in the summer of 1971, I was 22 – and baby-faced, with it – and he was the most famous person I'd ever met. I knew I was not the first journalist to have been granted an interview with the great man there, in the rather sparse dressing room of Bristol's Colston Hall, and I reckoned he was probably sick of giving the same old answers to the same old questions from the same old people, so I decided to win him over with a bit of self deprecating charm. 'Thanks for seeing me,' I said, smiling encouragingly. 'You must be pretty tired of meeting people like me. . . '

He didn't smile back. But fixed me with a stare that, I thought, was unlikely to be mistaken for anything much less than contempt. 'I have,' he said, enunciating each word separately, as if with a full stop in between, 'Never. Met. Anyone. Like. You. Before. In. All. My. Life.'

It was as if he suspected that I wasn't a real reporter. That some dreadful mistake had taken me away from a job for which I was much better suited and dragged me in off the street to waste his time for half an hour.

He couldn't have known it, but he was half right. I had, indeed, never meant to be a journalist. I had become one only because a succession of chance happenings had led, four years before, to my standing at the front door of my parents' house giving off the unmistakable stink of a man who had spent his working day shovelling horse shit. On that day enough had been enough and I had decided to get a proper job, far away from the mushroom farm which had given me my first employment after leaving school.

Among the 'proper' jobs advertised that week was one from our local paper, the delightfully titled *Weston-super-Mare Mercury & North Somersetshire Herald*, which wanted a trainee reporter for a six-month probationary period, possibly leading to a permanent apprenticeship. I had no intention of going for the permanent apprenticeship, but I reckoned the job could be a fun way of passing six months until something better came along.

How different things should have been. How different it would have been if years earlier my life had taken a different course.

What if... What if... What if Philip had not died?

Philip was my best friend. He had been ever since I first arrived to be taught at the little village primary school on top of the hill at Redhill, nine miles south of Bristol, where my Mum worked. His dad Sam was a labourer cum lorry driver, and his mum Ruth was a school dinner lady, and they lived in a council house just down the hill from the school, a happy and contented family just like us.

We were slightly better off. Both my parents were teachers (my Dad taught ESN or 'educationally subnormal' children – they'd be 'young people with learning difficulties' in these more sensitive times – at a local secondary modern school) and we owned our own solid three-storey semi with a huge garden opposite the church in the bigger and posher village of Wrington, a couple of miles down the road.

Two small boys from different backgrounds, but with so much in common. We could almost have been brothers, we thought so alike, though he was rather more serious than I, probably cleverer and certainly more hard-working.

We sat next to each other in the classroom, and spent playtimes racing our toy cars down the slope in the playground and seeing who could pee higher up the wall in the primitive brick-built box that was the boys' open-air lavatory. We rode imaginary horses past imaginary cowboy cacti, built strange creeping machines from cotton reels and rubber bands and, without really understanding why, made jokes about the knickers the girls stripped down to in our Music And Movement lessons.

We dreamed of travelling the world, he as a soldier and I as a sailor, and though we knew we would not always be together we somehow just knew we would always be friends.

He was just ten, and I was nine, when he died, blown up one weekend in his grandfather's garage when playing with a box of matches and a can of petrol which was not quite empty. He suffered appalling injuries but lived for three days. He was even conscious for a while, though that's something I'd rather not think about because they probably could not have found enough morphine to kill the pain of the burns that covered almost every part of his body. Frenchay Hospital had one of the best burns units in Europe, but how could they have taken away the terror he must have felt? On the first day a nurse told him not to worry because she would look after him. He replied – as he would, because he, like I am still, was one of life's optimists – 'I know you will.' Those were his last words and on St Valentine's Day 1959, in the late afternoon, he died.

I had just gone to bed when the phone rang on that Saturday evening and a sixth sense told me what news it was bringing. I heard my mother's muffled voice speaking briefly in the hall, two floors down, then her footsteps coming up the stairs, up the thickly carpeted staircase that led to the two big bedrooms on the first floor, and past the bathroom, and then up the bare wooden staircase to the attic where my sister and I had our bedrooms.

I knew what my Mum was going to tell me long before she reached my room, and not just because she was not singing like she usually did. She sat on my bed and told me and we both cried. She stroked my hair, then quietly left. 'Just remember all the good times you had together,' she said as she closed the door.

It never entered my head that I should not go to school on the next Monday, though I remember being aware that I did not know how I should react. The other children didn't know either, and most did not mention Philip at all but gave me sympathetic smiles instead, so I knew they understood. And Alexis Stacey, a slightly older girl who I had always been rather frightened of, picked up her books without a word and came to sit beside me, in Philip's place, so I would not have to spend the day next to an empty desk. Our formidable teacher, Mrs Eleanor Clark, had not thought of that. She was no doubt upset too, in her formidable teacher way, but she had not thought of such a simple gesture and how important it would be to a small boy stunned and desperately confused by the death of his best friend. It was an act of kindness that I have remembered all my life.

Philip was buried in the churchyard just across the road from the school but I was not allowed to go to his funeral. In those days children did not go to funerals, not even of their best friends. But I was invited to choose one of the hymns ('When I Survey The Wondrous Cross', which had always been one of Philip's favourites, and mine) and nobody could stop me watching from the classroom window as the hunched black figures made their way up the steep path to the little church that afternoon. And that polished wooden box the men were carrying – was that all that was left of Philip? And of our friendship?

My father is buried in that churchyard too now, and I sometimes go there to visit his grave, full of sadness and regret for a Dad who died too young. 'Hubert Edward Harris. May 7 1919 to April 20 1979. Remembered with love.' Just 59 he was when lung cancer killed him. I was 29, precisely 30 years younger, because I was born on his birthday. Probably the best birthday present he ever had, he used to say. 'Probably'? I think he was joking.

I don't cry these days at my Dad's grave. But I still do at Philip's.

It's hideously ironic that if Philip had not died my life would not have been what it has been. I would not have grown into the same man, and would not now be blessed with all the things that today I most value.

I would not have been sent to the same schools (I went to boarding schools largely because my parents believed the new friends I would make there would fill the void left by Philip's death); without those schools I would not have developed the rather bolshie never-take-things-at-face-value questioning character I had developed by my late teens; without that state of mind I would not have coped with being a journalist; without that job I would not have met my wife or had my children. And without them? Simple. My life would have been immeasurably poorer.

1

I WAS JUST A FEW DAYS short of my tenth birthday when I achieved the dubious distinction of becoming the first boy in our family to be sent away to boarding school. We were not the sort of family to whom private education came naturally and my parents must have hated the very thought of sending me away at such a young age. But me? I loved it! It was as if a door had been flung open and I was free to walk through, from the safety of the world I had always known, into a new one full of untold challenges and exciting things to do.

The school my parents had chosen for me was Walton Lodge – an establishment selected, as far as I could tell, because its boys, when Mum and Dad had sometimes seen them walking in crocodiles around the Victorian seaside town of Clevedon on Sunday afternoons, had seemed well behaved and happy, which was all they wanted for me.

I have no doubt that sending me away to boarding school at such a young age, even to a school only ten miles away from home and from which they were allowed to take me out almost every other weekend, caused my parents untold heartache. But I have no doubt either that it was a brave, sensible and loving thing to do. Philip was dead, and my elder sister Liz was at her own boarding school (she had failed her 11-Plus so otherwise would have gone to be a pupil at the school at which my father was a teacher, which nobody thought was a good idea). So, although there were, of course, other children of my age in our village, there was none I was especially close to, and none I particularly wanted to play with.

So at the age of nearly ten I set off for Walton, having precious little idea what to expect. I don't remember saying goodbye to my parents as they left me there that day, just that I felt immediately at home in my new surroundings. For a shy child, lacking anything remotely approaching self confidence, it was extraordinary and could only have been thanks to the welcoming atmosphere generated by the staff and pupils.

I made friends among the 100 or so other boys immediately. It was an exciting new world for me (the school was based in two enormous Victorian houses, with a garden and playground in between, and, across the road, a huge playing field complete with a wild 'jungle' area with trees to climb, bushes to hide in and rocks to jump off) and I spent my early days exploring every inch of it.

The hub of the school was a vast room which was our gym, our hall, our cinema, and our playroom. It was where we met for assemblies, and for a quiet time before meals; it was where we watched Laurel and Hardy and Woody The Woodpecker films, and where we played British Bulldogs (a violent game in which one group of boys tried to run the length of the room without being apprehended by the other) to celebrate the end of term. But most importantly of all it was where we passed the time, mostly away from the gaze of our teachers, in the all-too-rare breaks between lessons and other organised activities. There were lockers filling one end and one side – the lower ones, which doubled as seats, were for the younger boys; while those higher up, on the wall, were for the older boys, or at least the taller young ones. The lockers were where we kept everything that was important to us – books, records, Teddy bears, toys, radios and cakes baked by our mothers – and even though they did not lock there were very few occasions on which anything went missing.

We shared dormitories of about a dozen boys in each, all more or less the same age. With old fashioned iron beds, each beside its own wooden cupboard and hooks on which to hang our dressing gowns, they looked more like the sort of hospital wards where Florence Nightingale might have felt at home.

It was there that the enormity of the changes happening in my life occasionally caught up with me and threatened to overwhelm me. By day I was too busy to be apprehensive, too excited to miss my home or my parents, but sometimes at those first few bedtimes, hidden under the blankets, the excitement would evaporate and a strange loneliness would hit me. My new best friend Mark Brunt, in the next bed, would be instantly sympathetic (and almost telepathic) and would hold out his hand in comfort, and many were the nights in those early days when we fell asleep holding hands across the divide between our beds.

By day I was happier than I had ever been – which one of my fellow 'new boys' felt was not quite right. Paul Annette, whose father ran a very successful restaurant alongside the harbour in Bristol, was deeply homesick and was appalled to see that I wasn't. He threatened to phone my mother to tell her that I was not in the least bit unhappy and was therefore obviously glad to get rid of her. Lacking in confidence I may have been, but I knew enough to know that my Mum would be delighted to hear such news.

It was at Walton Lodge that I was first told I should be a journalist (although it was said in the same way as you might tell a toddler he should play for Manchester United just because he can kick a ball without falling over). As part of an English lesson we were told to write about anything we liked and, while my classmates turned out admirable efforts on country walks, football or what they did on their holidays, I hunched over my desk for a condemnation of the death penalty. This was at a time when murderers were almost always hanged, and the radio news at breakfast time would regularly contain sombre reports that at that very moment (hangings were always at eight o'clock on the dot) someone was being put to death in the name of the state while his family and friends gathered with a small knot of anti death penalty campaigners outside the prison gates. Even at the age of eleven I found all this profoundly cruel, and the idea of killing someone as punishment for killing someone else distinctly illogical, so I set my thoughts down on paper as several pages of angry prose. My story was written from the viewpoint of the condemned man, starting the evening before his death. How he kept looking at his watch, realising he would never see the hands saying nine o'clock again; how he had his last sleep, his last meal and his last pee – all routine things which to him had suddenly taken on a new significance as he did them for a final time. I had him pacing his cell; sitting on his bed with his head in his hands, terrified; crying for his wife and children. It was designed to show that hanging was wrong not just because taking a man's life is wrong, but also because everything that leads up to that final moment is a kind of torture beyond imagination – something that should never be sanctioned by a society that likes to consider itself civilised.

That's something I believe even more fervently now than I did then, and I am rather proud that I had those beliefs, and was able to put them into words, at such a young age.

Our teacher Mr Phillips was impressed and proved it by reading my story aloud to the class – right down to the final word ('Aaaaaagh!' as I fell through the trap door and had my neck broken). Afterwards he took me aside and told me: 'You should be a journalist when you're older'. To which I no doubt smiled shyly, knowing I had no intention at all of being a journalist, since for as long as I could remember I had wanted nothing other than to go to sea as a navigation officer in the merchant navy and that was something one piece of inspired writing was not going to change.

For a boy who wanted to go to sea there could have been nowhere better to go to school. Clevedon stands on the southern shore of the Bristol Channel, and has its own seafront promenade and elegant Victorian pier. But more importantly it has to be passed by every ship that goes to, or comes from, the docks at Bristol, Avonmouth and – today – Portbury. And in those days that meant a lot of ships.

It was not long before the deputy headmaster, Mr Humby, a giant of a man from Guernsey who loved the sea as much as I did, decided that I was responsible enough to be allowed out on the light evenings of summer to go and see those ships. I needed no further encouragement and suddenly I found that a whole evening's homework, or 'prep', could in fact be completed in about half an hour. After that I would grab the old brass telescope my grandfather had given me and, with my friend Paul Baker, set off through a gate in the school gardens to the footpath that led across the golf course, past the castle ruins and down towards the sea. It was only a ten-minute walk, and it brought us out to the coastal path that runs from Clevedon to Portishead and to the rocks little more than a stone's throw from the ships as they lay at anchor while waiting for the tide on which they would complete their journeys into port.

On a good evening there would be half a dozen ships at anchor there, and on a better one (which usually meant the dockers were on strike, so ships had to sit there like patients in a doctor's queue, waiting sometimes for days on end for the latest industrial dispute to be ended) there would be more than 20, all waiting to make their way up the estuary.

On the best evenings, when we came to the rocks shortly before high tide, we would be there in time to see the crews busying themselves on deck, to hear the rumble of the chains being dragged in and then to see the anchors as they were pulled dripping from the sea. Then we would watch as the ships slowly got under way, moving up the channel – sometimes aided by tugs if they were unusually big – and around Battery Point at Portishead in the distance. Or we would by chance time our arrival after all that had happened, but soon enough to catch the ships coming out of Bristol on the outgoing tide – probably the same ships as we had seen sailing in just a few days before.

These were the days before Britain's merchant fleet – and the docks that supported it – collapsed. There were scores of shipping lines, not just giants like Cunard and P&O but lesser known but, to me, equally exciting companies like Everards, Ellermans and the Anchor Line, whose ships would sail up the channel past the rocks upon which Paul and I sat. Ships from Russia, South America and the furthest corners of the world were exciting to see (especially when the crew waved, which for some reason the Russians in particular often did), and it was sometimes hard to believe that these vessels – frequently old and rusty and looking as of they would never survive a gale in mid Atlantic – had set off from some port thousands of miles away just to come past the rocks on which we were sitting on the southern shores of the Bristol Channel.

Best of all were the ships of the Bristol Steam Navigation Company – our own local ships. These ships – Apollo, Juno, Cato, Pluto and others (the whole fleet was named after Greek gods, and ended with 'O') with their distinctive yellow funnels – were special, almost friends. They were proud, smart little ships which generally plied a trade between Bristol and Dublin, or Bristol and Scandinavia, and I had watched them for years, ever since my parents first took me to watch the ships negotiating the Cumberland Basin after coming up the Avon and under Brunel's Clifton Suspension Bridge on their way into the docks of Bristol.

Mr Humby told us that if anyone asked us to justify our daily trips to the coast path we should say it was to help with our geography, and so it was. Just as Paul and I quickly learned to identify the funnel markings of almost every shipping line, so also did we learn where they came from and what cargo they were likely to have on board. So we learned about the timber industry in Scandinavia, coalmining in the Baltic states, farming in Argentina, heavy machinery manufacturing in the USA – and, when we delved further, apartheid in South Africa and poverty in Brazil. It was like having a living geography textbook passing before our eyes.

For a boy who longed one day to go to sea it was a magical time, and it was all thanks to a visionary teacher who saw a way of using a love of ships as a gateway into the geography curriculum.

Paul was an excellent cricketer. I wasn't. I did once score 17 in a match against another school, and I took a hat-trick with the first three balls I ever bowled (the first and last wickets I took in eight years of trying to play cricket), but generally sport and I made an uneasy combination. I made it to be left back and captain of the Second XI football team – no great achievement considering it was only a small school and there weren't many more than 22 boys big enough to get into two teams of eleven – and I played regularly in the First XV at rugby, but that was largely because, unlike my more athletic peers, I had the rotund physique needed for a prop forward. It wasn't that I did not enjoy sport, just that I was both physically and psychologically unsuited for anything smacking of even gentle violence. As my games master said in an end-of-term report on my prowess at rugby, I would have been a half decent player had it not been for my 'unfailing good humour'.

I was a cheery little chap, renowned, not just on the sports field, for my positive optimistic attitude to life. I was thriving and growing up fast – like those fast-frame films of dormant plants suddenly unfurling and bursting into a riot of leaves and flowers under a summer sun. I developed a liking for books (but only if they were about ships, so Percy F Westerman's seafaring tales were a particular favourite) and, as soon as I heard other boys' Billy Fury and Adam Faith records (so different from the style of old English 'I am a jolly ploughboy' type of folk music my parents often listened to on the radio) acquired a passion for pop music too. I was, I suppose, becoming a teenager. And that would mean a change of school . . .

Kelly College was different. The whole ethos and tradition of the public school system offended me then, and it offends me now. Maybe that is why in the five years I spent at Kelly I never felt I truly belonged there.

New boys, on their arrival, were left in no doubt what was expected of them – and most of it, in my estimation both then and now, was bollocks. For example, how we were to dress: Juniors must at all times keep all three buttons on their jackets fastened; middles were allowed to unfasten one button; seniors could unfasten two and – rejoice! – prefects could leave their jackets flying in the wind, fully unbuttoned. Or where we were to walk: Juniors could set foot on this piece of grass but not that, could sit here but not there. Middles could have access to more grass than juniors, but not as much as seniors, which in turn was considerably less than prefects. Monitors (a kind of senior prefect) could wear white shirts instead of the lesser mortals' blue, brown shoes instead of others' black and could walk, noses in the air, with their jackets flying open wherever they damn well pleased.

To a boy fresh from Walton Lodge, where every pupil had been respected for what he was, rather than for how old or clever or arrogant he was, it was a culture shock for which I was wholly unprepared.

For boys whose families were steeped in the public school tradition it was as natural as the overcrisp fried bread we had for breakfast. But for me, the first (and very probably last) member of my family to experience private education, it took some stomaching.

'Why?' I asked, on innumerable occasions.

'Because it's our tradition,' came the reply.

'But it's a stupid tradition.'

'Just do it.'

It was at Kelly College that I learned to ask questions and to refuse to accept anything just because I was told it – not such a useful skill for the merchant navy officer I hoped to become, maybe, but a vital one for the journalist I still had no intention of being. I did not appreciate it at the time, but I now know that without my time there I would never have acquired the questioning bolshieness which would be so useful when, just a few years later, I found myself stumbling by accident into the world of journalism.

Kelly College was all that you would expect of a public school – and it had a fine record of sending its boys into the Royal Navy, which is why my parents selected it for me. It was as close as they were going to get to choosing an establishment that suited my needs, since no public school worthy of the name would boast of sending its students into the merchant navy, which was in most people's estimation a very much inferior organisation.

Kelly was situated near Tavistock, a couple of miles from Dartmoor, and there were many of us who suspected it was in fact modelled on the prison just a few miles away over the moors. It had a great granite-built main school block, which looked down from a lofty position above the magnificent playing fields. This was the nerve-centre of the school, containing the chapel, library, dining room, assembly hall and most of the classrooms, but it was in our three individual 'houses' that we spent most of our free time.

I was placed in Newton House – generally considered to be the poor relation alongside the posh School House, and stately Courtenay House – which was based in an attractive white-painted country residence, complete with tall portico at the front door, but which had been spoiled by the addition of two ugly modern extensions. As new boys we were shown to the junior study, a modest room with personal lockers along the wall and two large tables, flanked by benches, on a highly polished wooden floor.

In the junior study we felt safe – but that feeling did not last long. On the first Sunday of their first three terms all boys had to complete the Cox Tor run – another piece of ridiculous tradition, but this time accompanied by a nasty bit of officially sanctioned bullying. Cox Tor was a hill, about four miles away, up which Kelly College's most junior pupils had been running for generations. In their first term they would carry a large rock, to be deposited on a cairn on top of the tor; in their second they would carry a smaller rock and in their third they would carry no rock at all but run just the same. And at regular intervals along the route bigger boys would poke at them with sticks, or lash at them with branches torn from the hedgerow, while all the while shouting threats and insults.

'Why?' I asked, not unreasonably, I thought.

'Because it's our tradition.'

'But it's a stupid tradition.'

'Just do it.'

There were three kinds of boy cut out for success at Kelly College: Sportsmen, academics and those whose voices had broken at an unnaturally young age. I did not belong to any of them.

Sporting prowess was never likely to put me on top of the heap. While I was reasonably good at tennis it was seen as a loner's sport and my relative proficiency at it probably only served to underline my reputation of being 'not quite one of us'. I played rugby after a fashion (I remember that when I received the ball from one of my team-mates I would pass it on as swiftly as I could to another, muttering 'I don't want the bloody thing' under my breath) and I played hockey and enjoyed it, but usually found myself in goal, where it was considered I would be least nuisance. And I made valiant attempts at athletics until I proved my incompetence by hitting myself on the back of the head with a javelin when I threw it while holding it sideways.

My lack of skill on the sports field would not have mattered had I been blessed with great intelligence and/or application in the classroom. But while I was (I thought) reasonably bright I was certainly not a hard worker, so managed to get through my school years without much troubling my teachers from my desk which was, invariably, out of sight and out of mind at the back of the class.

Even without sporting or academic prowess I might still have become a pupil of some importance if only I had not still looked like a little boy. Those few among my peers who grew up unusually early – broad shoulders, deep voices and proper stubble on their chins – were respected in a manner otherwise reserved for star performers in the rugby XV. Which meant that those of us with soft downy cheeks, round cherubic faces (mine was rounder and more cherubic than most) and high pitched voices were not. And for those whose soft downy cheeks, round cherubic faces and high pitched voices lasted till their owners were 16, as mine did, there was very little hope.

We – the stubble-less, sports no-hopers and thickos – were at the bottom of the school heap, there just to make up the numbers. Most of my teachers would hardly have known I was there, and I suspect none of them, even just a year after I left, would have been able to remember my name.

I'm not sure that many of my fellow pupils would have remembered me, either. I did make friends, but Cary Coombs, my best one, left after a year or so, leaving me to try to catch up and make friends among boys who had already made theirs. It was like starting a hundred metres race two or three metres behind the rest of the field. I was there and taking part but never quite managing to make up the ground I had lost. As a result, while I had several friends, none of them would have described me as their best friend, though that is how, for short periods, I might have described them.

Some people would have called me lonely. Or a loner. But at Kelly College I learned to enjoy and be content with my own company, not least because I was becoming increasingly dissatisfied with the world in which I was living, and with most of the people who lived in it with me. It was a world totally divorced from real life, a world in which everyone had money, had hope and had potential. And a world in which everyone was male. I could hardly be called a man of the world in those days, but I was aware enough to know that the real world of which I was not yet a man was not much like the one which had Kelly College at its centre, and I could not understand how most of my fellow pupils were so satisfied not to be a part of it.

It is one of the great failings of the public school system that it is so far removed from the real world. Public schoolboys are not taught that they are better than anyone else, but that is what most of them come to believe as they grow up, isolated and insular in their privileged surroundings. I like to think I never fell into that trap and that's something for which I thank my parents. As teachers in state schools (my father by then was teaching at a special school for problem children at Weston-super-Mare, and my mother had become headteacher of my old primary school at Redhill) they could not help but be in the real world, and they made very sure I stayed there too.

If I needed reminding I was reminded every third Sunday, when my Mum and Dad arrived to take me out – usually for a splendid roast lunch at my maternal grandparents' house in Bude on the North Cornish coast. As other boys' parents drove up in huge and gleaming cars almost fresh out of the showroom, mine turned up in the sort of vehicle not often seen within the imposing grounds of a British public school. A Morris Minor Traveller with bits of the wooden trimmings being eaten away by rot, a rusty Ford Zodiac, a humble Hillman . . . I confess I sometimes – foolishly, as I know now, because a man's car is no guide to his worth to society – felt ashamed as they rolled up in their latest old banger. Until they bought an even older car, which was so ancient it became a perverse status symbol, that is. I could hardly believe my eyes as they drove up the long winding school drive in an ancient white Sunbeam Talbot, with two huge chrome headlamps standing proudly on stalks on either side of an absurdly long bonnet. It was a magnificent vehicle – and so old and impressive that the other boys jealously thought we were about to take part in some vintage vehicle rally having left our other car at home.

My only other glimpses of the real world came once a week when, after our housemaster signed an 'exeat' ('Let him go out' in Latin) we were allowed to walk into Tavistock – not the most exciting of towns, but it had a coffee shop and a record store and some real people, a few of whom were young and female. Not that any of us ever spoke to any representatives of this strange species known as 'girls'; we just looked and admired (although we had precious little idea of what we were looking at or why we were admiring it). This was in the mid 1960s, not far short of the 1967 'Summer of Love', but the so-called 'permissive society' had made few inroads in Devon, or indeed in Somerset where I spent my school holidays, and society there was just as strict and buttoned-up as it always had been. Our knowledge of girls was what was gained from newspapers (not that you can glean much from the Times and the Daily Telegraph, the only papers we were allowed), magazines (ditto National Geographic and Readers' Digest) and record sleeves (ditto – though some would say that the photos on the front of my Francoise Hardy LPs would tell a boy all he ever needed to know about sex).

It seems extraordinary now that hardly any of us at Kelly College had a girlfriend until after we left school. And by then we were 18! But I am pretty sure that is the case. One boy did return from his summer holidays to recount full details of how he had got inside a girl's knickers at a party, and we listened to every word (several times, in fact) and were mightily impressed. It was only later that I discovered that some of the salacious biological details we devoured so eagerly were so inaccurate he had probably got no further than unbuttoning her duffel coat. No woman I've ever known has been built along the lines he described so avidly.

We didn't (and I feel I have to mention this, since public schools do have a certain reputation) have boyfriends either. In all my time at both Walton Lodge and Kelly College I was never aware of any of the boys being gay or – since that word still meant 'happy and light-hearted' – queer, which was the word we used at the time. Some must have been, of course, but those who were did an admirable job of keeping it to themselves. I believe it was because we were so aware that boarding schools were reputed to be hotbeds of homosexuality that we were determined not to live up to people's expectations of us. Anyone thought to be giving support to the reputation we laboured under would have been very unpopular indeed. It's sad that the gay boys must have felt so obliged to keep their sexuality under wraps; but probably not really very much sadder than the rest of us, in that sex-starved environment, having to do the same.

It was pop music that kept me going. I became obsessed with it. My main diet was the record collections owned by other boys in the junior study – the Rolling Stones, Everly Brothers, Beach Boys and, somewhat bizarrely, the Bachelors (a trio of clean-cut Irishmen who sang songs from the old English music halls) were our favourites. But I broadened my knowledge through my tiny transistor radio, which I took to bed and hid under my pillow so I could listen to Radio Luxembourg and – rather later – pirate stations like Radio London and Caroline well into the night. This opened up a much wider musical world than the one favoured by my peers, and I fast became an avid fan of American harmony groups like the Four Seasons, the Vogues and Jay and the Americans. I kept a small notebook in the inside pocket of my jacket, in which I listed my top ten favourite records of the week. Usually it bore little relation to the official BBC chart revealed by Alan Freeman every Sunday afternoon . . .

If pop music dominated my life at this time, it was not long before it was joined by another passion which has been central to my life ever since. It was on a Saturday during the school holidays and my Dad and I had been working together all morning, repairing the leaking shed roof just outside our back door. With the job finished we reckoned we deserved a reward. Neither of us had previously shown much interest in football (although my Dad did once, as a teenager, have trials with Aston Villa) so why we decided to go to a Bristol City match was a mystery then and has remained one ever since. But go we did, and suddenly we were hooked. We simply could not get enough of it – the noise, the excitement, the sense of belonging, the smell of the liniment as the players ran out onto the pitch from the tunnel just below where we stood – and after that first game (City beat Hull, as I recall) Dad and I went to Ashton Gate for Bristol City matches one weekend, and to Eastville for Bristol Rovers the next.

I always rather favoured Rovers then. I liked their old Eastville stadium with its weird flowerbeds behind the goal, and their old-fashioned blue and white quartered shirts which were so much more attractive than City's plain red, and though the quality of football they played in the old Football League Third Division (League One, as it is today) was nowhere near as good as that played by City in Division Two (today's Championship), the matches there were usually somehow more exciting.

Eventually, though, logic took over. It just made more sense to go to Ashton Gate, on our side of Bristol, than to Eastville, which was on the far side and could be reached only by driving right through the shoppers' traffic jams which brought chaos to the city centre every Saturday. So my Dad and I became devoted Bristol City supporters, following the 'Cider Army' through season after season of second tier football before glorying in unexpected promotion and holding our own in the old First Division (the Premiership) for four years before setting a new record for the speed of our fall to the brink of bankruptcy and right to the very bottom of Division Four.

Football, for me as a public schoolboy, provided a welcome glimpse into the real world, where real men had real passions, but missing it made it so much more difficult to go back to school at the end of the holidays . . .

I must not give the impression that I was unhappy at Kelly College. I wasn't. But I was not happy either. It was an experience which I knew I had to get through to break out, at the end, into a much more exciting and satisfactory life. And there were some great moments along the way.

Not many schoolboys, for example, get the opportunity to watch helicopters involved in an emergency rescue mission right outside the classroom windows. That was in 1963, one of the worst winters on record and one which meant I started the term a week late because the roads were blocked and the trains weren't running (in the end they had to bring the old steam locomotives out of retirement because they could cope so much better with bad weather than the new-fangled diesels which had replaced them). That January and February the isolated farmers on Dartmoor were in dire straits. Their animals were either trapped in snowdrifts in their fields or starving to death in their sheds because supplies of feed could not get through. And the humans were suffering nearly as badly.

The only answer was an airlift, and it was our good luck that the Royal Navy chose to use Kelly's playing fields from which to conduct the operation. Huge low-loaders brought in supplies by road – bales of hay, mostly, but also boxes of groceries and spare, warmer clothes – and dumped them in a corner of the rugby pitch. And as soon as it got light, and until it got dark, helicopters ran a shuttle service of aid to the farms in the hills – landing and taking off right outside the school windows every day for a fortnight. And we were supposed to concentrate on our lessons!

The school ran a Combined Cadet Force, in which all boys had to take part (unlike PT, which I managed to avoid by joining the choir). Almost everyone was made to join the Army Section, but after making an emotional plea on the grounds that I had wanted to go to sea since I was eight, I was allowed into the very small and much more select Naval Section (there was also an RAF Section, but that was so small and so select hardly anyone ever got into it, or even found out what it did).

Surprisingly, I did not feel foolish in my sailor suit. I looked upon wearing it as an essential step along the way to fulfilling my seafaring dream. So every Thursday afternoon I donned my bellbottoms, itchy tunic, sailor's collar and white belt and gaiters – not to mention the little round hat – and, after a few minutes' marching smartly around the parade ground, headed for the corrugated iron shed where we learned such essential skills as morse code, semaphore, knot-tying and basic navigation. And every couple of weeks we went off to Plymouth, about 20 miles away, where we became real sailors with the help of one of the naval bases there. We sailed yachts, we had trips around Plymouth Sound on high-speed motor torpedo boats and we navigated boats the size of large tugs into the open sea. Those were great days, not even spoiled by my steering a very solid little ship at almost full speed into Drake's Island when my 'crew' below decks deliberately misunderstood the orders I was giving from the wheelhouse.

It was with the CCF that on May 28 1967 – towards the end of my time at Kelly College – I went to a headland overlooking Plymouth Sound to witness Sir Francis Chichester arriving home at the end of his epic single-handed voyage around the world. As the 65-year-old sailor and his little yacht the Gypsy Moth IV came into harbour nine months and one day after leaving it, he became the first man to race solo around the world, and more than 25,000 cheering people and a fleet of thousands of small boats turned out to welcome him home. It would have been an unforgettable day for anyone with a love of the sea and adventure. For a teenager who loved those things but was also bored after five years confinement in the 'prison' walls of a public school the emotion of the day was almost too exciting to bear.

I did, against all the odds, manage to pass all my O-levels except chemistry (a subject to which I had had an aversion ever since my hair flopped forward and burned spectacularly over a Bunsen burner). Not good grades in most cases, but ten passes nonetheless and several more than had been expected by most of my teachers who had never quite grasped the fact that the quiet boy they had hardly noticed at the back of the room was in fact reasonably intelligent. The only question now was which subjects I should study at A-level. The answer, bizarrely, was maths and physics. Never mind that my best subject was English, or that I enjoyed geography and had little aptitude for science. Logically it had to be maths – partly because it would be more useful than English for someone sailing around the world on a merchant ship, but also because it was a subject that could lead to two A-levels (Pure Maths and Applied Maths) whereas every other subject offered only one. Physics was chosen not because I had any skill at, or interest in, it, but because it was the only subject bar chemistry that could be studied by anyone doing maths. Simple. All very logical. And all a total waste of whatever talents I might have had.

My next two years were a struggle. A-level maths did not come naturally to me although I enjoyed pure maths (or maths-for-the-sake-of-it as I came to describe it) and physics started as a mystery and remained so throughout my A-level course for which, as always, I sat at the back of the class keeping my head down and trying very hard to avoid catching the eye of Mr Webber our teacher.

It did not help that by then I had lost the motivation of studying for my future career as a merchant mariner. I still longed to go to sea but, with a maturity at odds with the rest of my behaviour at the time, I knew that it would not be many years before I longed for other things as well . . . and they would not be compatible with the life of a sailor. I knew that one day I would want a wife, children – and grandchildren eventually – and a home as stable as the one I had grown up in – none of which would be successfully maintained if I were to spend most of my time many thousands of miles away on a ship. It was not a sudden decision, in fact it was hardly a decision at all; it was just a realisation that crept up on me, slowly, so that by my mid teens I had come to accept that the dream that had been at the centre of my life for so long was no more.

But how was I to tell people? My whole family, all my friends, all my parents' friends and all my teachers knew that the one thing upon which I had set my heart – the one ambition I had had since I was about eight years old – was to go to sea. My parents, in particular, had encouraged me and made enormous sacrifices for me. How then could I break it to them that I now no longer wanted to do it?

The obvious answer, of course, would have been simply to tell them the truth, but at the age of 17 or so that is not so easy. So I went along with it, pretending that I still wanted a career in the merchant navy while secretly praying that something would come along to get me out of it. It did – but it was a very close thing! It was just before I sat my A-levels that my application to be taken on as a trainee navigation officer landed on the desk of Shell Tankers' personnel department. The letter I received by return was optimistic (or pessimistic, depending on your point of view) and outlined a few basic steps I would have to take before being invited for an interview. First was a medical examination, which was arranged for me in Plymouth. I felt I was on a runaway train from which there was no escape. A kind of self-imposed, inescapable pressganging . . .

The doctor was very blunt but very sympathetic.

'You've passed,' he said. 'But . . . '

The 'but' was that, while my vision was good enough to be taken on then – that day, that minute – I was showing early signs of a kind of colour blindness that might deteriorate quite rapidly so that within just a few years I could be thrown out of the merchant navy as visually unfit. What use, after all, is a navigator who can't distinguish red from green, who can't tell whether a ship in the distance is coming or going?

'I'm sorry,' he said.

'Oh,' I said, trying to look miserable but feeling euphoric inside.

I'd done it! Thanks to that kind doctor, who was working so hard to ease my disappointment, I had found a way out of my predicament. And not only that: The way out I had found would ensure I got the undeserved sympathy of my whole family, all my friends, all my parents' friends and all my teachers . . . I walked out of the medical centre trying to disguise the spring in my step.

A few months later my parents drove me away from Kelly College for the last time. I felt great relief and joy and not the slightest trepidation at all. I was free. The only question was what on earth I was going to do for the rest of my life. I didn't have a clue. But on that day, with the imposing granite building disappearing – both literally and figuratively – into the distance behind me, I just didn't care.

2

THE YOUNG MAN produced by Kelly College was nowhere near fit to be let loose into the outside world. I was shy and lacking any kind of social skills and, worst of all, I didn't know what I wanted to do with my life – and wouldn't have had the talent to do it even if I had. Goodness knows what the boss of the mushroom farm saw in me when I went to him asking for a job!

The mushroom farm was the largest in Europe at the time, and by far our biggest local employer. It was the obvious place for any 18-year-old to go looking for work and they offered me a job on the spot. My job, they told me (and they made no pretence that it was much of a career for a public schoolboy with A-levels in Applied Maths and Pure Maths and some experience of steering small ships around Plymouth Sound), would be to shovel evil-smelling horse shit from a huge pile in the yard and put it into big wooden trays which I then had to lift and stack inside a shed the size of an aircraft hangar. It would be hard physical work, they said, and I would finish each day stinking like a farmyard and would probably never be able to get the grime from under my fingernails or wash the taste from the back of my throat. What they didn't tell me was that, in just a couple of months, I would learn more about real life than I had learned in five years in the privileged confines of one of Devon's finest schools.

I was put into a team of six men – all much older than I and all perfectly entitled to take the piss unmercifully out of the new posh-talking recruit who was joining them among the manure mountains. They were rough and tough men, elephant-skinned through working in the open air all their lives, and they could have teased me, bullied me, shunned me, laughed at me or scoffed at my first pathetic efforts at manual labour. But they did none of those things. They called me 'Young Un' because that's what I was, and sometimes laughed when I did something daft like using a shovel when I should have used a pitchfork, but once I'd proved I could fill a box with shit almost as well as they could, and with their help lift it high above my head onto the stack inside the shed . . . well, once I'd done that they accepted me as one of their own.

It was back-breaking, muscle-aching, stinking work but being part of a team of such decent men made it more enjoyable than it had any right to be. I was a working man, earning a working man's wages and doing a job well enough to earn the respect of both my workmates and my bosses.

We worked mostly at the main depot at Langford, five miles down the road from Redhill, but were sometimes diverted to a smaller site near Congresbury which had the great advantage of being opposite a pub. Lunchtimes there – washing down the sandwiches we had brought from home with a pint or two of Courage bitter – were where I had a crash course in holding my own in the saucy repartee of the English working man. They spoke of football, women, television and not much else and at the start I sat with them marvelling at their ability to be so happy with – apparently – so little. Then I began to chip in with a few comments of my own (on football and television anyway, since I still had little knowledge of women worth sharing with them) until, after just a couple of weeks, I was able to join in and play as full a part in their lunchtime banter as I was in their morning and afternoon shit-shovelling.

What I learned there, in that pub and in the yard among the heaps of manure and wooden boxes, amounted to the best education I could have had. In the space of a few weeks I learned not just how to do a dirty manual job, but how to talk to and like – and respect – men whose ambitions stretched no further than to do that dirty manual job well. I learned that such men (and by implication their wives and all their families too) were decent, admirable and useful people who were essential to the sort of society in which I wanted to live. And, what's more, I learned that such people could talk to, like and respect me.

It was no good kidding myself though. My parents hadn't made all their sacrifices just so I could spend my days filling wooden boxes with the waste of the nation's horses. Sooner or later – and I knew it had to be sooner – I would have to make a decision about not just a job but a career. And it wasn't helping that, as they had warned me, I was getting home smelling so much like a farmyard that my mother eventually made me change out of my stinking work clothes on the doorstep before allowing me into the house. This, though I was enjoying it hugely, was no life for me. So after two months, with much regret, I made the decision to look for a job that might be more suitable. And certainly less smelly.

It was advertised in that very week's local newspaper. 'Wanted – Junior Reporter'. Well, that was something I hadn't really considered. No more than I had half-considered being a vet, a TV cameraman, an accountant or a whole host of other jobs for which, I realised, I was totally unqualified. But they seemed not to be asking for any great skills of any sort. Just a few O-levels, an inquiring mind and the ability to enclose with my application 1,000 words on a subject of my choice. 'For an initial six months,' the advertisement said, 'possibly followed by an apprenticeship.' I didn't much like the sound of an apprenticeship, even only in 'possibility' form, but the idea of having a proper job for six months – and a job that was probably reasonably interesting and distinctly unsmelly, at that – was really quite attractive. So I went to my bedroom and wrote, in my very best handwriting, precisely 1,000 words on pirate radio stations and why Harold Wilson's Labour Government was being totally unfair in closing them all down.

By return of post I received a letter inviting me in to meet John Bailey, the editor of the *Weston-super-Mare Mercury and North Somersetshire Herald*, at his office in Waterloo Street, Weston, and suddenly I lost my appetite for working with my unlikely friends on the mushroom farm. I handed my resignation letter to the foreman, thanking him for giving me my first job, assuring him that I'd enjoyed it, expressing my regret that I could stay no longer (all of which was much more sincere than he probably knew) and giving him a week's notice. He looked genuinely disappointed. 'I'm really sorry,' he said. 'You could have had a future here. I was going to promote you to forklift truck driver.'

Forklift truck driver? Promotion after just two months? Me? If I'd known that I would probably not have decided to leave. But it was too late. I was committed – even though the only thing I was committed to was the vague chance that Mr John Bailey, Editor, might, just might, offer me a job that I wasn't sure I wanted.

On my last day I worked just as hard as I always did, filling just as many boxes and lifting just as many of them onto the stacks in the shed, and at the end of it I went round the men, shaking each one by the hand, saying goodbye and thanking them for being such good mates. Some of them reached out and hugged me and all of them wished me well.

'So tell me, Young Un, what are you going to do with yourself?'

'I'm not sure, but I think I'm going to be a reporter.'

John Bailey was a short, round little man who in another life might have been a bank manager. He had a pleasant face, almost smiley, which put me instantly at my ease. 'So how long have you wanted to be a journalist?' he asked, coming to the point at last after a few minutes' chatting about the weather, the traffic and the rubbish blowing around the cobbled yard below his first floor window.

'For almost as long as I can remember,' I replied – which was true only if I was suffering so badly from amnesia that I could remember back no further than a week.

'You can write,' he said, as he studied my pirate radio treatise over the rim of his glasses. 'I don't know much about pop music myself, but I found this rather interesting. Well done.'

'Thank you.'

'When would you like to start?'

'Pardon?'

It really was that simple. I was taken on as a junior reporter, to start the following Monday, and would be expected to work from 8.30am to 5pm five days a week, with an hour for lunch and, if I was lucky, time off in lieu for all the jobs I would be expected to do without complaint in the evening and at weekends. In exchange for that my new employers would give me £8 a week, five weeks holiday every year, as many notebooks and pens as I might require and a commitment to start training me immediately and to go on doing so if, after six months, I was deemed suitable for an apprenticeship.

The *Weston Mercury* was one of the most old fashioned newspapers in the country. It did have news on the front page, but that was just about the only concession it made to the modern world. Its headlines were too small, its pictures too few and its higgledy-piggledy appearance was proof that it was some years since it had been troubled by anyone with a flair for design. But it was a fabulously successful newspaper, both in the amount of profit it made for its two elderly owners, the Frampton brothers (known to all of us as Mr Jack and Mr George), and in the enviable position it held in the local community. People respected and trusted it – loved it, even – and weren't joking when they said that if something wasn't in the *Mercury* it hadn't happened.

It would have been absurd to expect me to enjoy being a reporter. I was too shy, too scared of talking to people I didn't know and too frightened of using the telephone. But I loved it immediately! Shyness, I was probably not the first person to discover, is all in the mind, and even someone as timid as I was can successfully pretend to be otherwise if he can hide behind the trusty shield of his job. So – while Richard Harris, gauche 18-year-old with next to no experience of adult life, was still more reserved than was good for him – Richard Harris, journalist and representative of Somerset's finest newspaper, was more than willing to take on the world.

I would not have lasted five minutes had it been otherwise. Les Stokes, the elderly chief reporter who dished out the jobs to the rest of us and was not half as gruff as he liked to make out, made no concessions to age or experience (or lack of it). While he and his deputy Gordon Wilsher concentrated on stories from the Town Hall, the rest of us – half a dozen trainees – were expected to do almost everything else. And 'everything else' to a newspaper like the *Mercury* meant a richly varied diet of everything from lost dogs, golden weddings and speeding drivers to beauty contests, giant tomatoes and courting couples getting stuck in their cars on the beach when the tide came in. We reported everything in a flat, no-nonsense style, with neither embellishment nor adjective, because that's what the *Mercury* had been doing for 125 years and there was no need for it to change now. The editor's instructions were simple: 'If a story is not interesting no amount of flowery language will make it so; if it is, it doesn't need any help from you.'

I certainly didn't need 'flowery language' when, after just a few weeks in the job, I was sent on my first big story – a murder. Murders in Weston were singularly rare occurrences, and an innocent and respectable 17-year-old being stabbed in the heart for no reason as he walked home from a night out in one of the sea-front pubs was the biggest news the *Mercury* had had to report for years. And it was entrusted to me! Les called me over to his desk as soon as I arrived for work, gave me as many details as he knew (which were not many) and told me to go and speak to the lad's parents.

'And make sure you bring back a photo,' he called as I left the office with a sick feeling in my stomach.

It was only a five minute drive to Locking Road, where the family lived, but that was long enough for me to ask myself a whole range of questions. Like: What sort of shit job is it that's making me do this? What do you say when you knock on the door of a mother whose teenaged son has died in a pool of blood on the pavement not ten hours before? What, in the unlikely event that she doesn't slam the door in my face, should I ask her? By what right am I knocking on her door in the first place? How do I face Les Stokes when I have to tell him she refused to speak to me? Should I just drive around the town for a bit before going back to the office and saying the family sent me packing? Oh . . . and how the hell do I make sure I bring back a photo?

In the event she made it easy for me. She invited me inside, into the neat living room where her husband was sitting, next to the kitchen where a teenaged daughter was making a pot of tea. They were all stunned, moving in the way that distraught people do, just a little bit more slowly than they would have been if the police had not come knocking on their door with the news at four that morning. 'This gentleman's from the *Mercury*,' she announced. 'He's come to ask us about Michael.'

I – not much older than the son she had just lost – told her how sorry I was, how I didn't know what to say, and asked her if she would like to tell me about him. She told me what a great son he was, how she was proud of him, how he had never been any trouble, how he had had his whole life before him . . . and her husband just sat in his chair nodding gently while I wrote every word down in my notebook. She shed a few tears and so, I confess, did I.

As I left that house I felt that I had done my job and had, in a strange way, also helped them to start coming to terms with their loss. I didn't feel that I had intruded and I didn't feel that I had cashed in on their grief. I felt that I had been the man they had needed, a total stranger to whom they could begin to articulate their feelings at a time when they so badly needed to do so. I had probably adopted the role more usually filled by the vicar, but it was still early and he probably had not even heard yet that one of his parishioners had been so savagely killed.

I was sitting in my car, taking a few deep breaths, when I remembered: 'Shit! The photo!' I couldn't go back and disturb them again, not so soon after saying goodbye – but I couldn't face Les Stokes without it either.

I need not have worried. The mother was already calling to me from the front door. 'Do you think you'd like a photo of him?' she asked. I told her that, yes, I thought we probably would, so she gave me three fat photo albums and a couple of framed prints off the mantelpiece just to save me having to decide immediately which was the best one.

'I'll bring them back as soon as I can,' I assured her.

'I know you will,' she replied.

When I walked into the office I felt as if I had successfully completed some bizarre initiation ritual. I had completed my first death-knock and done it, I thought, pretty well, without adding to the pain already being felt by that traumatised family. Les Stokes was visibly impressed, but raised an eyebrow when he spotted the photographic haul under my arm.

'I'm sorry,' I told him, feeling inadequate. 'I couldn't decide which one we would want so I brought them all.'

'Don't apologise,' he said. 'It's very clever. We've got all the photos . . . and that means nobody else can have them.'

I hadn't realised until then that, small newspaper though we were, we were still in competition with our larger daily brethren in Bristol and maybe those in Fleet Street too. They would all be wanting a photograph of the innocent boy so cruelly stabbed to death on the street of a quiet seaside town, but now they wouldn't be able to get one because we already had them all and when they went knocking on the family's door there would be none left.

'Well done,' said Les. 'We'll make a reporter of you yet!'

I basked in the glory of that moment – for several days, right up until I heard the editor bellowing from his office. 'Richard, step in here please.'

My heart sank, as hearts do when their owners hear the editor calling. It usually meant trouble. I walked out of the reporters' room and round the corner to the office where John Bailey was sitting with either a smile or a grimace (I couldn't tell which) on his face. 'I've had a letter from the mother of that murdered boy,' he said. 'You'd better read it.'

It's amazing how quickly your brain can wind back the clock when needed, and in a matter of seconds I had replayed the whole scene – from knocking on the family's front door to leaving the house with my bundle of photos – and still couldn't pinpoint where I had gone wrong. There must have been something though . . .

I began to read it. 'Dear Editor,' it said. 'I would like to thank you for sending your reporter to see me and my husband last Tuesday after the tragic death of our son Michael. We very much appreciated his kind comments and his sympathetic approach to his job, which cannot have been easy for him. Please pass on our thanks to him. He is a real credit to your paper.'

John Bailey looked at me and this time he was definitely smiling. 'Well done,' he said.

Their side of the bargain meant that, in return for my hard work, my employers would do rather more to train me in the art of journalism than just sending me out into the world with a notebook and a pen to see if I would sink or swim. The first sign of this was my enrolment for Monday evening shorthand lessons at the local technical college – shorthand being not just a useful tool for a reporter but an essential component of the Proficiency Test, the only professional qualification a journalist has.

There are certain compensations to being the only man in a class of 16 mostly giggling young women, but when I arrived for my first lesson I wasn't sure what they were. Sexual equality was still many years away, and the idea of a man learning shorthand alongside a bunch of trainee secretaries was, it seemed, just as mirth-inducing as a woman going down to the shipyard for a day's welding. I didn't get the wolf whistles, maybe, but I did get every other ribald comment known to man, or indeed woman. And it didn't help that to qualify for my weekly Pitmans shorthand lessons I had first to endure an hour's obligatory typing tuition – a series of QWERTY keyboard exercises set to big band music. Since every journalist I have ever known has been happy to get by with a typing style requiring no more than three fingers and, for the more advanced, one thumb, I could find no value whatsoever in the 60 minutes I had to spend fighting with the ancient Remington manual typewriter the college provided me with. Except that that was how I met Carol.

When I said that I was the only man in a class of 16 mostly giggling young women, what I meant was that 15 of them were giggly and the 16th wasn't. Carol was the classy one. The elegant one. The one who, because she didn't know any of the others and at 19 was a bit older than the rest, was forever slightly on the outside, just a little aloof. She was tall, slim, blonde and long-legged and an LACW (Leading Aircraftwoman) in the RAF. She lived with her parents in a bungalow in the village of Locking, a couple of miles outside Weston and a short walk from the RAF camp where her father, a retired squadron leader, ran the post office. I offered her a lift home.

The next week I offered her a lift to college and a lift home and, even though I laughed when she fell into a flower bed and got covered in mud as we arrived at the tech college together for the first time, we were soon very good friends. The Monday evenings we spent together started with our typing and shorthand lessons and continued, very often late into the night, with some beers in the Criterion pub and a burger (always well done, for her; less so for me) from the Wimpy Bar just up the road from the *Mercury* office. One night ended so late, and with so little petrol left in my car long after all the filling stations had closed, that she had to wake up her father to fetch the spare tankful he kept in his garage. 'He won't mind,' she whispered, as he tottered out in his dressing gown, key in hand. He probably didn't, but he did mutter 'We weren't so damn daft in my day' as he passed me in the dark.

We saw each other often, visiting pubs, going to the cinema, taking trips into the countryside and, just occasionally, watching Bristol City together – all the things that I most enjoyed doing. I even taught her to drive (illegally, with neither L-plates nor insurance) and the fact that we never became lovers, or indeed even boyfriend and girlfriend, is something that I remember with regret now as a wasted opportunity. One night, as we scurried out of a cinema in Bristol, holding each other close under an umbrella and looking for somewhere to eat, she told me: 'I'm ravishing.'

'I know you are,' I replied.

Then, seeing the quizzical look on her face, I hastily added: 'But if you're hungry I think you mean you're ravenous.'

That was as close as I ever came to telling her I fancied her. Maybe I didn't want to spoil what we had by making some clumsy move that she might not have welcomed. Maybe I didn't have the confidence to compete with the airmen with whom she spent her days. Maybe we had come to know each other far too well to turn our friendship into something more. Maybe she would not have had me even if I'd tried . . .

Carol had lovely legs but not even they could compare with the 22 on display by the West Juniors ladies hockey team. It was one of the perks of being the *Mercury*'s most junior reporter that I was given the job of spending a week covering the West of England ladies' hockey tournament on the beach lawns next to the sands. All the South-West counties had entered senior teams – Cornwall, Devon, Dorset, Somerset, Gloucestershire and Wiltshire – and the tournament was completed by the inclusion of a junior team made up of the best young players from all six of them. My favourites, naturally, were the West Juniors and in particular Julie, their energetic and beautiful 17-year-old captain.

There wasn't much in it to interest the *Mercury* itself, but we had an arrangement with the national papers and assorted news agencies that every evening we would phone them with the scores and a brief digest of the day's events. So that was my job – to watch the matches, record the scores and do the phoning. My workmates viewed it as a chore, as something to be done by the reporter at the very bottom of the newsroom pecking order. Who were they kidding? Just a few months earlier I had been locked away in the stifling all-male surroundings of Kelly College, where the sight of a woman's naked legs would have been a topic of lewd conversation for several days, and yet here I was being paid to watch dozens of very attractive young women wearing very short skirts and doing some pretty provocative things right in front of me. Some chore! And Julie, taking her captain's duties admirably seriously, made it her job not just to join me on the touchline to watch the games she wasn't involved in, but also to act as her side's unofficial PR spokeswoman for me in her team's hotel afterwards. It was, needless to say, desperately hard work and I received genuinely sympathetic looks from my colleagues on the few occasions I felt it necessary to return to the office.

I don't recall getting such sympathy when I was sent to interview a visiting showbiz star at Weston's Playhouse theatre. Sooty, a glove puppet Teddy Bear which for years had had its own series on children's television, was appearing there in a summer show, and on the basis that I was the youngest reporter and therefore probably still had a full set of Sooty Annuals on my bookshelf, I was given the job of covering the event. Harry Corbett, Sooty's inventor, scriptwriter, voice and owner of the hand which brought the puppet to life, was, I discovered later, a notoriously difficult man and he did nothing to allay that reputation when we met in his dressing room.

I asked him if he was enjoying his time in Weston.

'You'll have to ask Sooty,' he told me.

I asked him if the show contained any surprises.

'It's no good talking to me, young man,' he said. 'Please address your questions to Sooty.'

'Do you like our seaside?' I said, hardly believing that I was talking to a piece of stuffed yellow cloth mounted on the hand of a cantankerous old man.

'Oh yes,' squeaked Sooty. 'I've been on the pier and had an ice cream and candyfloss and all sorts.'

And so it was that I spent half an hour interviewing a puppet – or, indeed two puppets, for when my conversation with Sooty started to dry up Corbett fetched out, on his other hand, Sooty's girlfriend Soo, a talking panda.

There was no such entertainment to be had on the long winter evenings I had to spend at the parish council meetings which provided the staple diet of a paper like the *Mercury*. At Brean, a little holiday village just south of Weston, where the council chairman was an ex journalist, the meetings were held in the clerk's house, and the views of the reporter were frequently sought if members could not agree on a planning application, hedge-cutting timetable or some other matter of local interest. Here we sat squeezed together on sofas in front of an open fire, with coffee served on a silver tray, and maybe a small whisky to welcome Any Other Business. But Brean was a happy exception. Other councils met in cold, invariably draughty village halls – or, worse, in primary schools where we had to sit at the back on an infant-sized chair – where reporters were tolerated rather than welcomed.

So it was not that I was under any illusion when I realised, four months into my six-month trial, that this was the career I had been looking for. I had stumbled upon it by accident and had started doing it only because I could think of nothing better, but what I had chanced upon was, I knew, the job I was cut out for. It could be boring, frustrating, worrying and sometimes even frightening, but it was also interesting, exciting, fulfilling and extraordinarily varied. It was, I had no doubt, the career for me. I just prayed that John Bailey felt the same.

The signing of my indentures was turned into a little ceremony in the editor's office. John Bailey was there, naturally, and put on his jacket for the occasion, my Dad took time off from his school to come and sign the consent form and both Mr Jack and Mr George were in attendance to wish me well.

They had had plenty of practice, of course, for the *Mercury* had long relied on a staff made up almost entirely of keen young reporters, mostly recruited straight from the local grammar school (in those days very few journalists had been to university) who learned their trade locally before going on to try their luck on newspapers which were bigger and which would pay them more. I was the fourth apprentice on the books at that time: Nigel Kirton, the oldest, would soon depart for the Swindon *Evening Advertiser*, Chris Carter would go to the Bristol *Evening Post* and Richard Wyatt, closer to my age but with his future in broadcasting already worked out in some detail in his head, would eventually get a dream move to BBC Radio Brighton, which he used as a stepping stone to a long-term career as anchorman in local TV news in Bristol. As one qualified and moved off the top end of the ladder, another was taken on at the bottom, and so we were soon joined by the likes of Nigel Dando (whose sister Jill joined the paper several years later and went on to become one of the nation's favourite TV presenters before being murdered on the doorstep of her home in London in April 1999), Nick Walker (who ended up working on the Daily Telegraph after a spell on regional daily newspapers in Bristol) and Stuart Bonney (a Geordie who would one day make a fortune with his own PR and publishing business in Newcastle-upon-Tyne).

At the top end of the journalistic staff there was no such turn-over. John Bailey, Les Stokes, Gordon Wilsher and the sub editors Mike Thomas and Ray Dwerryhouse had, it seemed, all been there for ever and would remain so, and the chief photographer Graham Wiltshire, his deputy Ted Amesbury and their young darkroom assistant David Kenneford were all local men who had no intention of moving.

It is not surprising that there was always some tension between those happy to make the *Mercury* the pinnacle of their careers, and those of us who saw it as the first step along the way to something – and who knew what? – else. That tension was never more noticeable than after one of us went to college . . . and came back with news that the *Mercury* way was not the only way of doing things.

It was not just that our paper was one of the very last to be printed on an old flat bed press (even then most used the faster and more efficient rotary presses, while a progressive few were already into the burgeoning web offset technology that brought the first colour photographs to the nation's newspapers). The whole way of producing the *Mercury* was outdated – and sometimes laughably so.

Most newspapers (as we found to our surprise when we met reporters from others) were laid out according to a masterplan, which decreed – at least roughly – what they should look like. In very simple terms it might have meant having the main story, under the biggest headline, spread over three columns at the top; next to it might be a big photograph, with the story relating to it filling one column down the side; the page would be anchored by a story of medium importance across the bottom, under a headline smaller than the one at the top but bigger than the others on the page; and the rest of the page would be filled with shorter stories of less importance and therefore smaller headlines. The idea was not just to make the page look attractive, but to guide the reader's eye around it so that nothing was missed.

Not so the *Weston Mercury*! Here Mike Thomas and Ray Dwerryhouse took the reporters' copy and, after checking it for mistakes and potential libels wrote a headline for it and marked it up to be set by the compositors – across one, two or three columns – all without their having the faintest idea of where that story might eventually appear in the paper. By the end of the week their desks were suffocated under heaps of bits of paper, the proofs of all the stories they had subbed earlier on, which, armed with scissors and a paste pot, they proceeded to place, jigsaw-fashion, onto a dummy page, wherever they fitted best. The importance of a story was therefore of much less significance than whether it matched any of the holes available for it and the size of the headline depended on what the sub had specified two or three days before, not upon where the story was to appear on the page.

The *Weston Mercury* never won any newspaper design awards. But it was frequently held up at journalism college as an example of how things should not be done.

Young reporters going to college was something the senior staff tolerated without enthusiasm – just as long as they did not come back wanting to use any of the fancy modern ideas they had been taught there. Take, for example, something as important as a story's intro – that vital first sentence which either succeeds, or too often fails, to engage the readers' interest long enough to stop them turning the page. Writing an intro is a real skill, which many reporters struggle to master all their lives, so it is hardly surprising that colleges devote a lot of time to it. 'Keep it short and keep it simple,' is the rule, which is precisely the opposite of what we were told on the *Mercury*, where 'short' and 'simple' were two words which failed to find a place in the sub editors' vocabulary.

An intro such as 'A gang of children smashed 25 car windscreens when they went on a drunken rampage in Weston last night' might have won approval from a college lecturer, but back in the real world of the *Mercury* reporters' room it would have been thrown back at us until it read something more like: 'An estimated 20 young people, some as young as ten and all according to police reports aged under 14, ran through the streets of Weston last night – from the Old Pier all the way to Oldmixon, via the railway station – damaging the windscreens of 25 motor vehicles, all of them parked by their owners who knew nothing of what had happened until they returned to the scene several hours later and found piles of smashed glass on the road.'

It was an old fashioned way of writing for an old fashioned paper. But, though we frequently scoffed at it, we didn't mind. We knew that, despite some of our outlandish modern ideas, we were valued by our employers and somehow had a feeling that working on a newspaper as outdated as the *Weston Mercury* was giving us an unrivalled foundation in the job of being journalists.

My budding career as a journalist might have been cut short almost before it had begun. For it is no exaggeration to say that on July 10 1968 I could easily have died. It had been raining steadily all day, but until tea-time we had no hint that what was about to hit us would be anything particularly out of the ordinary. But then the summer evening turned dark, the wind started howling and the gentle rain became a deluge – rain like I had never experienced before, and haven't since. It went on for hours and in the late evening, after her shift at Bristol Maternity Hospital, my sister Liz rang home to say she was trapped in the Bedminster area of the city, with the floodwater advancing up the street towards the phone box she was in.

Her fiancé Chris, who lived a mile up the road, where his father owned a garage, and I – still thinking that what we were experiencing was just a particularly heavy summer shower – decided we would drive in and fetch her. Simple, we thought.

We got just a few miles before we had to turn back because the flood water at Lulsgate Bottom, just past the airport, was too deep for the little car we were in and we had no wish to add to the number of vehicles already stranded there.

By now it was the sort of challenge that two young men could not resist – especially when one of them had a father who owned a huge breakdown truck, with axles so high that it would take a flood of monumental proportions to stop it. We climbed into Big Bertha and set off for Bristol once more, making stately progress past all the much smaller vehicles which had come to grief, many with their drivers still inside, with their feet on the dashboard as the water lapped around their bottoms.

As we reached Bristol it became clear that this was no ordinary flood. People were hanging out of their upstairs windows while their furniture floated out of their front doors and into their gardens; a few were paddling up the streets in inflatable boats; some – braver, or perhaps more foolish – were playing on the higher ground, in their wellies.

And through it all Big Bertha, with her huge wheels, kept going. Until we reached Bedminster, half a mile from where Liz had been. There, even Big Bertha could go no further. So Chris and I abandoned her and continued our mission on foot. Thigh-deep, waist-deep, chest-deep . . . the water kept rising and we kept going, determined not to be beaten. Bedminster Road, the main street, was a scene from a disaster movie – a cacophony of burglar alarms, shop windows smashed under the weight of thousands of gallons of water, dummies from the fashion shops floating on the flood like grotesque corpses, television sets bobbing down the street like boats on the ocean . . . And it was all in the dark because the street lights had failed.

We found our way to a police station, and climbed the stairs in the hope that Liz might have found refuge there. Hundreds of people were there, sitting on the floor, frightened and soaked to the skin, and looking like refugees from a battlefield. But Liz was not among them. We went outside and continued our journey and stopped only when the water got up to our necks.

We made our way back up Bedminster Road and gradually we reached higher ground so that the water fell to our chests, our waists, our knees, and the comforting shape of Big Bertha loomed out of the dark.

It was only when we got home in the small hours of the morning that we discovered that soon after her first panicky phone call Liz had found her way to the police station, and from there had been given a lift back to the hospital. She had not been able to tell us because the telephones, like so much else on that dreadful night, had ceased working.

Much later, after we had had time to think back on what we had gone through, Chris and I realised just how foolish we had been. One of the first affects of any major flood is that the water lifts the manhole covers – so the streets had become a potential deathtrap for anyone crazy enough to walk up them as we had done. It was only through sheer good fortune that neither Chris nor I had fallen through an open manhole and disappeared without trace into the miles of sewers beneath the stricken city.

Seven people did die that night and thousands were forced out of their homes as rivers and streams burst their banks and flooded the valleys around them. Normally tranquil streams were transformed into raging torrents that swept away trees, cars, bridges and, in some cases, houses. In Somerset alone 67 bridges were either destroyed or badly damaged.

Most places had more than five inches of rain in 24 hours but the Mendip hills – which seemed to attract the very worst of the weather – had nearly seven inches in just 6½ hours and Chew Valley Lake, the main reservoir fed by water from the Mendips, gained 471 million gallons overnight.

High up in the Mendips the water made an improvised reservoir behind old lead mine workings at a place called Velvet Bottom, only for the 'dam' eventually to collapse and send the whole lot cascading at once down Cheddar Gorge, in a torrent of water, mud and rocks that smashed its way through many of the shops and cafes in the village at the bottom.

In Bristol, an old lady was saved only after a 12-year-old girl climbed up the outside of her house and lowered her down to a waiting boat on a rope of knotted sheets; in Congresbury, halfway between Redhill and Weston, where the main street was under six feet of swirling water, three men had to be rescued by policemen who swam to them with ropes; and at Cheddar 12 workers were trapped all night in the famous caves after the rising water blocked their exit.

Weston was cut off by flooding and landslides, and parts of Burnham-on-Sea and Clevedon, North Somerset's two other reasonably sized towns, were under more than two feet of water. In other towns and villages firemen could do nothing to help because they could not get their fire engines out of their garages.

The next day, after just a couple of hours sleep, I arrived at work keen to write a report about my experiences in the Great Flood. But John Bailey would have none of it. He was already writing his own first-person piece on how he had struggled to drive through 18 inches of water on his way home to Weston from a meeting in Winscombe six miles away.

'Eighteen inches? The water was up to my neck in Bristol,' I told him.

'We don't cover Bristol,' he told me quietly.

3

QUITE WHY THE CARDIFF COLLEGE of Food & Technology was chosen to be the centre for all journalist training in the South-West of England and the Midlands is something I never discovered. We were in the college but never really part of it, so although membership of the Students' Union was forced upon us, we did not enter fully into anything like student life – partly, maybe, because the other students were Welsh, and it was very clear that the people of Cardiff were not yet ready for another invasion by the English. And anyway we were all older than the other students and, being in work, considered ourselves to be rather above them. Not that it bothered us. We were there for only eight weeks a year, on a block release course, and found all the fun and comradeship we needed among ourselves. We didn't live together – or, indeed, anywhere near to each other or to the college in most cases – because our accommodation had been found by our various employers, and they had chosen it on the basis of cost (ie cheapness) without much recourse to a map. But, after spending all day together at college, we often got together again in the evenings, which we spent socialising in a modest way around Cardiff's bars.

The *Mercury* found me a room at the home of Mrs Paju – a Welsh lady married to a former Estonian seaman who had once turned up on his ship at the docks in Splottland and never gone home – who lived near the castle and tried (without success, fortunately) to get her daughter interested in me. Richard Wyatt had stayed in the same house the previous year and had recommended it for me on the basis that I would be kept well fed, well entertained and well cared for. I have often wondered why he was so keen that I should stay there. He either (a) disliked me much more than I thought (b) had enjoyed much more at the hands of the Miss Paju than

I was prepared even to contemplate or (c) thought I would find endless fascination in the sight of her father picking his toe-nails while watching television in a language which, even after many years in an English-speaking nation, he still could not understand. I found the house much less agreeable than Richard had, and made a point of spending as little time in it as possible.

It wouldn't be right to say that I was out of my depth at college (not as much as I had been out of my depth at Kelly College, anyway) but there is no doubt that I often felt over-awed by those of my classmates who came from bigger papers, bigger towns or were older or more worldly-wise than I – a situation made worse when the *Mercury*, and by inference Weston-super-Mare, was held up for ridicule, as it very often was. We were encouraged to swap tales of how we did things back home and to bring in examples of our own papers so they could be analysed and criticised, and it was often to the *Mercury* that the lecturers turned when they wanted an example of some journalistic absurdity.

I was, though, fascinated by the subjects we studied – Local Government, Law and Newspaper Practice – and by how they could be adapted to be of use in my work back in Weston. In those subjects I was no better and no worse than most of my fellow students (though perhaps I could turn out a half decent news story more quickly than most of them) but in shorthand I was king! It was not something for which I deserved particular credit. Some people can paint, some can play football and for some reason I could do shorthand, right from the moment I went to my first lesson at Weston Tech. I had an aptitude for it and, while others struggled to get anywhere near the 100 words a minute required by the Proficiency Test, I passed exam after exam until I peaked at a magnificent 170 words a minute.

A much bigger test of our nascent journalistic skill came early one morning when our senior instructor Peter Saunders told us to take our notebooks and collect our coats because we were going out. 'Come back with as many ideas for stories as you can find,' he said. 'You've got two hours.'

The idea was for us to walk around the city looking for anything that might make a news story – the first test of that elusive talent known as 'news sense' – and I'm happy to say that this was one occasion that the much maligned *Weston Mercury* came up trumps. Those of my colleagues who worked on bigger papers, or on papers based in much bigger towns than Weston-super-Mare, were not used to having to go out looking for news. In their experience news was something that usually came to them and when it didn't they did not really know what to do. They seemed just to wander around aimlessly, apparently waiting for someone to be murdered, or a bank to be robbed in front of their eyes, while those of us who worked on very small papers knew that in the absence of a shotgun wielding bank robber we could make a news story about anything from a lost chihuahua upwards. That is what newspapers – or newspapers like the *Mercury*, anyway – were all about and what made the job so satisfying.

I returned from Cardiff to discover that John Bailey had had an idea. Each of the junior reporters would be assigned his own patch – part of the *Mercury*'s circulation area to call his own. We would spend one day a week, and more if necessary, working there exclusively, building up contacts and using them to find as much news as possible. I had been given Burnham-on-Sea, a small seaside town about ten miles south of Weston.

It was another of those happy accidents that changed my life.

I had been to Burnham before, of course, and knew it as a rather sleepy place, renowned for little more than the fact that it had two lighthouses – one, a tall stone-built construction standing incongruously well inland in the middle of the town; the other a strange little square job built of wood and mounted on nine legs on the beach. It was the sort of town to which people went to retire, with a faintly genteel air which its single seafront amusement arcade did little to spoil. I didn't imagine it would be a hotbed of news. Indeed, I didn't imagine that very much ever happened there at all.

My job would be to make myself known to as many people as possible – vicars, councillors, shopkeepers, undertakers, hoteliers, policemen, teachers – and get them to agree to meet me regularly so they could tell me about all the interesting things happening in their community. I found the people of Burnham very welcoming, almost flattered by my presence in their town, and soon identified the half dozen or so who were worth calling on every week. An awful lot of tea was drunk, but it worked, and every week I returned to the office with an impressive array of local news – enough, anyway, to satisfy John Bailey that his idea was paying dividends.

One week I received a press release from the British Safety Council telling me that a Burnham schoolgirl had made it through to the regional finals of the Miss Beautiful Eyes competition, a national event intended to promote eye safety in the nation's factories. I made it my job to go and find her. It did, after all, sound marginally more interesting than calling on the secretary of the local Mothers' Union for yet another cup of tea and digestive biscuit.

Tina Lewis, the girl with the beautiful eyes, lived in a café in the main shopping street. The Seaspray – a couple of notches up from a greasy spoon and a favourite with the town's young people – was run by her dad Norman, a big Welshman with a loud voice and a twinkling sense of humour, who did most of the cooking, and her mum Rina, a vivacious and attractive Italian woman who served the customers. Mrs Lewis, in particular, took a shine to me immediately, plied me with frothy coffee (a welcome change from the tea everyone else served me), gave me steak and kidney pudding for my lunch and apologised for the fact that Tina, at 17, was still at school. Would I like to come back in the evening? Well yes, of course, though not necessarily for yet another hot drink.

That evening, as arranged, and with her mother hovering with a very large smile on her face by the milkshake machine behind the counter, I met Tina and, confusing lust with love, fell in love with her instantly. It wasn't just her eyes that were beautiful. Even in her school uniform, she was dazzling from head to toe. She had beautiful eyes (obviously), glorious long dark hair, a lovely smile and (I imagined) a wonderful body. She had a bewitching laugh, and a laudable way of pretending that she did not know how attractive she was. Unfortunately she also had a boyfriend.

However I had to be positive. I had got a good story and a rather fetching photograph for my newspaper, had met some more Burnham people who would surely be able to furnish me with the necessary local news as the weeks went on, and I had found a friendly café which served very tasty steak and kidney puddings which I would not always be asked to pay for. I resolved to have lunch there every week, and if occasionally I had to return late in the day and was able to feast my eyes on the lovely Tina, then that was just a perk of my job.

I looked forward to my weekly visits to Burnham in general, and to the Seaspray in particular, and the more I got to know Tina's parents the more they seemed to like me. Tina seemed to like me too, but it was clear there would be no shifting her from her boyfriend – even though he was only a schoolboy and I was a working man with money, a car, a bright future and the ability to get her picture into the local paper as often as she might wish.

As the summer approached the Lewises started making plans for the influx of tourists (there was a holiday camp just outside town, many of whose visitors could be expected to wander in to the Seaspray at some stage during their stay). The café was given a springcleaning lick of paint, some of the oldest equipment was thrown out and replaced by something newer . . . and the search began for the extra staff who would be needed. Norman's usual policy, being Welsh, was to recruit a couple of nice Welsh girls, students or somesuch, who would spend their summer working in the café and sleeping in the flat upstairs. The previous year – either because he could not find any would-be waitresses from his homeland or because his geography wasn't up to scratch – he had ventured a few miles across the border and found two girls from Herefordshire, which of course is just about in England. Both of them had worked at the Seaspray for the whole summer of 1968 and had found boyfriends among Burnham's biking community. One of them had never gone back to Herefordshire and the second would soon be returning to Burnham for another summer, which, I was told, was very good news for everyone, me included. 'You'll love Pat,' said Mrs Lewis. 'You'll love Pat,' said Mr Lewis. 'You'll love Pat,' said Tina. 'No I bloody well won't,' said I, not appreciating being told, by people who barely knew me, whom I would or would not like, let alone love.

I was sitting in my usual corner of the café, drinking coffee and talking to one of the locals, when there was something of a commotion behind the counter. Mrs Lewis was getting excited. I looked up from my coffee and saw the reason: A tall young woman in a brown trouser suit was coming through the door with a diffident smile and a suitcase. This must be the famous Pat. 'Nothing special,' I thought, and went back to my coffee.

Yes, you've guessed it. I married her. Or at least I did, much, much later. For now, though, Pat was just the new waitress. No more than a pleasant girl who smiled at me when she served me my steak and kidney pudding and who looked at me with something amounting to suspicion when she saw the special place I so obviously had in the Lewis family's affections.

It was Mrs Lewis who told me more about her: She came from the market town of Leominster, where her father was vicar, and wanted to go to college to train as a nursery nurse. The previous year Pat and her school friend Averil had come down together, and Averil had met Lewie and Pat had met Bill – both of them bikers and regular customers of the Seaspray. At the end of the summer Averil had stayed with Lewie in Burnham, but Pat had returned home and her relationship with Bill seemed to have fizzled out. But nobody was quite sure how completely it was over . . . and nobody would have been at all surprised if it unfizzled itself now that she was back in town. And, in case I had missed the point, everybody loved Pat, and so would I once I got to know her, Mrs Lewis said.

That was a view not necessarily shared by Pat herself, so – unknown to me – she and Tina made it their business to find me a girlfriend. On the very flimsy basis that anyone as lovely as Tina must have some equally beautiful friends, I agreed to go with them one Saturday night to meet Heather who lived in a village near Cheddar in the Mendip hills. I discovered immediately that my evening might have been better spent staying at home and watching Match Of The Day on television with my Dad, as I usually did. Heather was unattractive in almost every way it was possible to be unattractive – a fact which was obvious to me as soon as I set my disappointed eyes on her and which was confirmed the moment she opened her mouth. Not only was she not good to look at, her needlessly loud voice and cackling laugh meant she wasn't good to listen to either.

It was a long and painful evening, most of which I spent sitting on the floor at Heather's feet, wishing I was almost anywhere else but there. There were three women in that room and not one of them was any good for me. Tina, though gorgeous, was infuriatingly unavailable; Pat, though pleasant, had the spectre of last year's boyfriend hanging over her, and anyway I was determined not to like her just because I didn't want to give Mrs Lewis the satisfaction of being right; and Heather, though clearly there for the taking (I probably flattered myself), was someone I would be happy never to meet again in all my life. My head was aching from the constant barrage of noise from Heather's mouth, my bum was aching from too long sitting on the hard floorboards and my heart was aching with the frustration of it all, so when Pat got up to go to the lavatory I took the opportunity of a brief respite by moving, temporarily at least, to take her place in her big soft armchair, which had the great benefit of being as far away from Heather as was possible in that small room. She returned all too soon, obliging me to act the gentleman by letting her have her seat back. I leapt up out of it with an enthusiasm I did not feel . . . and exploded my trousers in spectacular fashion. The zip burst open, the belt snapped and the waistband button catapulted across the room . . .

On such small foundations are great love affairs based! Pat was (I discovered later) rather impressed by the way I coped with the embarrassment that focused everyone's attention on my nether regions, and she was more impressed still when on the way home Tina asked me what I thought of Heather and I politely refused to confirm that she was indeed the most appalling and unappealing young woman I had ever met in my admittedly limited experience of the species.

It was that evening, though I did not know it at the time, that Pat decided that I might, just might, be worth getting to know. I had clearly come to the same cautious conclusion about her because it was only a few days later that I (a dog-hater) found myself on Burnham beach with her, walking Jasper, the Lewises' spaniel. I found, to my surprise, that Pat was more than just pleasant. She was much better looking than she had ever seemed in the confines of the café, and she was easy and interesting to talk to and most of all she was fun. I'm ashamed to say though that it needed a few more walks before I plucked up the courage to ask her out . . . and even then it needed my sister's wedding to spur me into action.

In those days weddings were not the lavish affairs they are today. Liz's comprised a ceremony at Wrington church and a simple afternoon reception in Redhill primary school (which both she and her fiancé Chris had once attended, and which was joined onto the school house where I still lived with my parents). No disco. No ceilidh. No lively party into the night. And, as far as I was concerned, no hope of anything other than a huge anti climax – especially since Carol, who had agreed to give me some support for the big day, had something else to do and therefore could not keep me entertained in the evening.

So what to do? Simple – find myself a girlfriend! But who? Simple again – Pat! Neither of us knew what we were letting ourselves in for . . .

The one thing Liz was worried about on her wedding day was that some of Chris's family – especially his large number of unruly cousins – would think it a good idea to pursue the happy couple, as they had pursued many others over the years, as they drove away in their car after the reception. She had even asked me to do whatever I could to prevent such a thing happening. So as Liz and Chris emerged from the house in their smart going-away outfits and made their way to their car, I stood in the middle of the road outside, listening for the telltale sound of any other starting engines. And when a car came up behind me, full of cheering and leering cousins, I did what I had been asked to do. I stopped it. The best way, I reckoned, was to sit on it – very firmly on its bonnet so that it could go no further without causing me a very nasty injury. And sit on it is what I did, forgetting that the car might still be moving and that, being a Wolseley, it might have therefore placed its barbed W-shaped emblem just where the smooth and gleaming bonnet had been a split second before. I sat not on the bonnet but on the emblem, and as my sister and her new husband drove off, safely unpursued, I drowned out the sound of their goodbyes with my screech of pain. Putting my hand to my buttocks (in much the same way as a shot sheriff might put his hand to his smitten chest in a John Wayne western) I felt for the wound. My hand came away sticky with blood.

I ran into the house, pulling off my trousers as I went, past an anxious Carol, past the two startled bridesmaids who were standing in the hall, and upstairs to my bedroom. The damage was serious – a large gash right at the top of my thigh, less than half an inch from where it would have put a very painful stop to any thoughts I might have had of fatherhood.

But I had a potential new girlfriend to meet and not even a barbed W was going to stop me. So just four hours later, with a tetanus injection in my buttock and a complicated bandage bound around me from my waist to my thigh, I arrived to pick up Pat from the Seaspray. On my first date with my future wife I went tenpin bowling, in great pain and wearing a bloodstained nappy.

Away from the Seaspray and away from Mrs Lewis's tiresome attempts at matchmaking, I was better able to appreciate Pat for what she really was. Thanks to our walks on the beach I already knew that I liked her, that I was comfortable with her and that she made me laugh. But now she took on another dimension. She was gorgeous, with sensational long legs that she did not mind displaying to their full advantage beneath a very short skirt. I could not believe my luck, and wondered how I had been so blind and why it had taken me so long.

Things were going well and no longer did I go to Burnham only on workdays. There was, though, the small problem of Bill, her last year's boyfriend. She told me that for some reason the sound of a curlew reminded her of him still, and there was no doubt that she became too quiet and thoughtful for my liking when she heard it, which was often. The countryside was full of the bloody things, each one determined to call out as I passed, just to remind me that I had a rival for her affections. He was always there at the back of my mind (probably more than he was at the back of hers) and I was convinced that, though our blossoming romance was progressing nicely, she would go back to him instantly if he ever gave her the slightest encouragement. All of that though changed one night on Brean Down, a wild grassy headland that sticks out into the Bristol Channel midway between Burnham and Weston. This was our favourite spot and we walked there often, in the daytime, at dusk and in the dark. The trouble was that, like everywhere else, it seemed, the curlews loved it as much as we did. Which meant that, though we kissed and we cuddled and we talked and we played, Bill never seemed very far away. But that night, in the dark, as she snuggled her face into my chest she said very softly the words that remain the best that anyone has ever said to me: 'You can forget about the curlews'. If they were making a film of our love story that would be the moment when the slushy music would reach a crescendo and fireworks would light up the sky behind my head. But as it was I just smiled and pretended that I had not heard her. I said 'Pardon' just because I wanted to hear her say it again.

It was surprising how many good and genuine reasons I managed to find to go to Burnham that summer. Never had the town been so well served by its local newspaper. Driven by a desperate longing to be with Pat, I searched everywhere for the news that would give me a reason to leave the office . . . and I usually found it. Most people, I discovered, had something about them that was worth putting in a newspaper – or a very parochial newspaper like the *Mercury* anyway. Most people have done something, been somewhere or known someone that's interesting enough to merit a few paragraphs in their local paper – even if they don't know it. The trick is to persuade them to tell you about it, and you can usually do that if you have enough time. I was lucky that my editor did give me enough time, and I repaid him by returning to him with countless stories of the goings-on of that lovely little town. He admired my dedication to my job and never once suspected that it was for any reason other than utter devotion to my career.

My routine was always the same – lunch served by Pat in the Seaspray, then a couple of calls on whoever was going to provide me with the news (and my excuse for being there) that day, then back to the café for a coffee or two until Pat finished her shift. Mrs Lewis, basking in the satisfaction of a successful matchmaking, frequently let her finish early so we could spend the rest of the evening together. And on days when I could find no reason to be in Burnham for the *Mercury* I still went there as soon as I could after work and spent my evenings there . . . and I didn't care how many curlews I heard.

Sometimes, of course, work did get in the way of my love life. As I slowly climbed up the *Mercury* ladder I was given more responsible jobs, including coverage of some quite serious court cases, which I enjoyed

Richard Harris

Our 'summer of love'

enormously. My first experience of the British judicial system had been at Weston Magistrates' Court where my job was to fill my notebook with the details of every person who nicked a bar of chocolate from Woolworths, every driver who strayed too far above the speed limit and every visiting Birmingham holidaymaker who thought Somerset cider was a harmless boys' drink until he woke up in a police cell next morning with a sore head and a summons for being drunk and disorderly. These were before the days of the Crown Prosecution Service, so prosecutions were conducted in court by two of the town's most experienced policemen – Sgt Murdo Chisholm for most and, for the more serious ones, Supt Gerald Lockyer – and I built up a good rapport with both of them, so that they whispered in my ear if a case was going to be worth my staying for or whether I might be better advised to nip out for a coffee in Forte's ice cream parlour around the corner.

It was Mr Lockyer who was prosecuting the case of a young man accused of a minor indecent assault on a schoolgirl. The lad denied even being in the area at the time of the incident so the girl, sweet and shapely in her school uniform, had to be called to give evidence. 'Can you see the man who did it?' Mr Lockyer asked. 'Yes, it was him,' she replied quietly, pointing without a moment's hesitation to me on the press bench. I shrunk horrified into my seat, pretending to busy myself with my notes but knowing that, as my face flushed red with embarrassment, every eye in the room was upon me.

It's at times like that that a young reporter is grateful for all the contacts he has made. Mr Lockyer knew me well, and I was on speaking terms too with both the court clerk and the chairman of the magistrates, so there was probably no real danger of my being led, screaming my innocence, to the cells. Mr Lockyer smiled at the girl and said gently 'I don't think so – why don't you try again?'. She did, and after looking around the courtroom pointed instead to the lad in the dock (who, incidentally, looked absolutely nothing like me). 'No, it was him – sorry,' she said.

Further embarrassment came at Wells Assizes, to which I was promoted after avoiding all the many legal pitfalls awaiting a young reporter at a magistrates' court. Wells is a glorious little city, boasting lots of quaint and narrow streets, ancient buildings and one of the finest cathedrals (around which flows a water-filled moat, complete with dazzling white swans) in the whole of Britain. It was a pleasure to be paid to spend a day there and I had many happy days exploring it, and writing amorous postcards to Pat, while waiting for any cases to be dealt with which might be of interest to the people of Weston.

On one of my earliest visits I found myself in the cheery company of Clive Jackson, a roly-poly man of about my age, who managed to hold down a job as a reporter on the *Cheddar Valley Gazette* without ever taking it wholly seriously. It was good to see a friendly face in the austere surroundings of the ancient Assize Courthouse – not least because I was still new to this more intimidating level of the judicial system and was desperate not to put a foot wrong.

I was there for a major fraud trial involving a man from Weston and Clive was there for the sentencing of a Cheddar woman who had plunged a broken beer glass into the face of a man in a pub, but the first case on the list was that of a petty criminal from Shepton Mallet. No one from Shepton Mallet was of any interest to the readers of either the *Mercury* or the *Cheddar Valley Gazette* but Clive and I both decided we would go into the courtroom to watch, if only to find out more about the court process so that we would be better able to follow proceedings when the cases we were interested in eventually came on.

The case was fairly uninteresting, until the defence barrister got to his feet and started telling the judge of the problems that had turned his client, the defendant, from a decent and respectable citizen into the sort of middle aged offender who was on every policeman's list of suspects whenever any crime was committed within five miles of Shepton Mallet town centre. It all started, he said, with an accident in the hapless man's youth, which had resulted in his receiving a nickname from his schoolmates which had distressed him so deeply that he had taken to drink. The drink led him into a downward spiral of drugs, vandalism, theft and minor violence and now here he was facing his umpteenth burglary charge.

'He recovered quite well from the accident in his youth, Your Honour, but the sad fact is that he has never – not even today, 25 years later – fully recovered from the nickname that was so unfairly bestowed upon him,' the barrister said. 'It was not the accident, but the nickname that brought him here today and I ask you to take that fully into account. I would ask Your Honour not to send this man to jail because of an unfortunate nickname, but to give him a chance to prove that he can put all that behind him and live the useful life he might have lived had he not been given it in the first place.'

Clive and I were all agog. Novices though we were, we reckoned that we'd grasped the point that it was all to do with the nickname. But we, just like everyone in that courtroom, wanted to know what the nickname was.

There was only one person who had the power to find out. And he came up trumps. 'Are you ever,' the judge asked, 'going to tell us what the nickname was?'

We braced ourselves, knowing that this was to be some sort of defining moment in the case. 'Er . . . if Your Honour pleases,' said the barrister. 'It was One-Ball Hancock, Your Honour.'

There followed the sort of silence which comes only when a lot of people are determinedly trying not to make a sound. Not a grin passed anyone's face, not a chuckle escaped their lips. But as I sat there in that hushed courtroom, squeezed close to the ample frame of Clive Jackson, I felt his body begin to tremble. Soon his giggles racked his whole body, his fat was wobbling convulsively and I was conscious that he had ceased breathing lest something audible should escape from his mouth. And, of course, as he giggled, so did I. We soon exploded into a series of snorts and coughs, which did nothing to disguise the fact that we were tittering like naughty schoolboys in a manner that did our professionalism no credit at all.

The day I had been dreading came in August, when Pat left the café and went back home. Leominster was only 70 miles away but to me it seemed like the end of the earth and I was convinced that our own Summer of Love was over. The chances of our relationship surviving were, I reckoned, remote.

Wanting to make the most of every last minute we had together, I offered to drive her home and she agreed . . . but warned me not to expect too much from her parents. When Bill had visited the previous year, she said, they had given him a distinctly cool welcome – and I should prepare myself for the same. I was, after all, a journalist (even then a profession many people viewed with a certain distaste), while Bill had been a highly qualified electrician, with a good job in a power station; my hair was a long and unkempt mop, while his had been neatly trimmed around his ears; and I was wearing old cord jeans, while he had taken the trouble to wear a suit for the occasion. The only thing I had in my favour, it seemed, was that I didn't ride a motor bike.

But that was enough. The Rev Gerald Rainbow and his wife Kitty seemed to take to me immediately and against all the odds accepted me as a suitable boyfriend for their younger daughter. Not that it mattered very much. As I kissed her goodbye at the vicarage door I was convinced that it would be the last time I would see her and as I drove away from Leominster later that afternoon the tears were streaming down my face.

I was, I'm happy to say, wrong. It was indeed the end – or an end anyway – but only in the sense that it was the end of the beginning of our relationship. The simple carefree days of Burnham, were gone, and were being replaced by something that was more difficult, more satisfying and somehow more grown-up. I had not dared to hope that Pat felt the same about me as I did about her, but it soon became clear that she did when she invited me back to spend a weekend at the vicarage. And another weekend. And another. By the time she moved to Bristol, to train as a nursery nurse at the Church of England Children's Society's home in Wick House, Brislington, I had become a regular visitor at Leominster Vicarage, and was still being made welcome by her parents, whom I liked just as much as they seemed to like me.

I was, of course, still on my best behaviour – not least because I was not used to living in a vicarage. Until then I had only been vaguely aware that Pat was the daughter (and indeed the grand-daughter) of a vicar, but staying in that house made it something I could not ignore and I was unsure how I was supposed to conduct myself. Did it matter that I could hardly keep my hands off her, I wondered? Or wanted to kiss her all day long? Or, when her father wasn't looking, run my hands up those great legs that she still enjoyed showing off under her very short skirts?

Her move to college in Bristol should have made our relationship very much easier since it was so much closer to my home. But we had reckoned without the Church of England Children's Society, which imposed conditions upon its students which were specifically designed, it seemed, to frighten off all except the most ardent of suitors. Pat had to be back by 9.30 in the evening, except twice a month when she could stay out till 11.15pm (but strictly only to go to the theatre) and once a month when she was allowed to go to a dance, and only a dance, as long as she was back by 12.30am. And she was nearly 20 years old!

We made full use of the limited number of late passes but not for the reasons her bosses intended, and she became adept at lying to them about the films we had not seen and the dances we had not attended.

4

BY THE TIME I RETURNED for my second spell at the Cardiff College of Food and Technology that October I had changed. I was more confident (both in myself and in my worth as a reporter) and more outgoing – and our course lecturer Peter Saunders noticed it immediately. 'I was a bit worried about you last year,' he told me over a pint in the pub one evening. 'You were too quiet and subdued. But not now. What's happened? Have you found a good woman or something?' I told him that yes, while I could not say whether or not she was particularly good, there was no doubting that she was a woman.

I had decided at an early stage that I would not be going back to Mrs Paju and instead found a place in a huge and rambling establishment beside the railway line in Senghenydd Road where I was joined by the two people with whom I had got on best the previous year – Rosie Staal, a lively and cuddly blonde from the *Western Morning News* in Plymouth, who was a dead ringer for Mary Hopkin, a young Welsh singer who was enjoying great success in the pop charts at the time, and Marilyn Rowse, also from Plymouth, who was Scottish, married and much more mature and responsible than the rest of us.

Our lodging house was run by Mrs Thomas, a sociable middle aged lady who for some reason accepted only two types of people as lodgers in her home – young journalists and minor performers from the local theatres and variety clubs. It was a strange mix, but great fun, not least because we (who were booked in for two months) knew neither with whom we would be sitting down to eat in the evening nor for how long they would be staying. This merry assortment of magicians, tap dancers, comedians, balladeers and female impersonators were a joy to us three journalists who, being trained to ask questions, made no secret of our interest in what life on the lower rungs of the showbiz ladder was like.

And one of them was a fire eater. It was around two in the morning when his lady assistant came into my bedroom. I woke up when she opened the door and then listened wonderingly as she cursed at the end of my bed and groped for the light-switch. It was one of those pull-the-string things that you usually get in bathrooms and it was a while before she found it and tugged it . . . and spotted me just coming to my senses in bed, not knowing whether to scream for help or to thank whoever was looking after my luck that night.

'Oh,' she said, 'I thought this was my room.'

I – not being at my conversational best in the small hours of the morning – muttered 'No, it's mine', rolled over and went back to sleep.

Now, I have no idea whether she really thought it was her room (very probably she did, because all the doors in Mrs Thomas's house looked much alike) or whether she had something else in mind, like teaching me the finer points of some of her boss's fire-eating tricks. But I was a bit sleepy and I was prepared to take her word for it. In fact I didn't even give it much thought until the next day . . .

I should have known though that when I encountered her over the next day's dinner (the theatrical people slept in late so didn't join us for breakfast) it would be before a packed and appreciative audience.

She was blonde, 25-ish and quite nice looking in the sort of way that people are who appear in working men's clubs in Wales, and she fixed me with a mischievous look in her eye from the far side of the table. 'Was that your room I was in last night?' she asked.

I had to agree that, yes, it was; that, no, I hadn't minded being woken up; and that, yes, wasn't it a funny thing that she had mistaken my room on the first floor for hers on the second.

By now Pat was a major part of my life. It was too early to say we were in love, but we had certainly got past the stage of being casual boyfriend and girlfriend. So at every opportunity (which meant every weekend, and on some midweek evenings as well) I drove back across the Severn Bridge, from Cardiff to Bristol, to spend time with her. If we were lucky her days off coincided with mine, and she would usually come to spend the weekend with me at my parents' house, or I would go to hers in Leominster; if we weren't we would simply make the best of whatever time the Wick House curfew allowed us. She was beautiful and sexy (though she seemed not to know it, which, of course, just made her more so) and it wasn't just her sensational legs and short skirts that attracted admiring looks. One day, on a day out in Devon, we had to stop at traffic lights and a man got out of the car in front, walked back to us, stuck his head through the roof of my open-topped Triumph Herald convertible, looked her up and down, said 'Mmmm, not bad' and returned to his car in time for the lights to turn green.

She had an easygoing charm that enchanted anyone who met her and everyone seemed to like her – my friends at the *Mercury*, people from college, my family and total strangers she met when I took her with me when I was covering Saturday afternoon village fetes – and she seemed to like everyone in return. She was also, though I gave it little thought at the time, a perfect partner for a reporter. She seemed to have an intuitive understanding of what it was to be a journalist – the unconventional working hours and the not knowing where I was going to be from one day to the next – and didn't baulk when some unfortunate family lost everything but their budgie in their burning house and I dared to call it 'a good story'.

By the time my course came to an end I was supposedly ready for the Proficiency Test, for which my editor would enter me once I had completed my indentures. We knew, because our tutors told us often enough, that it wasn't the most difficult of examinations. All it required was a working knowledge of the law and local government, the skill to write a news story in simple and succinct English, the ability to write shorthand at at least 100 words a minute . . . and a dirty mind.

A dirty mind, we were told, was a vital gift for any journalist because double entendres were traps waiting for us around every corner and it was best not to have our readers sniggering at our innocence and naivete by writing, for example, of amateur musicians spending all day playing with their organs, schoolgirls being entered in dancing competitions or master craftsmen having the biggest tools in town. We were told to read and re-read everything we wrote – and then to read it again as if we were actors in a Carry On film. Only then should we consider it clean enough to be passed on to the sub editors.

For a bit of fun at the end of term we were encouraged to bring in from our own papers examples of stories – or, more usually, headlines – for which such basic rules had clearly been forgotten. I confidently submitted the headline from a *Mercury* story about a planning application for a block of flats in Weston's main shopping street – 'GIANT ERECTION IN THE HIGH STREET?' – and sat back certain that the prize for the rudest would be mine. Sadly it wasn't. I was trumped by Rosie, who triumphantly produced a headline which she swore had appeared in the Western Morning News above a tragic story of a young woman who died from septicaemia after falling into a gorse bush: 'BRIDE DIES FROM PRICK ON HONEYMOON'.

Back at Weston, with my training behind me, my indentures finished and my Proficiency Test passed, I knew it was time to move on. The *Mercury*, fun though it was, was no place to spend much more of my life. I had established that I enjoyed being a journalist, and was reasonably good at it, so I wanted to test myself on a bigger, more challenging paper. The usual choice for young *Mercury* reporters was one of the two daily newspapers in Bristol, the *Evening Post* or the *Western Daily Press*. It would obviously have been possible for any of us to apply for jobs anywhere else in the country – on daily papers in Coventry, Sheffield or Newcastle, for example – but what was the point when they were no better than the ones only a few miles up the road? For newly qualified journalists living in North Somerset, working in Bristol had two great advantages – we already knew the patch quite well and we could go on saving money by living at home (a major consideration, for journalism has always been a scandalously poorly paid profession in which many of the best practitioners are paid a good deal less than teachers, police officers or even nurses).

So I had a choice, and the obvious one was the *Evening Post*, a good, solid, dependable evening paper selling nearly 200,000 copies a night, whose editor, Gordon 'Fatty' Farnsworth, was known to be a pleasant and decent man who treated his staff so fairly that none of them had a bad word to say about him either while they were working for him or afterwards. The alternative was the *Western Daily Press*, about whose editor Eric Price there were many people who had much to say that was bad. Eric Price was famed as an arrogant and demanding – but inspirational – leader, who after working at the Daily Express under Arthur Christiansen, one of the giants of the newspaper industry, had brought his methods to the West Country to rejuvenate a newspaper which was fast slipping into terminal decline. The result was that this ailing old paper had been turned into the fastest growing regional newspaper of the time – a paper that, though selling only a relatively modest 80,000 copies a day, was recognised as one of the best in the business.

Price was an exceptional editor, but perhaps not always a very pleasant man, and the stories of how he treated his staff were legion. One which was going round at the time concerned a reporter who, after spending most of his day working on a story, had to watch while a furious Eric Price read it, rejected it as 'fucking rubbish', tore it into small pieces and threw it out of the first floor window so that it spiralled away in the breeze onto the street below. Only later, while watching the evening news on television, did Price discover that it had in fact been quite a good story – so he despatched the hapless reporter into the street to gather up the pieces of his previously unappreciated work.

I have no idea whether the story was true, but within a few weeks, after gaining first hand experience of the man, I was more than willing to accept that it might have been.

For some reason – confounding all those who believed that, given a choice, I would always opt for a quiet life – it was to Eric Price that I wrote asking for a job, knowing that a job on his paper was so highly sought after that he never had to stoop to advertising for staff.

He invited me in for an interview. I was terrified. I sat opposite the great man, as aware of his fearsome reputation as I was of the fact that if he could be persuaded to offer me a job it would be the making of me as a journalist. He studied my carefully crafted letter, made some comment about my working for the *Mercury* being 'a good start', then settled his eyes on my CV.

'Two maths fucking A-levels!' he exploded. 'What use is that? You're a journalist not a fucking accountant!'

I was dumbfounded, spluttered some sort of futile explanation and wished I could be magicked back to the gentlemanly John Bailey in the cosy confines of the *Mercury* office.

'Ha!' said Eric Price, grinning. 'So when can you start?'

So much for the gentlemanly John Bailey! He was livid when I told him I was leaving for the *Western Daily Press*. He took out on me all the years of frustration of seeing all his young protégés leaving him almost as soon as they had qualified. 'You're all the same,' he shouted (the first time in four years that he had lost his temper with me, though I had seen him do so many times with others). 'You let us train you and you let us pay to send you to college and then you repay us by walking out on us at the very first moment that you're able to. Whatever happened to loyalty?'

I gently thanked him for giving me my first break in journalism and for all he had done for me since, and told him I would be sorry to leave, but I reminded him that for the past four years I had been doing a damned good job for him and had never once complained that I was being paid only peanuts for the privilege. Now, I told him, I had the chance not just to work on one of the best regional newspapers in the country, but to be paid considerably more to do it. We parted on good terms as I knew we would, and he wished me well.

5

AT THE WESTERN DAILY PRESS they made no concessions to my inexperience. The news editor, Norman Rich, took the encouraging view that if Eric Price thought I was good enough to be given a job no further questions needed to be asked about my competence.

One day I'd be at the docks where the men were on strike over an unpopular sick pay scheme and the next I'd be talking to the manager of a schoolboys' football team who couldn't find any opponents to play against because they came from one of the roughest parts of town and nobody wanted to be on the same pitch as them; one day I'd be despatched to a suburb where vandals were throwing windfall apples at a courtyard of old people's bungalows (the council solved that by chopping the trees down) and the next I'd find myself talking to a teenaged mother who, though she had never smoked before, had become Bristol's champion pipe smoker by keeping a single bowlful of tobacco alight for an apparently praiseworthy 40 minutes and 20 seconds. Within a few weeks I returned to Burnham, where the government had decreed that a new county boundary should run right through the middle of the holiday camp's ballroom, and very soon was back in Weston too, where the council was threatening to shoot the pigeons that were attacking the holidaymakers on the prom.

The great joy of the job – and the great joy of journalism itself – was that one day was never like the one before.

Norman was as unalike Eric Price as it was possible to be. He was kindly and unflappable and blessed with an apparently unlimited patience which was quite unusual in a news editor; a lovely Yogi Bear of a man, not far short of retirement, whom it was impossible not to like. I did though have one minor concern: Although I believed he had confidence in me I was never quite sure why, when I asked if I could go for my mid-evening break, he replied, without fail: 'Yes please' as if he couldn't wait to be rid of me. It was, I think, either a rather feeble joke or a very clever way of worrying me just enough to make sure I didn't get complacent.

Norman was responsible for anything happening within the city boundary, while Peter Gibbs, his younger and more thrusting deputy, was in charge of the more rural parts of the circulation area. Between them they organised a department of 20 or so reporters – not counting those based in district offices in such places as Bath, Swindon, Trowbridge and Yeovil – all of whom seemed to enjoy the job as much as I did.

Because it was a morning paper we mostly arrived for work after lunch, by which time our *Evening Post* colleagues on the other side of the newsroom had already done most of their day's work. We continued until 10.30pm (or whenever our work was finished), with just a pint-and-meat-pie break in the firm's social club just around the corner half way through the evening. It was the social club, where we rubbed shoulders on a not-quite-equal basis with Eric Price and his senior executives, that reminded me how different life was from that which I had enjoyed at the *Mercury*. The very idea of a newspaper having its own social club was mightily impressive to a young man who had begun his career in a newsroom which did not even have a kettle with which we could make a cup of tea. It was a symbol that I had moved a few rungs up from the bottom of the ladder.

An opportunity to move a few rungs even further up arose very soon after I started, with the sort of story guaranteed to attract the appreciative attention of my new employers. The vicar of Redhill – an elderly man who had seen service as chaplain at Parkhurst prison on the Isle of Wight before moving into semi retirement and fully fledged alcoholism in Somerset – suddenly walked out on his wife to start a new life, or what in his drunken state was left of it, with the lady violinist who had been his girlfriend more than 40 years before. It was a cracking story, the sort certain to get big headlines in my new paper, and no doubt even bigger ones when followed up, as it was sure to be, in the *News of the World*. There were only two problems: First, the Rev John Hurford and his wife Sue were family friends; and, second, I couldn't help feeling that the pain that this decent couple were going through was their business and nobody else's. It was a hard decision because I knew that writing that story could make my name on the *Western Daily Press*, and I confess that I nearly did so. But in the end I decided to keep my mouth shut, so DRUNKEN VICAR RUNS

OFF WITH CHILDHOOD SWEETHEART was one headline that never saw the light of day.

It was not long before I was entrusted with working the late shift, starting at 5.30pm and going on to 1.30 the next morning, more than two hours after all the other reporters had gone home. I found it exciting starting work in the late afternoon, and driving into Bristol just as most people were driving out, even though in the summer I frequently had to make the journey through a maze of country lanes to avoid the nine-mile queue into the city on the A38 (the M5 motorway at that time was not even a twinkle in some traffic engineer's eye). I was often followed by two or three cars full of holidaymakers, to whom I offered my services as a guide when I saw them stationary at the end of our road. 'You have a choice,' I'd tell them, 'you can either sit in this queue for the next four hours or you can follow me and I'll get you into Bristol in 20 minutes.' Most viewed me with great suspicion and chose to sit in the queue, but a few of the more adventurous ones decided it was worth taking a risk even with someone as unsavoury-looking as I.

The late shift was my favourite. I loved arriving for work in Bristol at a time when most other people were going home, and setting off for home in the small hours of the morning when the streets were silent and deserted. It was (though I don't remember appreciating it at the time) quite a compliment that someone with so little experience was entrusted with such an important shift. Being late reporter meant that, from about 10.30pm, I was in sole charge of news coverage of this, one of the country's most prestigious newspapers, and there was no one to shield me from the excesses of the irascible Eric who was leading his team of subs on the floor below.

Anything that happened late at night, anywhere in our huge circulation area from Gloucester to Exeter, and from Hereford to Weymouth, was down to me. My evenings were spent making the 'calls' – ringing round all the area's major police, fire and ambulance stations every hour – and following up any incidents revealed by them. So I found myself talking to a woman cashier at a local cinema who had just been robbed by a man armed with a revolver, trying to piece together a story of a huge fire at a plastics factory and writing about a sailor who had gone missing after setting off from Bristol in a small boat – a worrying one, that, since the sailor in question was our own business editor (he later turned up safe and well in a Somerset pub, unaware of the lifeboats and helicopters searching for him).

It was not always so exciting, of course. Although I had learned the basic rule of doing the calls – if you simply asked 'Is anything happening?' you invited the answer 'No'; but if you invented some imaginary incident and asked 'What's all this about a pile-up on the A38 at Highbridge?' it at least made them open the incident report book to check – the plain fact was that on some nights simply nothing happened. On those nights I busied myself drinking coffee from the office hot drinks machine, writing love letters to Pat and hoping that Eric Price would not come upstairs demanding to know why I was providing him with so little news.

Occasionally he did come up. Once when a fellow reporter had come back late from an important council meeting and was trying to bash out an urgent story for the front page whose deadline was but minutes away, Eric appeared in the newsroom, storm-faced, and stood over the wretched man, leaning on his desk as he desperately tried to type out his story. He said nothing, but expressed his impatience by noisily kicking the side of his metal desk before snatching the first sheet of paper from the typewriter mid sentence. He took the paper to the subs downstairs but was back within minutes for the second sheet, again kicking the desk and again looking with disgust at the unfortunate reporter. He snatched the paper . . . and the reporter fell from his chair onto his knees on the floor, sobbing quietly. Eric stepped over him, walked back to the subs' desk without a word and left me to look after my broken colleague.

As reporters we didn't see much of Eric (I was encouraged to call him by his first name, although he referred to me as 'Mr Harris') so we were not as aware of his threatening presence as were the subs downstairs, who worked much more closely with him. The trouble is, it wasn't long before I was one of them.

'Mr Harris?' said the booming voice on my phone.

'Yes, that's me.'

'Come down here, you're a sub editor.'

'Pardon?'

'This is Eric Price. You're a sub.'

'Oh hello, Eric. No, don't you remember? You took me on a few weeks ago. I'm a reporter, not a sub.'

'No, you're a sub. You were a reporter. Now you're a fucking sub. Now come down here.'

I went, and discovered that Eric had that night sacked a sub for some perceived incompetence, only to discover that he then did not have enough to get the next edition out. So he found himself another one – me. It soon became clear to both of us that I was not cut out to be a sub editor. The first story I worked on, a nib (news in brief), was of a ten-year-old boy hit by a bus. My headline said: 'BOY, 9, HURT'.

I found no pleasure in being a sub. After so long enjoying the variety and freedom of being a reporter, the idea of being chained to a desk correcting other people's copy did not appeal to me one bit. And being one of Eric's subs, working in silence among a group of unhappy-looking men, one of whom was a grandfather-type whose sole function appeared to be to act as a target for the editor's paperclip-throwing, looked like having no perks at all.

Fortunately Eric saw that I was never going to make it and, after a fortnight, sent me back whence I had come. When I walked upstairs and re-entered the newsroom the first face I saw was Norman's. I could have kissed him.

It was my good fortune that these early days of my career were at a time when newspaper owners set great store by the quality of their journalism, and invested in it accordingly. Or, to put it another way, it was before newspapers were taken over by a new breed of accountants and hard-headed businessmen, most of whom saw journalists as being responsible only for a negative figure on their balance sheets. It would not be long before newspaper managements, in their enthusiasm to reduce costs, decided it was a good idea to cut back on the one department which, as they saw it, was nothing more than a needless drain on their resources. In their book it made great sense: Journalists cost money and contribute nothing to the bottom line, so get rid of as many of them as possible and pay the ones who remain as little as you can get away with because if they don't like it there are plenty of others who will; marketing people sell lots of advertising and are solely responsible for any profits that are made, so take on more and more of them on contracts loaded with bonuses and annual incentive payments. It apparently never enters their heads that while casual purchasers of a newspaper might occasionally buy it because of the advertisements they hope to find in it, most committed regular readers buy it for the strength and variety of the editorial it contains. Nor do they ever consider that those regular readers might just be deterred by the fact that the quality of the news coverage suffers if there are fewer journalists to gather it, process it and present it on the page.

Fortunately my time on the *Western Daily Press* coincided with a healthy investment in editorial. We were encouraged to go out looking for news, just as we had been on the *Mercury*, and enough of us were employed to enable us to do that job in the way we had been trained to.

I had been at Bristol for only a few months when Peter Gibbs called me over and told me he had a special assignment for me. My job would be to spend a week in Dorchester, the county town of Dorset, where I was to find at least three stories a day during a promotional push to improve the paper's circulation there. He gave me few clues how this was to be done, or where I should look for news in a town I had never even passed through before. But it was the sort of challenge I enjoyed and I had a rough idea of how to go about it – I had, after all, done much the same sort of thing with some success in Burnham-on-Sea (only this time I wouldn't be looking for a girlfriend).

The doubts set in when I arrived in Dorchester. It was a pretty town of picturesque ancient buildings, with an attractive sloping main street in which were found a museum, a historic courthouse and – in the days before chain stores took over every high street – an interesting array of little shops, but what it did not have, as far as I could tell, was anything whatsoever happening. I drove down the main street and up again, and twice around the road that served as a ring road and my spirits sank as I looked in vain for something – anything – that might be newsworthy. Three stories a day? I'd be lucky to find one in the whole week!

It was on my third lap of the town, as I looked for somewhere to park my car, that I spotted a small industrial estate and, standing incongruously next to it, a row of well cared-for little cottages. In desperation I parked my car, walked to the first of the cottages and knocked on the door – all almost before I had decided why I was doing it. An old lady with a round face and hair tied back in a bun came to the door, smiling and wiping her hands on a pink floral apron. I told her who I was and that I hoped I wasn't disturbing her.

'I hear you've been complaining about the noise from the factories,' I said with as much confidence as I could attach to something that had no basis whatsoever in any kind of truth.

'Oh no, my lovely,' she replied in a thick clotted cream accent. 'Somebody's told you wrong. It's not the noise. It's the smell.'

And so the first of my stories from Dorchester that week was of a group of mostly elderly residents, living in a row cottages which had stood for centuries, who were now complaining about the smell from one of the factories on the new industrial estate which had been built far too close to their homes.

The Accidental Editor

That gave me the confidence to tackle my special assignment with an enthusiasm that must have impressed my masters back in Bristol. I found that the local grammar school had taken possession of a live 4ft crocodile to help the children in their biology lessons, that a mother whose ten-year-old daughter had been knocked down by a car was campaigning for extra road safety measures outside her school, that people on a housing estate were having to walk a mile to the shops because the council was too mean to tarmac the muddy path they wanted to use as a shortcut, that the museum was having to keep most of its best exhibits in cardboard boxes because there wasn't room to display them to the public . . . and every day there were all the usual fires, road accidents and minor crimes that routinely provided newspapers like the *Western Daily Press* with so much of their news.

I returned to Bristol feeling I had done a pretty good (and an enormously enjoyable) job, though I did not expect much in the way of praise from my notoriously hard-to-please superiors. However I had reckoned without one of the qualities that made Eric Price such a good editor. He was not, after all, just a blustering bully who reckoned he could get the best out of his staff by making them fear that they were forever only one mistake away from the sack; he tempered that with a surprisingly human, almost fatherly, side to his nature which in this case meant a few muttered words of thanks for the job I had done.

A few of weeks later I was sent away again – this time to Lyme Regis, a gorgeous little Dorset seaside town, with a quaint harbour and beach nestling under huge fossil-encrusted cliffs. Compared with Dorchester, working in Lyme Regis was easy. Because of its very nature – a small seaside resort with a bit of fishing thrown in – it was much easier to identify the people I needed to get to know. So it was to the boss of the fishing fleet, the owners of the fossil shop, the skippers of the pleasure boats, the secretary of the local hospitality group and the chairman of the council's tourism committee that I turned, and they – flattered, just as the people of Burnham had been, by the appearance in their community of a reporter whose newspaper was clearly interested in their activities – provided me with an impressive supply of news stories which, at the end of every day, I dictated to the copytakers in head office from the phone box beside the picturesque little harbour. Was there anywhere better to spend a week in high summer, being paid to do a job I loved?

I never found out whether I was sent to Dorchester and Lyme Regis because the news desk had by then decided I was the best man for the job, or whether it was just a way for them to find out if I was up to working in a strange town on my own initiative. Whichever it was, the result was the same.

Eric Price called me to his office – the first time I had been in it since my interview – and I could not work out what I had done to warrant my dismissal. I thought I had been doing rather well, and as far as I was aware had not committed any outrageous mistakes or landed the paper with any libel suits or summonses for contempt of court, but there was clearly something . . .

'We need a man in Yeovil,' he said. 'Would you like it?'

I knew where Yeovil was – on the road to both Dorchester and Lyme Regis, for a start – and that it was a busy and fast-expanding industrial town, that it was set among lovely countryside and picturesque villages, and that it was where Yeovil Town FC, then England's top non-league football team, played on a famous sloping pitch. I also knew that of all the company's district offices Yeovil was one of the plum ones in which to work, perhaps second only to Bath.

'To work with Jeff Berliner?' I asked, knowing he was the *Western Daily Press*'s very experienced and highly regarded reporter there.

'No,' he said. 'Instead of. He's leaving. Got some fucking PR job with the police. So it would be just you. Do you want it?'

'If you think I'm up to it.'

'I wouldn't have fucking asked you if I didn't.'

6

BRISTOL UNITED PRESS'S office in Yeovil was in a seedy-looking building next to a pub in an unattractive street just off the town's main shopping quarter. Downstairs was the distribution area, run by office manager Ken Andrews and his wife Betty, to which copies of the *Western Daily Press* and *Evening Post* were brought by van from Bristol before being delivered to all the local newsagents; upstairs was where I was based, alongside Trevor Kavanagh, the *Post*'s reporter, and Eddie Wood, a photographer shared by the two newspapers.

We were an unlikely trio. Trevor was a rather serious man, a few years older than me, already blessed with a wife and a couple of children, and displaying none of the qualities that would one day make him one of the most influential and highly regarded journalists in the country as political editor of *The Sun*. Eddie was a good humoured Geordie, in his fifties, who had worked as a news photographer for so long, under so many editors and with so many reporters, that he could have done my job just as well as I hoped to do it myself. The three of us worked well together, though we never became especially close. Colleagues rather than friends.

My contact with Peter Gibbs on the newsdesk in Bristol was at best sporadic. Early every afternoon I would let him know of the stories I was working on – something I did on the phone if I had some good stuff to offer him or by sending him a message on the huge teleprinter in the corner of the office if I hadn't and wanted to avoid listening to his facetious comments about the paucity of my news-gathering talent.

The teleprinter was a magnificent machine which sat inside a plywood box like an enormous typewriter salvaged from an industrial museum. Its keys were so big and stiff it needed a real effort to type on them, the manual equivalent of walking through a muddy field in ill-fitting wellies, and it was, I thought, potentially very dangerous. Your pounding fingers could easily slip into the gaps between the keys, and if they did there was a very real chance that they could twist and break (something I managed to avoid, although on several occasions I went home nursing sore fingertips). In those days, long before the invention of computers and e-mails, the teleprinter was the only way of sending our copy to the news desk unless we chose to go to the trouble of phoning our stories over to the grumpy copytakers, which we rarely did because they were never glad to hear from us and always asked: 'What's up with the printer today, then?'

My contact with Eric Price was even more infrequent. He was not normally the sort of editor who would phone with praise for a good story – just damnation for a bad one. 'Mr Harris? No fucking by-lines for a week,' he would say, usually in the small hours of the morning after the first edition that he had just produced was found to contain a story of mine which he felt was badly written, incomplete or just plain boring (or, on a particularly bad day, all three).

He imposed strict rules on grammar and punctuation and more than once phoned me in the middle of the night to complain about a poorly placed comma or a mis-spelled village name. It was he who taught me most of the rules of writing which have stayed with me, to the point of pedantry, ever since: 'Over means above or physically higher than, so if there are 14 apples there are more than, not over, a dozen fucking apples,' he would say. Or: 'Fewer is for numbers and less is for amounts – so it's fewer people eating less cake, fewer cars using less petrol or fewer editors causing less fucking fuss.' And it wasn't just for the rules of English grammar that he was a stickler. Woe betide anyone who adopted the modern style of referring to a senior councillor as a piece of furniture. 'A chair is something with four legs and it's usually made of fucking wood,' he would thunder. 'If you mean chairman say so.' And any reporter daft enough to describe a local celebrity as 'well known' could expect the same: 'If you need to tell people that someone is well-known he is not, so you fucking shouldn't.'

It was noticeable though that – after insisting that councils, clubs or schools were singular entities and should therefore attract verbs and pronouns in the singular (as in 'Yeovil Town Council is increasing its rates') – he fell remarkably silent on the subject when it came to pop groups and football clubs. 'The Beatles is at No. 1' is clearly absurd, for example, and 'Bristol City is winning 6-0' sounds just plain wrong, and not just because they (or, indeed, it) rarely achieved such a feat.

Quite when I realised I was in love with Pat I don't know. But certainly by the time I moved to Yeovil she had become such a joyous fixture in my life I could not envisage any kind of future without her. She was the missing piece that completed the jigsaw of my life. I felt incomplete without her and wanted to be with her all the time (something I made a good stab at achieving, despite the fact that I was working strange hours in Yeovil and she was working equally strange hours at college 40 miles away in Bristol).

On her 22nd birthday, March 21 1972, I asked her to marry me. We spent the day on Exmoor and I might have proposed to her there had my insides not been turned to jelly by the knowledge of what I had decided to do. Instead, we had reached almost the end of the day and we were nearly back in Bristol . . . and, though I thought I knew what her answer would be, I had still not summoned up the courage to ask her. But then, in my car parked on the shores of Chew Valley Lake, one of Somerset's most romantic beauty spots, with the sun going down and the birds swinging in to their night-time roosts, she snuggled up to me and told me, not for the first time, that she would always love me. I seized my chance.

'Does that mean you'll marry me?'

'Yes,' she said (and it was only later that I discovered she wasn't quite sure what I'd asked her but, hoping it was some kind of proposal, said 'Yes' just in case).

I kissed her and gave her an engagement ring on the spot. It was made from an old piece of silver paper salvaged from the remains of a chocolate bar that I found in the ash tray.

We had no immediate plans of when to get married – apart from the sooner the better – or of where to live after we had done so. It was obvious, though, that I would probably have to move from Yeovil, partly because I didn't want to start married life working the evening shifts of a morning paper, and partly because we wanted a home of our own and the price of even the cheapest houses in Somerset was well beyond what a reporter could afford. For now though we were happy to continue as we were, enjoying the thought of our futures together and confident that whatever happened, and where, we would be happy. And anyway, I would enjoy my time in Yeovil until something better came along.

My patch was much more interesting than Trevor's. His was firmly based in Yeovil and the villages in the immediate vicinity. Mine extended much further, and took in the whole of South Somerset, not to mention the Dorset towns of Sherborne, Shaftesbury and Blandford Forum, the coast around Charmouth and Lyme Regis, and enough of South Devon to include a little village called Tipton St John, near Sidmouth, which had nothing special about it except that it was where I was born. To get around in this huge area I was given my first company car (a bright red Mini), which was quite soon replaced by a mustard-coloured Mini Clubman – a bit nippier and slightly more comfortable but still pretty cramped for a 6ft 1in man and his 5ft 10in girlfriend. It was a beautiful part of the world to work in, so I tried never to do anything over the phone which I could do by driving to do it in person instead.

Yeovil was a wonderfully newsy town, which made it no great challenge to a reporter (either that, or I was very lucky or hugely talented).

A tearful husband came into my office, for example, asking if I could help him find somewhere to live because, after giving up his job (and therefore his tied cottage) on an isolated farm for the sake of his wife who was so lonely there, he now had nowhere to go with her and their three children. A vicar told me he had been asked to exorcise a house where a young wife was being worried by ghostly noises in the attic while her husband was out – only to discover, after his particularly macabre death, that the noises had been made by the husband as he pleasured himself in a rather strange solo sexual practice involving the ropes and pulleys that eventually slipped and strangled him. Brave men were always, it seemed, jumping into swollen rivers to rescue people from crashed cars, running into burning houses to drag the helpless occupants from the flames or chasing robbers down the street on bicycles, and on one memorable day I arrived for work to discover that a ton of rubble had crashed through our own office roof thanks to a team of incompetent demolition workers on an adjoining site who sent a 20ft high wall tumbling the wrong way.

Sometimes of course news just did not happen and I would sit in the office wondering what on earth I was going to do to satisfy the news desk's three-stories-a-day requirement. Thank goodness, then, for village by-passes! I learned early on that in any village with a main road running through it (and there were many of them in my patch) you would find an action group campaigning for a by-pass and only too keen to talk about it to their local newspaper; and in any village which once but no longer had a main road running through it, you would find at least one shopkeeper complaining how he was about to go out of business because the new by-pass had taken away all the trade he had depended upon.

While I liked the buzz of big hard news stories I also enjoyed the challenge of the sort of softer stories which are often referred to as 'human interest'. The *Western Daily Press* had an excellent outlet for such stories, a daily column called Mr West's Diary, to which all of us were expected to contribute once or twice a week. I was happy to do my bit.

It was here that I was able to place my stories about some of the endlessly interesting people who helped make the community what it was – clever, colourful, lively, busy and sometimes just plain weird people.

The place was awash with such people if you took the trouble to look. There was a painter called John Bell, for example, whom I almost literally stumbled across while on a walk in the woods where he had been living rough for three years, ever since giving up a high pressure job in the City. 'I suddenly realised that painting was more important to me than anything else in my life,' he told me from the engine-less remains of the old van which he called his home.

There was a delightful man who came back to the village where he was remembered only as the lad who had once delivered their milk, and who didn't mind at all that his former customers now, in insisting that he join them for a pint or two down the pub every night, made no allowances for the fact that in his 20 years away he had risen to a new job as the Bishop of Paraguay and North Argentina.

There was the musician who was eking out a living from making dulcimers in his garden shed and the titled lady who let a passing tramp sleep in her garage, while providing him with blankets and regular cups of tea to make his stay more comfortable.

There was the choirmaster who bought one church's scrap organ for next to nothing, and spent three years renovating it before installing it amid much ballyhoo in his own. And best of all there was the Rev Dougie White who found love for the first time at the age of 65 and never tired of telling me how wonderful was this new thing called sex that he had discovered and how it was a mystery to him how he had managed to live without it for so long. As if to emphasise the point, his 25-year-old wife (one of his ex choirgirls) presented him with a daughter on their first wedding anniversary and he sped to the maternity hospital in his 100mph bright red sports car to share a piece of their wedding cake.

The chance to get to know such people is the joy of being a journalist.

I do not claim to have been an outstandingly good reporter. Good reporters – and I have seen a few of them, and been in awe of every one

– are those who can walk through a town and be greeted on every corner by someone who calls out their name, either to pass the time of day or, just as often, to give them a story. I never worked hard or long enough to develop those sort of contacts, and relied instead on half a dozen trusted people whom I got to know very well, and who in turn seemed to know enough of everyone else's business to keep me reasonably well informed of what was happening around the town.

What I did have, I like to think, was an impressive news sense, so that I could spot a potential story and develop it even before some of my colleagues and/or rivals knew it was there. One such was the ancient privy.

All of us are taught to read through the piles of local council minutes which are routinely delivered to every newspaper office, just in case, somewhere lurking deep inside, is an idea for a story slightly more interesting and out of the ordinary than a retired gentleman wanting to build a conservatory on the back of his house. All of us are taught to do it, but very few of us ever do. But on one quiet afternoon when the teeming rain made the idea of actually walking round the town looking for news particularly unappealing, I found myself skimming through the committee agendas which had arrived through the post that day. It was a mind-numbing job, but on about page 96 I saw that a couple from a village just a couple of miles outside Yeovil were asking for a council grant to help them renovate an old outdoor lavatory they had discovered while cutting back the brambles at the bottom of their garden.

To call it a lavatory was, as I discovered when I went to see it the next day, doing it something of a disservice. It was a splendid example of a 300-year-old stone-built privy, with five seats side-by-side so that mum and dad and three kids could all crap together in a bizarre example of a family outing. And, better than that, the couple who owned it, and who needed public money to restore it, were a delightful pair, a surgeon and his wife, who only too readily appreciated not just the absurdity of it all, but also why a reporter from the local paper was so interested in it. With their help I kept the story running for weeks, especially when they took up my suggestion that, since it was now being part-funded by the ratepayers, they should have an official opening, decorate it with bunting and invite the public in to have their photographs taken while sitting on it.

I was busy in the office one evening writing the latest instalment of my privy saga when the phone rang. Unusually, it was Peter Gibbs. 'Have you heard about the murder in Yeovil?'

That was a difficult question to answer because I was, after all, the man on the spot and I would have heard about it if I had been doing the routine calls to the emergency services as I should have been. But there was no point in lying, and anyway I reckoned my reputation was just about good enough to bear one such mistake.

'Er no,' I admitted. 'Where?'

'It's in a pub somewhere. Called the White Hart. Do you know it?'

'Er yes, I think so,' I told him, picking up the phone and walking with it towards the window overlooking the street, where not even I could now fail to notice the ambulance and three police cars which were parked, with their blue lights flashing, in haphazard fashion outside the pub next door. 'I think I know where it is. I'll get onto it straightaway.'

An hour later (if I had taken any less time he might have realised that the pub with the 'murder' was much nearer than I was prepared to admit) I was able to phone Peter and tell him that I had been there and established it was in fact not a murder, but a particularly nasty stabbing, and that the victim was in hospital and his attacker was under arrest so, because of the sub judice laws which restrict what can be reported once a suspect is in the hands of the police, there wasn't really very much we could publish.

'Good work,' he said.

At three minutes to eight on the morning of Wednesday July 5 1972 I was awoken by a pounding on my bedroom door. June Knight, the rather fierce middle-aged spinster who had taken me in as a lodger, had come with a cup of tea – an unheard-of occurrence, not least because I usually liked to sleep well past the time that she left the house for her job with the local council.

'You'd better wake up and listen to the radio news,' she said. 'There's been a fire.'

I did as I was told.

The fire was the main item on the BBC's national news: 'At least six patients have died in a fire at a psychiatric hospital in Dorset. The fire broke out shortly after 2am in a ward at Coldharbour Hospital in Sherborne. Firemen are still at the scene and it is feared more bodies might be found as they sift through the wreckage.'

I was there within an hour and the scene that greeted me was as near to hell as I ever want to get.

Thin wisps of smoke still coiled slowly into the sky but the hospital itself did not seem too badly damaged, not if you disregarded the small sections of roof that had caved in and the blackened bricks where the smoke had found a way out through the windows smashed by the heat. But the expressions on the faces of the firemen, and the nurses who gathered in small tearful groups beside the snaking hoses, and the dreadful smell – all these told their own story. Firemen were working there still, but they seemed to be doing it without making a sound, as if in deference to what had happened. It was the silence that was the most horrifying thing of all.

A small knot of reporters whom I had met before – from the local weekly papers, and regional TV and radio stations – were already there and I was relieved to be able to join them. As the morning went on we were joined by a posse of men from the national newspapers, and by reporters I had only previously seen on the BBC and ITN national news, and I was appalled by the callousness and sick humour they brought to the job (it took just a few hours for me to discover that it was their way of dealing with something that was too unspeakable to deal with in any other way, and by the end of the day I found to my dismay that my humour had become just as sick as theirs).

There was no hastily convened media centre, as there would be today, and no hospital press officer or PR executive from the health authority. Just a few shattered hospital staff doing their best to cope with something for which even their worst nightmares had not prepared them.

Some of them brought us coffee in cardboard mugs, and told us 'Six so far' when we asked how many patients had died. Halfway through the morning a furniture removal van drove slowly up the hospital's main drive and pulled to a stop beside the fire engines, and when they opened the doors at the back we saw that it was loaded with empty coffins. And there were many more than six.

There are times when a reporter can only stand and watch and feel guilty for not being able to do something more useful, so we stood and watched and counted as the bodies were brought out and placed into the waiting coffins which were then re-stacked inside the van. Seven, eight, nine . . . Fourteen, fifteen . . . Twenty-two, twenty-three. Christ! The dreadful counting lasted all morning and into the afternoon and, by the time we had finished and the firemen were satisfied there were no more, we had reached thirty.

Thirty men, helpless men with various levels of mental handicap, had died that night, probably behind doors locked for their own 'safety', and as we tried to make sense of what we were witnessing we looked for someone to blame. The fire brigade for not responding quickly enough? The Government for starving hospitals like this of the money they so badly needed? The hospital authorities for not installing sprinklers and smoke alarms? The staff for not being sufficiently watchful . . .?

And then we discovered that there had been just one nurse on duty in the ward when the fire broke out and the rumour went round that he had been outside, having an unofficial smoking break. The poor man! The national paper reporters in particular needed a scapegoat and they had found him. Or, at least, they had found out about him. Actually finding him was proving much more difficult, for the hospital managers were very sensibly refusing to give us his name, say where he was or even confirm that he might have had something to do with how the fire had started. The national reporters pleaded, bullied and tried to bribe, but the hospital stood firm and it was clear that the unfortunate nurse was not going to be produced to them like some animal on its way to the sacrifice.

So I decided I'd had enough. I had spent all day there, my notebook was overflowing with so much information there was not a newspaper in the world big enough to print it all and I was sickened and tired by what I had seen. I rang Peter Gibbs and told him that I felt there was no point staying any longer, phoned my story to the copytakers from a phone box near the hospital's main gate, got into my car and headed for home. At the last minute I decided to take the scenic route – along some of the loveliest of the lovely country lanes that link the pretty villages around Sherborne – because after such a day I needed something to remind myself that, for all its pain and tragedy, there was still great beauty and peacefulness in the world. As I indicated to take the turning to the left I looked in my mirror and saw a convoy of four or five cars all doing the same. The hacks from the nationals had seen me leaving and were following me, thinking that as a local reporter I had found out where the 'guilty' nurse lived and was on my way to talk to him. They thought I would lead them to him but they were wrong. I led them to my home.

A month later the nurse was in the congregation for the memorial service but nobody wanted to talk to him by then because it had been established that he was not to blame, that the fire had been started by one of the patients failing to stub out a surreptitious cigarette in the middle of the night. The magnificent and ancient Sherborne Abbey was packed with a congregation that included national politicians, local councillors, health administrators, nurses, relatives of the dead, people from the town, uniformed representatives of the emergency services and not half as many reporters as had been at the scene of the fire. And right at the back, as if hidden out of harm's way, were about a hundred patients from the hospital, some of whom had been in the stricken ward but had survived.

It was a stiff and formal service, the sort of thing the English church thinks it is rather good at, but which so often is curiously devoid of emotion, but then came the last hymn, Kumbaya – chosen because it was the only one that the patients knew and could sing. As we reached the second verse an astonishing deep roar came from those dozen or so pews at the back of the abbey. It was out of tune, and several beats behind the melody being played on the organ, but those men at the back, handicapped as they were, had at last recognised something that they could sing and they were singing it for all they were worth, as if in tribute to the friends who had not made it through that terrible night. The rest of the congregation stopped singing and let those poor, tuneless, desolate men have the moment to themselves. It might have been because we sensed it was the right thing to do, but I suspect it was, more likely, that with the hairs prickling on the backs of our necks, the lumps in our throats would have made it impossible to sing even if we'd wanted to.

Occasionally the outside world contrived to intrude on life in South Somerset, and I found myself having to react to stories of international significance. For example, when General Idi Amin, reviled president of Uganda, took control of British interests in his country and kicked out thousands of Asian workers, several hundred of them were sent as refugees to a disused military base a few miles from Yeovil. The council officer given the job of preparing for their arrival was a likeable man with, not surprisingly, no experience to qualify him for such a task. He set to work, enjoying the challenge of such an unlikely assignment, and, working virtually round the clock, managed to get the camp cleaned, repaired and painted with about a day to spare. Just one thing, I remember, defeated him: While he had managed to find ready supplies of clothes, food and bedding, he had no idea whatsoever where he could obtain the 50,000 condoms the Government had assured him would be needed.

On another occasion I had to delay my regular Thursday night visit to the Sherborne folk club to call in on a man whose son, according to the Press Association news agency, had been taken hostage in the Middle East. He was a widower, a man in his late seventies, whose upright stature and impeccable politeness was evidence of the many years he had spent as a high ranking army officer. He invited me in, and insisted I had a gin and tonic, and told me he was so proud of his son he was always happy to talk about him, even to strangers like me. He was a lovely old man but as our conversation progressed I realised he had not understood why I was there. Worse than that, he had no idea that the son of whom he was so proud was in any sort of trouble.

So how do you tell an old man, living alone and with not a care in the world, that his only son is at that moment in the hands of armed terrorists so unpredictable they might choose to kill him at any time? The answer is that you don't. Or rather, more accurately, I didn't. I simply suggested that he might like to ring the Foreign Office, and tried very hard to do so without causing him too much alarm. And then I wished him luck, said goodbye and drove away cursing the incompetence of any government that could tell a news agency that an oil worker's life was in danger but not take the trouble to tell the man's father first.

Yeovil's own local paper, the *Western Gazette*, provided a comprehensive local news service, but even reporters from that excellent organ sometimes missed angles to stories which deserved to be more fully explored. So I followed up its stories, just as reporters from the national papers frequently followed up mine. That's the way newspapers work – big fish feeding on medium-sized ones, which have already fed on small ones.

On my desk I had a box file full of cuttings taken from the local papers, all of which I intended to follow up sometime when I was not too busy. This had its dangers, and sometimes I got caught out, and found that I had left it so long that the story had been overtaken by events.

In August 1972, for example, the *Western Gazette* had a story of a local musician who had just spent a week in London after winning a recording contract. I tore the cutting out, put it in my file and made a mental note to get in touch with him sometime when I fancied a trip out to Shaftesbury, where he lived. His name was Peter Skellern and by the time I got round to seeing him his record was high in the pop charts and he had become one of the most sought-after singers in the land. Eddie and I went to his house, where his wife made us tea and he played us not just his hit (*You're A Lady*, a plaintive love song accompanied by Peter's piano and a brass band, was one of the most distinctive records of the early '70s) but also the planned follow-up, of which he wanted our opinion. As Eddie and I heard *Our Jackie's Getting Married* our eyes met and it was clear we both felt the same: It was dreadful! It was a jaunty little number, sung in the broad accent of

Skellern's native Lancashire, but it had none of the charm of its predecessor and stood absolutely no chance of being bought in enough numbers even to make the lower reaches of the pop charts.

'What do you think?' he asked.

'Er . . . it's different,' I said.

'Yes, different,' said Eddie, for once stuck for words.

Skellern looked at us with a smile and pressed us no further. I thought then, and I have become more certain since, that, with *You're A Lady* having done its job by bringing him to national attention, he did not give a damn whether he ever had another hit record (he had a couple, as a matter of fact, but *Our Jackie's Getting Married* wasn't one of them). He had his future musical career already mapped out and none of it depended on getting into the charts ever again.

Jim and Gladys Rowswell were a couple who gave me what turned out to be one of my most problematic assignments. They were a delightful old couple, he 70 and she 68, who lived in a small village near Crewkerne and had done so, in the same house, for 44 years.

The trouble was that their home was a large detached council house and they were using only one of its three bedrooms at a time when there were countless young couples with two or three children who could not be found a council house at all. The solution adopted by Chard Rural District Council was to ask the Rowswells to move into a smaller house, allowing one of the homeless families to move into theirs. And – worse – when the old couple refused to leave the house which had been their home for all their married life, the council saw fit to begin legal proceedings to evict them.

It didn't require much effort to get the right sort of tear-jerking quotes from them – 'A good home is all we have lived for, and all we want is to be allowed to die here,' said Gladys – and it required none at all to feel desperately sorry for them. And yet . . . And yet I couldn't help feeling that, though it had approached the problem in a particularly brutal and hamfisted manner, the council was justified in what it was trying to do. How could it be right for a couple and their three children to have to be put up in a cheap and unsuitable bed-and-breakfast because the house that would have been ideal for them was being occupied by two stubborn old people who needed only a fraction of it?

A bit of sympathy from the council, a more compassionate approach and the right person being sent to talk to them over a cup of tea, would, I was convinced, have persuaded the old couple to agree to move – and to move quite happily, what's more – but because of its heavy-handed tactics the Rowswells dug their heels in . . . and became a cause celebre that attracted the attention of Eric Price.

My own feelings did not matter, and anyway even I could see that, justified or not, the council had presented me with a great story. Eric went further, and started a campaign to get the council to change its mind, demanding from me a new story every day (always heavily slanted in the Rowswells' favour) which was backed up with regular condemnation in his leader column.

In particular he turned his attention to council chairman Nora Davies, a small-time local politician who was totally unequipped to deal with such a situation. In my view, Mrs Davies, whom I got to know quite well, was doing her best in very difficult circumstances and her only failing was that she lacked the steel to stand up to the council officers who were advising her so badly. In Eric's view, it was purely Mrs Davies' intransigence that was the cause of all the trouble and he took every opportunity to tell her so. Imagine how delighted he was when I discovered that her family owned a stall which sold fruit and vegetables to passing holidaymakers from a lay-by on one of the main roads to the far westcountry and that – even better – it was rumoured to be operating without planning permission! Eric was going to skewer her, well and truly, and she would have no choice but to rescind the Rowswells' eviction notice (no, I couldn't see the connection either, but he was convinced that the one would follow the other). I went to the lay-by and found the stall, but was frustrated to find that it was Mrs Davies's son selling the potatoes, onions and tomatoes, not the lady herself. And, according to him, although the stall was undeniably owned by the Davies family, in reality he ran it himself and his mother had something even less than a passing interest in it. Eddie Wood took a photograph (if only to prove to Eric that we had indeed been there) and we returned to the office with the bad news.

That, we thought, was that. But the next day the *Western Daily Press* published Eddie's photograph of the Davies family's fruit and veg stall – with Mrs Davies superimposed on it, as if she had been there when we called. I could only shake my head sadly, disappointed that an editor for whom I had such high regard could stoop to such tactics, but when I had calmed down enough to express my feelings to Peter Gibbs I didn't need him to tell me that the mighty Eric would not lose much sleep over my discomfiture.

But still the campaign went on, and still the council proceeded with its plans for the old couple's eviction, every step of which I reported in great detail while feeling growing sympathy for the council in general, and Mrs Davies in particular, in the face of Eric's increasingly personal attacks.

I was there the day the Rowswells accepted defeat and moved out of their house – and I was there to welcome them into their new home, a smart little old folk's bungalow a quarter of a mile down the road. I had great pleasure that day filing a story in which I quoted a delighted Gladys saying: 'I think I shall like it here after all. Once we settle in it will be quite pleasant.' After all the huge front page headlines of his vitriolic and ultimately unsuccessful campaign Eric gave my happy ending to the saga just a small single column headline on an inside page.

By now Pat and I were more convinced than ever that our future together lay in some place other than hideously expensive Somerset, and I even came to accept that it might have to be in the north of England, which to me meant somewhere north of Gloucester. Although, after being born in my grandparents' house in Devon I had spent the first four years of my life in Birmingham, I had never ventured any further north, even on holiday. So to further my education Pat – whose family had originally come from the North-East – took me to stay with one of her aunts in Durham, where I was surprised to find that the lovely countryside had not been lost beneath one almighty slag heap, and we even spent a fortnight on a camping holiday in Scotland which opened my eyes to the beauty to be found in the far north of these islands (and, probably more importantly, allowed me time to grow the beard which I have never shaved off since).

By now, also, Pat had qualified as a nursery nurse, left Wick House and, after three weeks looking after the new-born son of an elderly colonel and his wife in the New Forest, found a job as nanny with a barrister couple who lived in a sumptuous old world cottage in Compton Martin – the north Somerset village which by coincidence boasted what had long been our favourite pub. Simon and Sue Darwall-Smith (who both went on to become judges) were excellent employers who paid Pat quite well, provided her with a car and tried to allow her whatever time off from looking after baby Belinda that she needed to coincide with mine.

We made sure the Darwall-Smiths knew that Pat was not likely to be their nanny for long, and I studied the job advertisements in the *UK Press Gazette* every week with great interest. I wasn't asking much – just a job which would move my career onto its next phase (although I really had very little idea of what that should be), and be in a nice part of the world where we could afford a house. I had interviews for jobs in Ipswich and Hertford and was offered them both, but turned them down mostly on the grounds that, after the kudos and excitement of working on my own initiative on the *Western Daily Press*, they just did not feel enough of a challenge.

I hardly knew where Nottingham was when I applied for the job there. I knew it was somewhere up north, that it was the home of Robin Hood and that, like Bristol, it had two football clubs. I knew that the *Evening Post* was a good solid newspaper, published alongside the morning *Guardian Journal* just as the *Evening Post* was published alongside the *Western Daily Press* – and that while it was not one of the big league like the *Birmingham Post* or the Wolverhampton *Express & Star* (or even the *Western Daily Press*) it sold almost 150,000 copies a night and was almost certainly big enough to satisfy my ambitions. The job sounded promising too. Being a 'Feature Writer/Sub' would probably, I thought, give me the chance to build on my fortnight's ill-fated subbing experience under Eric Price while also allowing me to develop the feature writing I had dabbled with on Mr West's Diary. There was something else about that job advertisement too: 'Come to where you can still afford to live.' For a man looking for a cheap home so he could marry the woman he loved it was, at the very least, worth a look.

I liked the feeling of the *Evening Post* as soon as I entered its front office on the corner of Forman Street in Nottingham. The place was bright and well cared for, busy without being chaotic, and the counter staff were cheerful and friendly. And, what's more, they were expecting me. 'We'll let Mr Snaith know you're here,' I was told.

Bill Snaith was a dapper man of around 60, with a highly polished head, smartly dressed in a tweedy grey suit and enormously polite. In fact he was so polite that I, coming from Eric Price's four-letter-word environment, wondered if he could really be the editor of a thriving evening newspaper.

I had no doubt that he would offer me the job. Some people, I know, go to pieces at interviews and fail to do themselves justice; I'm the opposite and somehow always manage to give such a totally false impression of my abilities that any potential employer would be foolish not to offer me a job. So I was more than a little nonplussed when Mr Snaith told me that the job for which I had applied did not in fact exist.

'I'm sorry,' he said, 'but there was a bit of a misunderstanding. We don't have a vacancy for a feature writer . . . but we'd be happy to take you on as a reporter.'

I am sure Mr Snaith could tell how annoyed I was about being dragged 200 miles across the country on false pretences. There was, after all, absolutely no way I would have applied for job as a reporter on the *Evening Post* when I already had a better job as a reporter on what I considered to be a better newspaper.

'You might as well talk to Mr Ivory, our news editor, while you're here,' he said, rather apologetically.

Bill Ivory was a big crinkly-haired Welshman who, I thought, had a rather high regard for both himself and the position he held, and I knew at once that I would not have been able to work for him even if I hadn't already decided that I wasn't going to. We talked about Bristol, and how it was just across the water from his homeland, and about some of the big stories he had covered when he was my age, but he spent precious little time asking me about what I might be able to offer him. Then, to my astonishment, he gave me a pen and a notebook and led me into a little room where, he informed me, he was going to give me a shorthand test.

'I've got a certificate for 170 words a minute shorthand,' I told him with some pride, knowing that he was unlikely ever to have interviewed any other reporter capable of such a speed.

'That's what they all say,' he replied dismissively. So there, in that pokey little office, I found myself face to face with a news editor I didn't like, who was testing my ability to do the one thing that I knew I excelled at . . . and all for a job I had no intention whatsoever of accepting.

When I was handed back to Mr Snaith I was, frankly, sick of being mucked about and just wanted to get out, to meet Pat who had been sitting patiently in my car in the car park throughout my interview, and then to go home. But for the second time in our short acquaintance, Bill Snaith managed to surprise me. 'What would you say to working on our diary column?' he asked. I learned later that I had, as I expected, made an exaggeratedly good impression at my interview – so good that, while I was having my awkward meeting with Bill Ivory, Mr Snaith was scurrying around the office trying to find a job that might appeal to me.

Suddenly the idea of working in Nottingham was on again – and, if anything, more attractive than at any time previously. The job I had been offered would involve writing most of On The Square, the diary column that was the closest thing the *Evening Post* had to Mr West's Diary, and subbing the contributions of other reporters to it. I would also get the opportunity to work on other features pages and try my hand at page design if I had time. And, because it came under the auspices of the

Features Department, I would be working under not Bill Ivory, the news editor, but Wilf Berry, the likeable but unobtrusive features editor who was next on my list of people to meet. I told Mr Snaith I was interested but could hardly give him an answer until I had talked it over with my fiancée.

I phoned him next day to accept.

A few words of thanks from Eric would have been nice, or maybe a good luck message for the future, but when I sent him my resignation all I received in reply was a short note: 'Dear Mr Harris, I am in receipt of your letter. As you say you will leave on December 12. Yours sincerely Eric Price.'

7

MY INITIAL FAVOURABLE impressions of the *Evening Post* were well founded. It was a much loved newspaper – by the people who owned it, by the people who worked for it and, more importantly, by the people who bought it in so many tens of thousands every day. It had a pivotal place in the local community, both physically thanks to its huge offices and printing works on a prime site right in the city centre, and emotionally thanks to the part it played in the everyday lives of its readers.

T Bailey Forman Ltd was owned by the Forman Hardy family, which at that time was led by Col Tom Forman Hardy (known to all of us simply as The Colonel), a much decorated war hero who owned a farm and a country mansion in the picturesque village of Car Colston a few miles east of the city. The Colonel was a shy but kind man, a newspaper proprietor of the old school – running the business in philanthropic manner, more out of a sense of duty than to make a profit – and his benevolent hand could be seen in its every aspect. Although he was seen only rarely in the office, he was hugely respected by his staff, and showed us equal respect in return, and we had little doubt that, when the time to take over from him as company chairman came, his elder son William, who had been trained for the job since birth, would be just the same.

Almost equally respected, though perhaps not for the same reasons, was Christopher Pole-Carew, the managing director, whose delicate mission, it seemed, was to drag the comfortable old business into the modern world without ruining the ethos which had made it such a success in the first place. In his previous life as a naval officer PC, as we all knew him, had somehow managed to squeeze his 6ft 5in frame into some of Her Majesty's submarines, so none of us doubted that underneath his rather boyishly charming exterior there must have been a steely determination to get the job done. For now though he was all that we, as journalists, could have asked for – a managing director who, while never interfering in the business of the editorial department, made sure that there were enough of us to do the jobs we were paid (and paid very well, in comparison with other newspapers) to do.

For the third time in my career I was lucky enough to have been given a job in a company where the work of a journalist was appreciated and valued – at a time when, I knew, there were beginning to be fewer and fewer such companies about.

Important decisions had to be made though – not least when Pat and I would get married and where we would live afterwards. We chose Saturday April 7, simply because that seemed the first date by which we could reasonably hope to be organised, and decided to look for a house in the rural area to the east of Nottingham. In the meantime, with Pat still working for the Darwall-Smiths, I needed somewhere to live until we found and bought a house. Nottingham did of course have a good supply of comfortable flats that would have been suitable, but they were all very expensive and, even more crucially, demanded a minimum rental of six months. I knew I would be gone within four months, so had to settle for whatever I could get: A couple of damp and dingy furnished rooms, with a single gas fire, and a bathroom shared with all the other occupants of a house in the run-down Sherwood district. It was, quite simply, all that was available and today it would be where the most hopeless kind of unemployed people, or maybe illegal immigrants, would live; back then, it was my home, and it was only later, with hindsight, that I realised just how dreadful it was. It had carpets, but they were grubby and threadbare; it had furniture, but it was shabby and stained; and it had a double bed, but it sagged so badly in the middle that when Pat came to stay we had to pack the mattress with wool from a home rug-making kit to make it even remotely comfortable for two.

Compared with that, No 9 Toll Bar Avenue, Bottesford, was a little palace. It was a not-quite-new three-bedroomed semi, on a large private housing estate in a village which, despite far too much recent development, was still at its heart picturesque and tranquil. Bottesford was 18 miles east of Nottingham, at the head of the Vale of Belvoir in the very northern tip of Leicestershire. It had three pubs, a few shops, schools, a railway station, a regular bus service and a church which boasted, above the tombs of generations of Dukes of Rutland from the nearby Belvoir Castle, England's tallest spire. Toll Bar Avenue was on the western, Nottingham side of the village, a cul-de-sac cut off from a coal yard by an ugly grey metal fence.

No 9 was really no different from thousands of other houses built in the late 1960s . . . except in one respect: It had a huge garden. Legend had it that, because of an architect's mistake, it had been built in the wrong place, effectively straddling plots intended for four houses, not just two. Whether or not that was true, the result was that it was strangely set back from most of the others in the road, with a big open plan garden at the front and an even bigger garden at the back. We paid £7,400 for it and it became ours just a week before our wedding.

In those days the bride and groom had very little to do with organising their weddings. That fell to the bride's parents (who, fortunately for us, still also felt an obligation to pay for their daughter's big day). The result was that our wedding merited adjectives like traditional, conventional and – dare I say it? – even staid. I did wear a rather adventurous purple shirt (which caused one of Pat's aunts, who bumped into me in the town an hour before the ceremony, to enquire quite without malice: 'Isn't it time you went back and changed?') and at our modest reception in Leominster's Royal Oak Hotel my best man, Nick Walker from our *Mercury* days, made an unconventional speech in which he claimed rather too convincingly for several of my bride's elderly relatives that he didn't have a clue who I was, had never met me before that day, and was only doing the job because I had begged him to do so after bumping into him on the street outside. Apart from that our wedding was every bit as unsurprising as any featuring the younger daughter of a conservative vicar in an old fashioned English market town.

My soon-to-be-father-in-law had arranged for me to stay the night before the wedding with his curate, Godfrey Simpson, a young man who, with his round face and slicked-down hair, looked every inch the archetypal cartoon clergyman. Godfrey and I had absolutely nothing in common and clearly came from opposite ends of virtually every spectrum it was possible to come from, but we hit it off immediately. We laughed and talked late into the night and into the morning of my wedding day, and our only worry was trying to work out how he too could meet the woman of his dreams.

The next day the woman of my dreams solemnly walked, on the arm of her brother, up the aisle of the splendid 1,300-year-old Priory Church of Saint Peter and Saint Paul at Leominster. She looked (of course)

April 7, 1973

gorgeous in a traditional (of course) white wedding dress but as she stood so demurely beside me she wasn't really the girl I had asked to marry me. My Pat would have run down the aisle towards me, eyes sparkling and smiling broadly, and would have flung her arms around me and given me a big kiss and to hell with anyone who thought she shouldn't or who considered her skirt too short!

We were married in a simple but moving ceremony made all the more special by being conducted by Pat's father, and when I came to promise to love her until death did us part I had absolutely no doubt that I would.

Our marriage highlighted one small problem: Who it was exactly that I had married. Officially, of course, I had married Patricia Mary Rainbow, spinster of the parish of Leominster in Herefordshire. I knew that because it's what was said on our marriage certificate. According to me and to my family and friends I had married Pat, but according to her family my bride was known as Tricia (or, infuriatingly, to some of her relatives as Trisha). Not surprisingly. it required great mental agility to remember, when talking to relatives and friends, how I should refer to her.

'Pat and I . . . ,' I would say to my relatives and friends.

'Tricia and I . . . ,' I would have to say to her family.

And to make things worse I called her Paddy!

The reason for all this was simple enough: To her family (her parents, brother, sister and a huge assortment of aunts and uncles) and to a very few of her friends, she was and always had been Tricia. But when she went to school one of her teachers for some reason decided she would be Pat, and so she was for the rest of her school life and beyond. So, while defiantly being called Tricia at home, she was just as resolutely referred to as Pat by anyone who had known her as a schoolgirl – and, because that included her friend Averil who went with her to work at the Seaspray Cafe in Burnham-on-Sea, anyone who met her there (including me, and through me all my family and friends) knew her as Pat.

Given the choice I would have called her Tricia from the start, because it's a much prettier, warmer and more feminine name, and therefore much more appropriate for her. But Pat she was and Pat she had to remain until slowly, over the years, the number of people who called her Tricia (including any new friends, to whom she immediately introduced herself as Tricia) began to outnumber those who didn't. Today, decades on, she is almost universally Tricia, and if friends still call her Pat it is because they have been friends for a very long time indeed.

Which just leaves the question of what I should call her here: Pat, because that is how I have referred to her so far, or Tricia because that is how she gradually becomes known as our story progresses? With my apologies for confusing you, the lady whom you have come to know as Pat will now be known as Tricia. If I got used to the change, so can you!

Tricia came from a much larger family than mine. My father was an only child and my mother had just one sister (they had also had a brother, but he had died more than 30 years before) so I had only my Auntie Jean, her husband my Uncle Jim, the head of a Devon comprehensive school, and their four children, my cousins.

From Tricia came a much more colourful bunch! From her mother's side came Auntie Bo, a tweedy spinster from Durham, who at the age of 70 dropped everything to become a missionary among the headhunters of New Guinea; Uncle Bill, a gentle pipe-smoking retired naval officer from the Cotswolds, and his hyperactive wife Auntie Peggy, neither of whom ever talked about their horrific days as prisoners of the Japanese in Hong Kong during the war; Auntie Bunty, a brilliantly funny widow whose husband had died in Africa very soon after their marriage, and before their only child was born; and Uncle Cuthbert, a widower, who ran the family firm, Harrison & Harrison organ-builders in Durham. From her father's side came Auntie Freddie (yes, honestly – her father was Frederick and her mother Edith, so they called her Fredith), a rather fearsome lady who was married to Uncle Tom, a blunt-speaking Yorkshire farmer and lorry driver; and Auntie Mary, better known as Mary Stewart, the best-selling novelist, and her husband Fred (later Sir Frederick), a geologist who, as one of the best scientific brains in the country, served as a government adviser under a string of prime ministers while at the same time somehow being a highly regarded Dean of the Science Faculty at Edinburgh University. Extraordinarily, there was not one of this collection of uncles and aunts I didn't like and over the years I have thoroughly enjoyed being an adoptive member of such a family.

My relationship with Tricia's closer relatives was rather more difficult. While I got to know her parents very well, and like them very much (though I could never bring myself to do the dutiful son-in-law thing of calling them Mum and Dad) I never managed to do the same with her brother and sister. This, I accept, was more my fault than theirs, because I did not have the patience (or the will, if I am honest) to cope with the way they were. John was very, very tall and very, very thin – which, while nothing to do with the mental problems he so obviously suffered, just served to add to the isolation he must have felt. Years later he was diagnosed as being a paranoid schizophrenic, which at least meant that he could then receive treatment, but in those early days he was just the very odd brother of my new wife, a man whose difficulties had dogged him, yet been uninvestigated, since early childhood. He was loving and devoted to his family (me included) but he was also difficult, exasperating and impossible to have a normal conversation with, so I just didn't bother to try.

Ann had no such problems. She was, I suppose, a good-looking young woman (though nowhere near as attractive as her sister) who had been a nurse in London before returning home to marry the curate from a nearby parish whom she had met while buttoning up his trousers after giving him an injection in his bum. There was no particular reason that I didn't get on with her, or she with me, just that we had next to nothing in common. She had no interest in any of the things which, apart from Tricia, were central to my life – pop music and football least of all – and rarely bothered to read a newspaper or show much interest in what was going on in the world. I found it impossible to form any sort of rapport with her and, just as with John, in the end I just didn't try.

Just three days after our wedding, at breakfast-time on Tuesday April 10, a cheerful group of passengers – mostly women and children from the handful of North Somerset villages I knew best – boarded a plane at Bristol Airport, just up the road from Redhill where I used to live. They had chartered it to give themselves a bit of excitement during the school holidays and planned to be back at tea-time after a day's shopping and sightseeing in Switzerland. Most of them had never been abroad before.

Not many of them made it home. Their plane ploughed into a snowy, forested mountainside while coming in to land at Basle, somersaulted and broke up. Somehow a few people in the rear section did manage to escape almost unscathed and were able to race down the hillside for help, but of the 148 passengers and crew, only 40 survived. In one tragic moment men had lost their entire families, and scores of children their mothers.

When the coffins brought the victims home they came in a heartbreaking procession down the main road from the airport, through Redhill and on to the villages which had had the hearts torn out of them. One coffin came home to Redhill itself, but other villages were much worse hit. Axbridge, in particular, and Cheddar, Congresbury and Wrington all counted their casualties in double figures.

On our honeymoon in Majorca Tricia and I knew nothing of what had happened. Nobody, sensibly, had seen fit to telephone us with the news and I – as I always did when on holiday – made no attempt to keep up with what was happening back home. Like many journalists, I try to cut myself off from the world when I go away. Living with news every other day of my life, I like to take a break every now and again – which means no newspapers, no TV news and no radio. I reckon the world will be in much the same state when I get back as it was when I left it, and I'll have plenty of opportunity to catch up later with what's been happening while I've been away.

Sometimes, though, you just can't help it. You just can't avoid seeing the headlines of the British national papers on the foreign news stands, or you just can't miss the headlines you hear as you flick through the channels on the television in the holiday apartment.

That was how Tricia and I found out about the plane crash. As we returned to our hotel one evening we were confronted by the headline on a pile of English newspapers lying on the reception desk: 108 DEAD IN MOTHERS' OUTING PLANE CRASH.

They were almost all the sort of people who played a central role in the life of their communities – parish councillors, WI committee members, sports club organisers, church leaders and shopkeepers – all the people who, as a young reporter on the *Mercury*, it had been my job to get to know. When I eventually dared to go through the list of the dead I found that I knew more than sixty of them and one of them was Jean Bull, a dinner lady I had known since the days when I used to queue up with the rest of the children for our meals and free milk at Redhill School. We hadn't even had a chance to open the wedding present she had given us.

I was hit by a wave of different emotions – from horror and shock to panic (thankfully misplaced) that my sister might have been on the plane; and from grief for the villages which for so long had been so much a part of my life to irritation that my honeymoon should have been so dreadfully interrupted. And, I must be honest, I was frustrated that I was not there to report on the biggest story ever to have come out of North Somerset.

8

THE EVENING POST'S FEATURES Department was staffed by people much older than I, all of them determinedly winding down towards retirement. Wilf – a kind man, but one who would do almost anything to avoid even the mildest confrontation – was only in his late forties but had probably been looking forward to drawing his pension for at least 20 years. Harold Mount was a studious man of around sixty, a former Fleet Street sub who felt that his true talents had never been properly appreciated at the *Post* and was plainly aggrieved that he had never been formally recognised as Wilf's deputy (once, when he complained about this to the editor, he was denied both the title and the pay rise he wanted but offered as paltry compensation an office chair with arms, which succeeded only in insulting him and making him even angrier). The department's 'secretary' and odd-job woman was Jean Ward, a tiny gravel-voiced, chain-smoking fifty-something alcoholic whose routine was to do half a day's work before disappearing for a long lunch in the pub and returning afterwards unfit to do almost anything at all. In the mornings she was a pleasant, funny woman, but later in the day she became a drunken harridan who hated everyone in the office (except, on one occasion, when for some reason she grasped me in her scrawny arms, said I was the only one who understood her, told me she loved me and gave me a gin-reeking kiss).

I was the office junior in more ways than one, but never once regretted my move. After the considerable autonomy I had been allowed in Yeovil, I was allowed it again in Nottingham, being permitted – and indeed encouraged – to stamp my own mark on On The Square. I modelled the column firmly on Mr West's Diary and packed it with as many stories about interesting people as I could find. In my first week I featured a

The 'office junior' at work
COURTESY OF THE NOTTINGHAM POST

glamorous blonde milkwoman called Heidi ('I have noticed that a lot of men have started getting up early to pay their bills instead of letting their wives do it,' she told me), a man who was travelling to Australia to find the son he hadn't heard from for 25 years, and two brothers and their three sisters who had a combined age of 454.

The column was completed by various filler items contributed by the news reporters, who were each supposed to provide me with two stories a week but very rarely did so despite my regular complaints to Bill Ivory. Their attitude – supported, I have no doubt, by Bill himself, although he always denied it was so – was that I was the one being paid to write On The Square so I should just get on with my job and let them get on with theirs. And not only was I writing it, I was subbing it and designing the page too – just the sort of experience I had hoped for when I accepted the job in the first place.

We had been taught the basic principles of newspaper lay-out at college, and I remembered enough of it to design pages that were acceptable if not eye-catching and when I asked Wilf if I could branch out and work on some of the other pages – the pop music page, for example, or fashion – he was only too keen to let me have a go, if only because it reduced the workload under which he was struggling himself. I found that while simple subbing (going through other people's copy and making sure it made sense and was spelled right) was a bore, writing headlines and designing the pages was great fun and gave me a chance to exercise whatever artistic talent might have been lurking inside me.

And I still had my dirty mind! The features pages, possibly because so many of them were written by elderly ladies whose heads had never been troubled by impure thoughts, would have been a minefield for any unsuspecting sub editor. Our redoubtable lady columnist Ailsa Stanley, for example – a pillar of the community and a local magistrate – could not understand why I had re-written an article in which she told us that 'Nottingham women are sick and tired of having sex rammed down their throats'. And another columnist, a pet-loving lady who was allowed to sub her own copy (always a recipe for disaster!) failed to see why one week her column survived no further than the first edition before being pulled. Writing of how she spent evenings alone at home, she told thousands of boggle-eyed readers the length and breadth of the East Midlands: 'When my husband is away I like nothing better than sitting by a roaring fire playing with my pussy.' Our pure-minded women writers weren't the only ones to blame either. Even the *Evening Post* style book, written by a very senior journalist and intended to guide us in our use of the English language, had this advice: 'Never refer to children as "It". Even the very young have sex.' Which may well have been true in those increasingly permissive times, but it was probably not what he meant.

My new job brought me into contact for the first time with that obstreperous, bloody-minded, highly skilled and (often) delightful group of men known as The Printers. The *Evening Post* had already taken great strides forward, technically speaking, so that while the news pages were produced using old fashioned hot metal, the features pages were being used as trailblazers to pioneer the use of more modern technology. Our pages were set not on hundreds of little slugs of metal, as newspapers had been for generations, but on strips of photographic paper which had to be cut up and pasted onto a board, in accordance with the page plan drawn up by the sub editor. This meant that the sub and the compositor had to work much more closely as a team than they had ever needed to before – especially when the sub was, as in my case, a novice who needed as much help as possible from men who knew much more about the job than I did.

I found endless fascination there in the paste-up department, watching as my draft page plans, inexpertly sketched out like a child's map with a mass of untidy pencil squiggles, were transformed by these master craftsmen into full pages fit for the eyes of more than 200,000 readers. It didn't matter that more often than not my pages did not fit – a story would fall several inches short and fail to fill the hole I had allocated for it, or a picture would be too big, or a headline would be in the wrong sized type and look just plain silly – the comps would somehow rescue them and, displaying infinite patience, advise me on how best to avoid such a cock-up next time.

Until then I had believed that journalists were the only ones who could possibly feel anything like the passion I had come to feel for newspapers, but here were men who seemed to love the printed word just as much as I did. For them the ink of the old printing methods was almost literally in their blood, and the tragedy was that so many of them would within a few years find their great skills made worthless by the technological revolution that lay just around the corner.

It was in June 1973, just six months into my time in Nottingham, that the revolution claimed its first casualty. Christopher Pole-Carew announced something that everyone who had any knowledge of the technical side of the business had been expecting for some time. It would affect only the very last stage of the newspapers' production – the type of printing plate fixed to the press – but it had ramifications throughout the company, and indeed the newspaper industry as a whole.

Print workers were represented by two different unions, the NGA (National Graphical Association) and SOGAT (the Society of Graphical and Allied Trades) and they could not agree which of them should be responsible for the new Letterflex plates that would be replacing the rather older magnesium-etched ones. So, in an example of the obduracy that besmirched the reputation of the printing industry at the time, both of them refused to do it and, on the orders of their national leaders, they withdrew their labour. It was ironic that the action was taken not against the management, who in best T Bailey Forman style had gone out of their way to introduce the changes sensibly and sensitively, but against the unions, one versus the other.

Those of us who worked closely with the compositors and printers and therefore had a foot in each camp, found ourselves in the middle of a dispute which was nothing to do with us and which, it seemed, was wanted by nobody except a few union leaders in London. For those of us who wondered whether we should become involved in some way, and maybe take one side or the other, one of my best friends among the printers had this advice: 'Keep out of it! If you journalists join in you will just make it worse.'

So, in the spirit of the time, when unions seemed keen to take industrial action at the slightest provocation, the journalists did indeed join in and, as predicted, made things a good deal worse. The National Union of Journalists (NUJ) called a strike, although many members – especially those who worked closely with the printers – argued against it, not least on the grounds that nobody was entirely sure who it was in support of.

I, like a lot of others who believed that strike action should be a matter of last resort, not first – and, with the 'keep out of it' plea from my printer friend still fresh in my memory – carried on working, resigned from the union and joined the rival Institute of Journalists (an altogether less militant and doubtless less effective organisation) instead.

The pickets gathered in threatening numbers outside the office, but inside there was something like the old British wartime spirit. The unions could not have found a better way of instilling a sense of never-say-die teamwork among us, even though, not surprisingly, a few of those who had voted against the strike found themselves pressured to join it after all, and were soon to be seen shuffling embarrassedly on the fringes of the picket lines. One, a sub called Ellard Styles, who had originally been one of the most vociferous anti-strikers, suddenly switched sides and became an equally outraged picket – earning himself, among the rest of us, the telling soubriquet Turn Styles.

Violence was never far below the surface. And it nearly broke out on one of the rare days that Tricia gave me a lift into work and dropped me off at the gate. I emerged from the car to the expected jeers from the pickets and walked into the yard, turning to look back over my shoulder to see that she had got away all right. She hadn't. She was still stuck where she had stopped, with one of the *Post* strikers, the council reporter Carl Piggins (a man whom I had never much liked, partly on the grounds that he wore a bow-tie – something I looked upon as an irritating affectation) shouting and gesturing angrily at her through the car window. I turned and hurried back, not quite sure what I was going to do but fairly certain that it would involve violence of some sort. A young policeman saw me coming, quickly weighed up the situation and, disregarding the official advice that he was there just to watch and not take sides, decided he should intervene. He calmly walked over to our car and, ignoring the snarling Piggins, quietly told Tricia with a sympathetic smile 'I'm sorry madam, but you can't park there' as if he was doing nothing more challenging than controlling the traffic in some quiet English town on market day.

There were enough journalists still at work to cope with the demands of producing a newspaper every day, though, and those who were on strike were, in truth, barely missed. But in the production department things were very different. The few printers and supervisors who remained at work were enough to guarantee production of the *Evening Post*, which did not miss an edition throughout the five weeks of the dispute, but they could not do the same for the *Guardian Journal*, the morning paper produced in the same building, and its edition of June 19 was its last.

The death of the Guardian Journal brought surprisingly few changes around the office – not least because it was easy to accommodate most of its handful of journalists among the staff of the *Evening Post*. Ken Macmillan, the GJ's editor, was made deputy editor under Bill Snaith, the reporters were absorbed into the newsroom and the sub editors were simply added to those working on the evening paper. The only one who had no obvious place to go was Ian Scott, the GJ's abrasive features editor.

Ian was a highly skilled, and very ambitious, production journalist, with a great flair for design and an impressive knowledge of the technical side of the business. What he did not have was much semblance of man management skills, which resulted in an unparalleled ability to rub people up the wrong way. Although he kept his small office near the editor's in the executive corridor, he began to be a frequent visitor to our room, having adopted the title Features Co-ordinator even though as far as we knew no official announcement had been made to give it to him – or even to explain what on earth such a role involved or whether it put him above, below or equal with Wilf in the management hierarchy. We assumed that Bill Snaith did not want to upset either of them, so just let the two of them fight it out between themselves. It was in fact no fight at all. Wilf, the timid even-tempered man from Boston in Lincolnshire, was no match for Ian, the brusque street-fighter from Glasgow, and soon found himself unhappily subservient to him in every respect. Harold Mount, now finding himself down to third in the pecking order, became increasingly morose and Jean Ward took even more to drink.

Jean blamed herself for it all. It was she who had answered Ian's initial phone call, when he had rung years before to ask about a possible vacancy after leaving the *Leicester Mercury*, and she held herself responsible ever afterwards for what she saw as his unwelcome presence in our office. If she hadn't picked up the phone, if she hadn't been so polite, if she hadn't transferred him so efficiently to the editor's secretary . . . well, she thought, he might not have been here among us now.

Jean's dislike of him overflowed one afternoon when, after a particularly heavy lunchtime in the pub, she was even more clearly unfit for work than usual. Ian did what Wilf should have done years before, and told her that she was becoming a disruptive influence in the office, that her behaviour was not acceptable and that she would be sacked if it continued (all perfectly reasonable, except he should have told her in private, not in front of everyone else in the room). Jean stood up unsteadily from her chair, walked round her desk, fixed her glazed eyes upon him as best the alcohol would allow her to and jabbed him several times in the chest while reminding him that it was she he had to thank for getting his job in the first place. 'Never forget,' she said, very carefully so as not to appear as intoxicated as she obviously was, 'that I was the one who dragged you up from the gutter where you belong.' With that she took a step back to steady herself on her desk, missed . . . and fell in a spluttering heap of spindly arms and legs on the floor.

Ian sent her home and told her not to return until he called for her.

She retired soon afterwards, and died from a surfeit of alcohol not long after that.

Amid all this I was the only one who rather enjoyed the arrival of Ian Scott. Yes, he could be rude and over-demanding but, even though he did not have the people skills to achieve it, all he wanted was to get the best out of his staff. Given a choice between his uncompromising management style and Wilf's comfortable woolliness (which was not a style of management at all) I was happy to accept Ian's because at the age of 24 I was too young to think of winding down to my retirement and welcomed the opportunity to work under the sort of pressure that I felt was more appropriate to the office of an important daily newspaper.

Tricia meanwhile had very quickly found a job as a nursery nurse in a primary school in Sneinton, one of the most deprived districts of Nottingham. It was the first time she had used her qualifications for anything other than nannying and was the start of a career for which her personal qualities of patience, understanding, optimism and unbounded love of children – particularly those who laboured under all kinds of unimaginable handicaps – made her ideally suited.

We travelled the 18 miles from Bottesford into Sneinton together every day in our car (a cheap white Simca, which we had bought new as replacement for the company Mini I had lost on leaving the *Western Daily Press*), which she parked at her school while I walked the extra mile or so to the *Evening Post* offices in time to join in one of the Features Department's more bizarre traditions. For some reason which nobody could explain, the Features Department had always been the ones to sort the editorial mail. So first thing in the morning the editorial messenger – usually a retired man, but sometimes a lad fresh out of school – would arrive with all the post piled in a big wicker basket which he placed on a deep shelf which ran along one side of the room. Wilf, Harold and I, joined by the assistant editor Ron Dunstan (a gloomy little man who could not possibly have been as unhappy as he appeared), spent the first half hour of our working day solemnly sorting the letters into smaller wire baskets, one of which went to the editor himself, one to the news editor, one to the sports editor, one to the chief photographer and one straight to the rubbish bin . . . and helping ourselves to any freebies (anything from books and records to packets of vegetable seed and household gadgets) which the nation's PR companies had seen fit to send us. Nobody ever thought to question whether it was a proper use of our time.

Tricia, working in one of the most deprived districts of Nottingham

Although we rarely saw them – or indeed any members of the senior management team – we were constantly aware of the benign control of the Forman Hardy family who had run the business ever since one of their ancestors, a Lincolnshire printer called Thomas Forman, had founded it nearly 100 years before. The family had other business interests, ranging from the Hardy & Hanson brewery in the north of the city to a huge farm on the outskirts, but there was no doubt that the newspaper was central to everything they did. It gave the company a stability almost unheard of in the newspaper industry and provided for us, its employees, the comfort of knowing that we were working for people who truly understood and appreciated us. So when in 1974 William Forman Hardy, the elder son who had been destined from birth to take over the firm from his father, was killed in a motorbike crash on the A46 near Newark, it sent shockwaves not just through the firm but through the city as well. William was the future of the business, and without him there was no longer any certainty at all.

It was his younger brother Nicholas – fated to take over the family farm in just the same way as William had been groomed for the newspaper business – who was called upon, unwillingly I have no doubt, to fill his shoes. Nick was a quiet man of about my age, who was not surprisingly unsure of himself in the alien newspaper environment but who despite his lack of confidence eventually went on to do his best as figurehead of the firm. He had all his family's charm and good manners, and fair-minded commitment to his employees, but it was clear to all of us that his heart just was not in it. It was no surprise when, many years later, he accepted an offer from Associated Newspapers and sold the firm for £93.4 million.

It was the day after William's death that I spoke to his father, the Colonel, for the first time. I was running to catch the lift down to the office car park when the doors closed in front of my face a split second before I was able to push the button to keep them open. I thumped on the doors, in frustration rather than anger, and they slowly slid open, to reveal our company's broken-hearted chairman, shyly apologising for going without me. What do you say to an old man who's just lost his son, and the heir to his world, whom you've never spoken to before, and who probably doesn't know who the hell you are? And who, though clearly racked by grief, just wants to apologise for accidentally closing the lift door in your face? I muttered something about how sorry I was, he nodded and, for the most awkward half-minute of my life, we continued our journey in silence

William's death brought no immediate changes to the daily business of producing a newspaper, and life in the Features Department might have continued as normal had I not, just a year into our marriage, developed excruciating shooting pains up my back from the base of my spine. These, my doctor told me, were caused by a pilonidal sinus – more interestingly known as 'jeep driver's arse' because of the type of people most commonly affected by it – on my tailbone and the only remedy was for a surgeon to cut out a nest of ingrowing hair which had turned septic in some kind of congenital defect I had just above my coccyx. Within three weeks I was in Grantham hospital (we reckoned I got special speedy treatment because such a thing made a welcome change from the consultant's usual run of appendicitis and tonsil operations) having the infected part removed like a slice from a cake. It meant three months off work – not because it was a particularly serious procedure but because, being where it was, it was impossible to stitch the open wound together, and equally impossible for me to sit down.

When I returned to work I found they had learned to do without me, not least because Wilf thought I had cancer and would never make it back. On The Square was now being written exclusively – and, everyone agreed, not very well – by the news reporters and subbed by whichever of the features subs had time, and the other pages I had been interested in were similarly being handled by Wilf and Harold. I was content to become a simple features sub, especially since in my absence the department had started to take on extra features pages which were much more interesting than what had gone before. It was not the most exciting phase of my career but I was happy and had other things to think about. Tricia was pregnant.

9

ANTONY PETER WAS BORN on Monday April 7 1975, our second wedding anniversary, just in time for lunch. He was a fine baby (although I would have thought so even if he had not been). He made his screaming entrance into the world at Grantham hospital as I sat in wonderment and in tears beside the bed, holding Tricia's hand. This was a moment for which I had hoped for almost as long as I could remember – a lovely wife, a beautiful son, a proper family – and I knew beyond a doubt that choosing not to jeopardise the chances of it by going to sea was one of the best things I had ever done.

We took him home a few days later to a house well prepared for him, with a brightly decorated little bedroom containing an ancient wicker cradle which was among assorted baby equipment that Tricia – confident that she would one day be a mother – had scrounged when Wick House closed shortly after she left it.

I learned to change his nappies and bath him (which in those days marked me out as something of a 'New Man') but could only watch in awe as Tricia adapted easily to her new role. Being a qualified nursery nurse who had already looked after numerous other people's babies was something that concerned her, because she felt everyone expected her to do everything right, with no room for the sort of mistakes most new mothers are forgiven for making. But she need not have worried. Some things just come naturally and she was – and, more than 30 years on, still is – a born mother who would have excelled at the job with or without training. I'm certain that this was why Antony was such a happy and contented baby who rarely disturbed our sleep and who quickly settled into our lives without causing very much disruption at all.

With Tricia at home looking after the new baby I took to travelling into work by train. Bottesford was a pretty place, so walking through it was no hardship. I came to enjoy my 20 minute stroll to the station on the other side of the village, and enjoyed walking home even more . . . especially when, half way across the field beside the river by the church, I was met by a smiling Tricia pushing baby Antony in his pram.

We were happy in Toll Bar Avenue. We had decorated the house in best '70s style, with bright orange patterned wallpaper in the living room and a shockingly unsuccessful combination of deep turquoise and magenta in the bathroom, and I managed to complete a very few DIY projects before discovering that I was not really cut out for such things. Our garden was a greater success and it became a vibrant paintbox of colour in the summer, with a vegetable plot so productive that I frequently commuted to Nottingham clutching a pair of giant primo cabbages which I sold to my friends at work.

But neither of us was cut out for life on a modern housing estate. What we really wanted was a cottage in the country – even though we knew our chances of being able to afford such a thing was remote. We scoured the estate agents' pages of the *Evening Post* and our local weekly paper, the *Grantham Journal*, every week, but the only result was a disappointing confirmation that, unless we were willing to take on a property that was almost literally falling down, such places were well out of our price range.

At work things were changing fast, and in the Features Department most of all. The management, like newspaper managements all over the country, had realised that it was no longer good enough just to produce a newspaper – albeit a very good one – every day and simply expect people to buy it. Habits and loyalty like that were going out of fashion, and anyone who wanted no more than a bit of local news had only to turn on the television or tune their radios in to the burgeoning number of local stations. What newspapers had to do was offer their readers more for their money.

To satisfy this demand a series of tabloid colour supplements were introduced – ranging from the rather stodgy Business Review (we liked to call it 'authoritative' but it was hardly that, since a lot of it was written by me and I knew almost nothing about the subject) to one specialising in home furnishing, and from a cookery special to a glossy guide to the annual Nottingham Festival. Whether it was because I displayed some latent talent for the job, or that I was the only one who didn't try to find some excuse not to work with Ian Scott, I couldn't tell, but the result was that I was given the job of planning, subbing and, very often, writing these supplements. I found that, underneath his prickly exterior, Ian was a much more pleasant man than he seemed. He was also a great teacher, and I like to think I was a keen pupil, and with his help I quickly learned a huge amount about page design, production and – rather more difficult for someone whose colour blindness had saved him from a career at sea – the use of colour, which in those days was very much in its infancy in the newspaper industry.

I found unexpected pleasure in planning a project from scratch, from deciding what a supplement's contents should be, to writing it, subbing it and seeing it through to production. It was an operation done on a shoestring, so I became expert at obtaining the help of all kinds of outside agencies – such organisations as the British Potato Council and the Meat Marketing Board, for example, were very useful for providing recipes, and even helped when I had what seemed like the bright idea of running a feature entitled '101 Things To Do With A Sausage'; and the Dulux press office could always be relied upon to supply free articles about how best our readers should decorate their homes.

When I could find no one to provide the material for me, I simply found a reliable reference book and wrote it myself – but frequently under a pseudonym lest people, seeing too many Richard Harris by-lines, might think we were in any way short-staffed. And so it was I adopted such alter egos as Chris Pendle (a middle-aged DIY expert) and Naomi Wainwright (a mature lady with a cheerful eye for colour-coordinated soft furnishings). It was always great fun when, following publication of a Home Maker supplement, readers phoned wanting to talk to Ms Wainwright about her latest piece of advice on how to hang curtains or keep the cushions nicely plumped.

'Can I speak to Naomi Wainwright?' they'd say.

'Speaking,' I'd reply, in my deepest, most macho voice.

Suddenly the Features Department, which had until then been, if anything, under-employed, was being given more work than it could cope with. The first of the reinforcements came in the unlikely shape of Bill Tomlinson, a former *Guardian Journal* sub who was already past retirement age but who was being allowed to continue his working life largely on the grounds, it seemed, that he was one of Bill Snaith's oldest friends. Bill Tomlinson liked to think of himself as something of an intellectual, and as a result had an air of Noel Coward about him. He was happiest when discussing books which the rest of us had never heard of (and which, I suspect, he had seldom read) and, because he considered himself heir to the *Evening Post*'s great tradition of scholars – the writers J M Barrie and Graham Greene had both worked there at some time in their careers – looked upon the rest of us as a poorly educated bunch of ne'er-do-wells who deserved no place in his cerebral company. He was a journalist of the old school, who probably wore his jacket and tie even when in bed, and there were very many things about him that annoyed me, yet I liked him very much and usually found myself sitting with him for lunch in the staff canteen.

His saving grace was a sense of humour which was totally at odds with the sober old man he appeared to be. At some time every morning (it was impossible to forecast when, but it was always when the room was at its quietest) he would leap from his chair and chant whatever was that day's *Daily Telegraph* quotation from the Bible. To have one's concentration disturbed by a crazy old baritone intoning 'Let your light shine before men, that they may see your good works' is something that a hard-pressed sub editor can find either infuriating or hilarious. I alone in the staid environment of the Features Department found it hilarious.

For a rotund old man Bill was surprisingly sprightly and he had a habit of getting up from his desk and leaping into the air to see how many times he could click his heels together before returning to the floor and then, without a word, going back to his work; and sometimes he would walk up the corridor past the many windows of the Features Department, slowly bending his knees as he went to give the appearance to us inside that he was walking downhill. He once did it not knowing that he was being followed down the corridor by the managing director. 'Silly old bugger,' said Mr Pole-Carew.

One thing that Bill couldn't cope with was the thought of learning anything new. Which was something of a handicap when, very suddenly, in 1976 the *Evening Post* became the most talked about newspaper in the country by adopting technology that no one else in the industry had dared to use until then.

Overnight, it seemed (and certainly we had very little warning) we became the first journalists in Britain to have computers on our desks. The technological progress that engulfed the company meant that the old days of typewriters, paper and stubby blue pencils were gone for ever, muscled aside by a new age of computer keyboards and VDUs. Reporters were inputting their copy direct into a huge central computer, and the subs were formatting it – deciding upon the size and font of the type, setting it across one, two or three columns, and writing headlines – all on-screen. Computers were not then sufficiently advanced to allow pages to be designed on them too, so the subbed copy had to be printed out on photographic paper downstairs before being compiled into the page in the paste-up department.

Because the computer struggled to keep pace with the demands of the news pages, we in the Features Department had to agree to wait our turn while the hot news of the day took priority as we approached the first edition deadline. The idea was that we would not output our less urgent features material until after the first edition had been safely completed and the presses were rolling, but it was not unusual for one of us to 'forget', or genuinely to misread the clock, and clog up the works so that all the day's urgent late news was stuck in the system behind some full-page feature in much the same way as a stream of sports cars might be held up by a slow-moving low-loader on the motorway. Indeed I had the distinction of causing the longest ever delay to the first edition when I not only output a story at the prohibited time, but by accident set the whole thing in such large type that there was space only for one letter on each line, so the feature that should have taken about 60cms of photographic paper had in fact used up about 30 metres of the stuff by the time it finished disgorging itself painfully slowly from the printer downstairs.

Most of us found the changes enormously exciting, but not Bill Tomlinson. Although he no doubt enjoyed the pay rise we were given for the extra work involved, he simply refused to play any part in the new-fangled computer age, so – while the rest of us revelled in being in the vanguard of a revolution which was later to sweep the whole newspaper industry – Bill simply continued as he had before, subbing the TV listings, horoscopes, lighting-up times and whatever other hard copy could be found for him. He was like a museum piece, retained as a token keepsake as if to emphasise the enormous developments going on everywhere else in the company.

Among the many changes that coincided with the introduction of the new technology was the addition of still more features pages, which meant the recruitment of extra staff to write them. One of these was a freelance journalist called Janet Myles, who, while being mother to three young sons, had been making a living working part-time for various local publications but who had never before been involved with the *Evening Post*.

She was taken on to work from home, mostly on 'advertising features' – the editorial that supposedly gave some legitimacy to whatever the marketing department had decided was the latest good excuse to milk yet more money out of their advertiser clients. So, to accompany two pages of advertisements for nursing homes or disability aids, for example, Janet would write a half-page feature on how to care for your grandparents in their old age; or when faced with a page of adverts from garden centres she would create a feature on how to turn the flowerbeds of your semi into the envy of your suburban neighbours.

For a long time Janet's was no more than a mysterious name at the top of the copy (always well written) that I was subbing, and it was only when she joined the team writing TellyView, a daily review of the previous night's television programmes, that I got to know her. And even then it was only because I was the only one in the department who could manage to type with both hands while balancing the telephone receiver between my ear and shoulder. TellyView, for which those of us who wrote it were paid an extra £10 a time, was the first urgent job of the day in the Features Department. It had to be written subbed and output quickly enough not to risk causing any delay to the news pages which at that early hour of the day were still being worked on. That was no great problem for those of us on the rota who worked in the office but for Janet, who worked from home, it meant dictating her copy over the phone to whoever was willing and able to take it – which, because the copy-taking ladies with their posh headsets and touch-typing skills did not start work for another half hour, meant me.

She and I hit it off immediately and I even found myself looking forward to those mornings once or twice a week when I would spend the first few minutes of my working day with the phone crooked awkwardly under my chin, chatting and laughing with this lively young woman I had never met; and on the days when it was someone else's turn to provide the review I missed getting my day off to such a bright start with her cheerful conversation.

On only one occasion was she not her usual perky self. When I answered the phone to her – precisely at the expected time, as always – she was clearly not happy. Her voice was flat and breaking, and it was obvious she was having to make a great effort to control her breathing in an attempt to contain whatever it was that was troubling her.

'What's wrong?' I asked.

'My husband's left me.'

'Christ! When – last night?'

'No, just. He walked out the door a few minutes ago.'

'Oh shit!'

'Now are you going to take this copy or not?'

And so it was that Janet, left at home with three small children by a husband who had walked out on her before the end of the family breakfast, calmly – or as calmly as she could – dictated to me her review of what she had watched on television the night before.

I'm happy to tell you that it was not long before, at her children's school gates, she met a man who was in much the same situation as she was. Tony Waltham was a single father, a geology lecturer at Trent Polytechnic and, as one of the country's most admired cavers, by coincidence a man I had interviewed a couple of years before for On The Square. It was as Janet Waltham that the greatest friend I have ever had in journalism became one of the best and most popular writers working on the *Evening Post* during its most successful years.

For Tricia and me life was good and getting better . . . and on Monday August 2 1976, with Tricia disregarding the midwife's advice that things might go more smoothly if she saved the breath she was wasting on four-letter expletives, Juliet Susan was born, just in time for lunch like her brother. I was (of course) there for her birth, but was so excited by having a daughter that soon afterwards I left the maternity ward and went into town to buy her a dress. Later in the afternoon I returned home to fetch Antony, who arrived with me at the hospital to meet his sister clutching what remained of a bunch of sweet peas that he had picked from our garden and mangled mercilessly on the way.

Antony was not at all put out by having a baby in the house to vie for our attention. He adapted to the new situation immediately and loved his sister just as much as Tricia and I did. We were, in every sense, a happy family and I could not imagine that life could have got much better.

In fact it did. While I had everything I wanted at home, I was also getting more than I had any right to expect at work. The changes affecting the Features Department were continuing, with a steady increase in the number of colour supplements we were producing, most of which landed on my desk. Ian Scott seemed to view me as an able and enthusiastic lieutenant and raised no objection when I knocked on the editor's door and asked for some recognition of the extra work I was doing. I came out with a handful of compliments, a small pay rise and the title Supplements Editor, which helpfully placed me not in competition with the genial Wilf but, since colour supplements were something in which he just didn't want to get involved, in parallel with him. I suddenly became aware that, thanks largely to my being a willing worker who happened to have been in the right place at the right time, my career was going somewhere (though precisely where I could not tell) – and so far I was managing to do it without upsetting too many people along the way.

My new title, modest though it was to anyone who understood the newspaper industry, was enough to open the doors of people in the outside world. It gave me some extra clout when asking for favours from the press offices of the various organisations with which I had to deal, and sometimes even persuaded TV stars and pop singers to take me more seriously than they otherwise might have done when I asked them for quick quotes on everything from their favourite colour schemes (for Home Maker), their best ever drives (for Car Buyer) or their most reliable time-saving kitchen tips (for the cookery supplement).

My title's greatest success though came when I was planning the editorial content of the *Evening Post*'s Christmas supplement, which I was determined would stay as far as possible from such clichés as 'Countdown To The Big Day' and 'How To Carve Your Turkey'. As I sat at my desk in the summer of 1977 planning a publication that was still six months away, my thought process went: 'Christmas = Christmas trees = the big one in Trafalgar Square = a present from the Norwegian people = a land of mountains and fjords' (and, being honest, '= a country I have always longed to visit but know I never will because it's far too expensive for the likes of me').

Showing a deviousness few people suspected of me, I composed a polite letter to the press office of the Norwegian Tourist Board, asking if they could supply us with 1,000 words on the Trafalgar Square Christmas tree – where it was grown, who chopped it down, how it was shipped to London and so on – and, under my signature and my grand title of Supplements Editor, added a hand-written PS that I hoped sounded more helpful than hopeful: 'If you are unable to provide such an article for us we would be happy to send one of our own staff to Norway to write it ourselves.'

It was my great good fortune that my letter landed on the desk of the senior press officer at the Norwegian Tourist Board at precisely the moment that they were thinking of changing their approach to media activities.

In the past they had invited groups of national newspaper and magazine journalists a dozen or so at a time, to visit specific tourist attractions – the Viking ships in Oslo, for example; or Edvard Grieg's home on the outskirts of Bergen; or the tiny wooden church at Utne in the Hardanger Fjord – but they were not happy with the results of such visits, feeling that they deserved more space in more newspapers for their efforts, and were thinking of trying something new. My letter arrived just as they were discussing the idea of inviting just one journalist (from a major provincial newspaper rather than a national one) and inviting him or her to be their VIP guest for a week.

My letter saved them the trouble of looking any further, so on Friday September 9 1977, excited beyond belief that I was being paid to spend seven days in a country to which I had dreamed of going for as long as I could remember, I boarded SS Jupiter at Newcastle-on-Tyne, bound for Bergen, looking forward to a week among sparkling blue fjords, snowcapped mountains glistening in the sun, villages of pretty little wooden houses set among meadows full of late summer flowers . . . and lots of smiling beautiful blonde women. The idea that Norway might somehow fall short of that picturebook ideal never entered my head, and as the ship made its gentle way through the fjords to Bergen I knew I was right not to doubt it. The fjords were blue and sparkling, there was snow on the mountains, which glistened in the sun, and the villages that we passed were indeed made up of little wooden houses among meadows of bright late summer flowers. It was all as I expected, all as I had hoped for . . . so I couldn't wait to meet the representative from the local tourist office – a beautiful blonde, I was sure – who was to meet me at the harbour and be my guide for the two days I would be spending in Bergen before moving on across the country.

Anne-Marie was a brunette. A very nice, even beautiful brunette, who was slim and friendly and laughed a lot and took me to see where her parents lived in a white painted wooden house on the hill overlooking the harbour, but there was no avoiding the fact that she – like most of the women in Bergen – was not my fantasy blonde. It was she who brought it up in conversation over dinner at my hotel that night. Perhaps she sensed my disappointment. Everybody, she said, came to Norway expecting the whole population to be blonde, but in fact that did not apply to the west coast where the consequences of too much raping and pillaging and the kidnapping of too many brown-haired Anglo Saxon women from their homes in northern Britain 1,000 years before were still being felt in the local population's hair colouring. I started immediately looking forward to getting away from the west coast.

But in the meantime Anne-Marie, enjoying the opportunity to escape from her desk in the town's tourist information centre, took me on a funicular ride up the Ulriken mountain; had lunch with me in the restaurant looking down on the Bergen fjords; walked with me along the floodlit mountain paths which, in winter, become the locals' cross-country ski runs; guided me around the fish market and the shops in the wooden warehouses around the Hanseatic wharf; drove me for an afternoon at Troldhaugen, Edvard Grieg's atmospheric home on the cliff-side just south of the city; and on the third day put me on a bus into the mountains.

At Ulvik, a pretty little town on the shores of the Hardanger Fjord, I was met by a small fair-haired man who approached me, hand outstretched and smiling. 'Hello, I'm Odd,' he said, and I, resisting the temptation to reply 'Don't worry, I'm a bit peculiar myself', smiled back and confirmed that I was indeed the mysterious journalist from Nottingham, England, who everybody seemed to be making such an inordinate fuss of. Odd Hammer was the owner of the Ulvik Hotel and it was there that I spent two supremely happy days, going for walks, taking boat trips, visiting all kids of ancient sites and discovering that Norway was everything I had hoped it would be (or almost everything, since I had still not met any proper Scandinavian blondes) and I sent Tricia a postcard promising her that one day I would take her there.

I was reluctant to leave Ulvik because I could not believe anywhere would quite match it for beauty, tranquillity or friendliness, but my itinerary was set and I had next to take the train across the very roof of Norway – surely one of the very best railway journeys in the world – and go on to its capital. After the peacefulness of the Hardanger Fjord Oslo was a nightmare of pandemonium and bustle and I got off the train feeling every inch the country bumpkin making his first venture into the big city. I had not been told what to do when I arrived there, but my experience of the trip so far gave me confidence that sooner or later someone would appear to look after me.

'Hello Richard,' she said. I turned and saw a young woman in a heavy overcoat smiling encouragingly at me from under a big furry hat. 'Anne-Marie told me what you looked like,' she added, before I'd even had the chance to ask how on earth she had recognised me. This was Sissel and she was blonde – but disappointingly so. She was, I was sure, a pleasant and friendly woman (because every Norwegian I had met so far had been pleasant and friendly) but she had a sad and dowdy look about her which made her hardly the blonde of my imagination. Sissel apologised that she only had time to drive me to my hotel and dump me there, but told me her boss from the Oslo tourist office would be coming round later to take me out for dinner. She, though, would be back next day after breakfast to take me on a guided tour of the forests on the slopes of the mountains behind the city, where I would be able to meet the man who would be felling the Trafalgar Square Christmas tree (which, I had to remind myself, was the whole purpose of my trip).

Sissel and I spent a happy day in the mountains. She was lively and funny and, I decided, not bad looking, but her windcheater and tweed trousers did her so few favours she seemed older and more care-worn than her years. Still, she had a sense of humour and appreciated the absurdity of my travelling hundreds of miles by ship, car, bus and train to watch a man chopping down a tree and – like Anne-Marie – enjoyed even more the excuse to escape from her office for a few hours. By the time she dumped me back at the plush Grand Hotel, in the very heart of the city, we had become good friends and I found myself pleased to hear that the mysterious 'representative of the Oslo Tourist Association' with whom I would be having dinner later was her.

The trouble was that when I went down to the hotel's splendid marbled foyer to meet her that evening she was nowhere to be seen.

'Hello Richard,' said the gorgeous young blonde I had just walked past and tried to ignore. The old windcheater and frumpy trousers were gone, and she was now wearing a long skirt in the gold and orange colours of autumn, a matching waistcoat over a white blouse and brown leather boots (the very fact that the image of her is imprinted on my brain more than 30 years later gives some clue to the affect). Her blonde but dull hair now seemed soft and highly polished and her care-worn eyes were sparkling with life. The transformation was complete. 'Sissel?' I asked, stupidly. I had found my fantasy Norwegian blonde!

We went to a restaurant called Blom, a shadowy and romantic place, with dark wood panels lit only with candles, where a pianist in the corner played music which I recognised as Grieg's before she did. She told me that her job often involved entertaining visiting English journalists, but she had never much enjoyed it before. 'You're not like all the others,' she said, her eyes sparkling in the candlelight and her hand creeping towards mine on the table.

'The last person who told me that was a hairy rock star who didn't seem to like me very much at all,' I replied, trying to bring the conversation back onto safer ground.

I had, of course, found other women attractive in the four years I had been married, but I had not met one who so obviously fancied me in return – and certainly not one who could have stepped straight out of my dreams.

Afterwards we walked together through the quiet Oslo streets, and took the lift to the top of the tallest hotel where I took ages to finish what was probably the most expensive drink of my life. Neither of us wanted the evening to end, and when she kissed me goodbye she had tears in her eyes.

But that night I slept alone.

Which was just as well because at three o'clock I was woken by clanging bells, a pounding on my door and much shouting that the hotel was on fire and we had to get out. As I stood outside in the cold Oslo night, I allowed myself a wry smile. Thank goodness I had resisted the temptation to invite Sissel back to my room. Unlike the rest of us gathered there on the pavement, she would not have had a dressing gown.

My Norwegian adventure was not over though. I still had another day to spend in Oslo and a chauffeur-driven Mercedes was put at my disposal to make my sightseeing more easily accomplished. Kon-Tiki, the Viking ships, the polar explorers' ship Fram, Edvard Munch's disturbing painting 'The Scream' – all these I was expected (and, in fact, I wanted) to see.

Time was also allocated for the Mercedes to drive me to some of Norway's finest souvenir shops before, next day, I caught a train to Stavanger, where I rejoined the ship upon which my wonderful odyssey had started. I returned to Nottingham to write two features – one about the Christmas tree and one, for our new travel magazine, about my time in the Hardanger Fjord – which seemed to me to be a paltry pay-back for the time and money invested in me by the Norwegian government.

10

IT WAS THE MID '70s and Britain was in the grip of industrial unrest. The newspaper industry had no right to expect it would be any different and it wasn't. In the summer of 1978 the National Union of Journalists demanded better pay for its members and threatened to bring every regional and local newspaper in the country out on strike if it did not get it. I was not the only one who thought it was an empty threat – a useful, if heavy-handed, bargaining tool – because I could not believe any union would seriously consider taking action which would surely bring about the closure of some of the companies upon which its members relied for their jobs. It was a time when newspapers were struggling financially, with advertising revenue falling as fast as their circulations, and there was a real danger that many of them might not survive the prolonged absence from the news stands that a long-running dispute would bring about. Newspaper readers are creatures of habit, and once they get used to not buying a paper every day it can be almost impossible to win them back, so what the union was planning seemed destined, inevitably, to result in some titles failing to weather the storm.

All this seemed to be lost on the NUJ's London hierarchy, who, when they did not instantly see their demands satisfied, called an all-out strike. Journalists on the *Evening Post*, like those working on newspapers all over the country, were called to mandatory chapel (office branch) meetings and told to withdraw their labour. But compared with the rest of the country the position in Nottingham was rather different. We – those who were still in the union and those who, like me, had left it some years before – had no argument with our employers for a start; they had always treated us well and paid us considerably more than the going rate for a newspaper of the

Post's size. While even those of us in the IoJ sympathised with our 'brothers' on less successful papers, who were indeed being poorly paid and treated shabbily, and while there was perhaps a legitimate argument that in the interests of solidarity those on big papers should support their colleagues on smaller ones, the plain economic fact was that people were being asked – no, instructed – to go on strike for around 20 per cent less money than they were already earning. With most of the Nottingham journalists already struggling, even on their enhanced *Evening Post* salaries, to pay their mortgages and feed their families, the suggestion that they might join a strike with such an aim – and condemn themselves to who knew how many weeks without any pay at all – was frankly preposterous.

For those of us who were no longer in the NUJ there was no decision to be made – we would go on working. Most of those who were still union members had already made up their minds that they would not support the strike either – and if any of them needed any further persuasion it came with the crucial intervention of Christopher Pole-Carew, our managing director. Having skilfully negotiated the company through the introduction of direct input without a squeak of complaint from his journalists, he was not having his plans scuppered by people employed by someone else on a newspaper which did not treat its staff as well as he treated his, so he coolly announced that if anyone walked out on strike in support of a dispute which had nothing to do with his company they would be considered to be in breach of contract and therefore dismissed.

The chapel meeting was, I was told, a subdued, despondent affair, with even strong trade unionists arguing that the NUJ's tactics made no sense when applied to what was happening in Nottingham. Why not hold the *Evening Post* and its management up as an example, they asked, and tell the rest of the industry: 'Look at this – if you treat your journalists well and pay them appropriately they will repay you with their hard work and loyalty and will never feel the need to go on strike'?

Such arguments were enough for most of the hundred-plus journalists on the *Evening Post*, even if they failed to convince the NUJ's leadership, and when the vote was taken only a handful were in favour of a walk-out.

Some of us, including me, assumed that would be the end of it, and that, having taken a democratic vote, the *Post* chapel would be allowed by their union to get on with their jobs and their lives. But we had reckoned without the obdurate militancy of the NUJ head office, who despatched a hit squad of officials to address staff at another mandatory chapel meeting. They might have turned a blind eye if we had been some tiny weekly paper employing half a dozen rookie reporters in a small town a million miles from anywhere, but they plainly could not afford to let their plans be thwarted by a major newspaper like the *Post* – which, because of its work with new technology, was already being recognised nationally as the industry's trailblazer – so when their attempts at persuasion failed they turned to threats instead. Anyone who worked through the strike would be 'blacked', they said, and would never, in the closed-shop utopia that they were convinced was just around the corner, be able to work anywhere again – not even at the *Evening Post*, whose management, they were certain, would fall into line soon enough.

For the many young journalists on the staff, who were hoping to use their time at the *Post* as a stepping stone to jobs on the nationals, the idea of being 'blacked' carried potentially career-shattering consequences, but even so when another vote was taken only a very few more of them were in favour of going on strike. Some withdrew their labour immediately and formed a small picket line in the street outside, but the rest, respecting the views of the majority, returned unhappily to their work. I saw Robin Anderson, who had been the father of the chapel (or chairman of the union branch in the office), sitting at his desk in tears, torn between his commitment to his newspaper and his loyalty to the union he had served for so long. A day later he, not unexpectedly, joined the picket line, though he still looked just as unhappy and never showed any appetite for the excesses which were to come.

The more we worked the more incensed the union and its militant supporters became . . . and the more intimidatory were the tactics employed by them. I escaped most of it (maybe because I was known to be no longer in the NUJ, maybe because I lived a handy 18 miles from the office or maybe just because we in the Features Department had never been considered part of the journalistic mainstream anyway) but I heard tales of others suffering from abusive anonymous phone calls at home, being threatened by burly figures who turned up on their doorsteps in the middle of the night, and having excrement shoved through their letter boxes.

Within a week or so the number of journalists who had joined the strike had risen to 28 – which still left around 80 who hadn't. And those 28 were, as they knew they would be, sacked.

As news of the *Post*'s mutiny spread and Pole-Carew's unforgiving stance against the strikers gained ever bigger national headlines, the union mobilised all the forces it could to bring it to its knees. The picket lines, begun by just a few gloomy *Post* journalists, most of whom didn't appear to want to be there in the first place, were joined by groups of local trades unionists, and then by busloads of others from all over the country – miners, dockers, railwaymen, bus drivers, firemen, college lecturers, other journalists and a ragbag of people who just wanted to join in the fun even though most of them didn't seem to have the faintest idea what the dispute was all about – who in their thousands brought the centre of Nottingham to an angry, bitter and violent halt.

The pickets had us surrounded. The *Post* offices were built on an island in the middle of Nottingham, so it was possible for them literally to ring the whole building, shouting, chanting, booing, spitting and threatening anyone who dared to pass. They came on foot and in buses and they came in their cars, forming a slow-moving nose-to-tail queue which drove for hours around the island, making it almost impossible for the vans to get out to deliver the newspaper which we – the three-quarters of the editorial workforce who were still working – were still managing to produce.

At an early stage we decided that while we would continue to work, we were comfortable doing so only if we were doing our own jobs, not those left vacant by the strikers. So I continued working in Features despite the fact that my labour might have been much more useful in the depleted newsroom, from which most of the strikers had come.

Being a features sub, tied to the office, meant I missed most of the trouble, because once inside the building I could stay there until it was time to go home. For the reporters life was much more difficult, because they had to endure the barrage of hate every time they entered or left the building, which, being reporters, was often.

Of course it was not only the journalists who suffered. A baying mob of pickets, with no personal knowledge of the newspaper they were demonstrating against, couldn't tell whether a man walking up the road was a strike-breaking sub editor or a clerk from the accounts department so they shouted and spat at him just in case; and they had no way of knowing (or even caring, most of them) whether the frightened teenaged girl wanting only to go home was a blackleg reporter or a junior advertising rep, so they called her names and chased her down the street just the same.

I don't mind admitting that sometimes I was terrified, and I had to develop my own strategy when it came to facing the mob. It was an old lesson I had learned at school that first came to my aid. I vaguely remembered being told that, to rid himself of nerves before knocking on the door of the headmaster's study, a schoolboy should do something very vigorous – waving his arms around, or running on the spot for a couple of minutes – because it helped use up whatever chemicals his body was producing that made him feel sick in the stomach. I reckoned that what applied to a nerve-racking wait outside the head's study probably applied equally to a confrontation with thousands of angry pickets outside a newspaper office, so every day I accomplished my walk from the station to the office at something approaching a jog, probably knocking other pedestrians out of my way as I went, as if I just couldn't wait to get there, so that by the time I arrived in Forman Street outside the office my body had used up its sickness-inducing chemicals and I was as calm as the situation would allow. Bitter experience told me that from then on it was better to walk slowly past the jeering hordes, because hurrying made it look as if I was ashamed and attracted even more of their anger, and if I spotted one of the striking *Post* journalists – most of whom seemed to be taking no pleasure in being there – I would go up to them, forcing a friendly smile upon my face, for a brief chat to show that as far as I was concerned there were no hard feelings (which was, in fact, true, since, though I disagreed with them and thought they were misguided, I respected them for having the courage to throw their jobs away on a noble point of principle).

One Saturday afternoon a few of the strikers managed to evade the security men at the gate and got as far as the newsroom, where they staged a sit-in protest. Within minutes they were confronted by a posse of journalists, led by the imposing figure of Christopher Pole-Carew, who between them took great pleasure in throwing them – literally, and very violently – back down the stairs whence they had come. Saturday was my day off, so I missed it, but there was still blood on the walls for me to inspect when I arrived at work the next Monday.

The dispute lasted for many weeks – all through the summer and into the autumn – and it was a painful, horrible, upsetting time for people on both sides. And, I suspect, it was just as bad for our families, who could only imagine what we were going through . . . and probably visualised it to be even worse than it was. For Tricia and me relief came in our garden, where we took out all our anger, fear and frustration on the weeds, which – imagining them to be pickets – we pulled up with a viciousness not usually associated with what is normally such a relaxing pastime.

The national strike ended, as most strikes do, with both sides claiming victory. But in Nottingham there was no such happy conclusion. There the 28 sacked journalists remained sacked, and all it meant was that the unions were able to focus all their efforts on stepping up their fight against the *Evening Post* in an attempt to get them their jobs back. The pickets remained, just as angry and just as intimidating, and the only change was that a few of them were now waving 'Reinstate the 28' placards instead of their fists (I often thought how useful it was that 28 of them that had been sacked – 'Reinstate the 27' just wouldn't have had the same ring to it). Not that the 28 were very much involved any more. With the financial backing of the NUJ they had set up their own weekly newspaper, the *Nottingham News*, and were far too busy producing it – and making a pretty good job of it – to spend very much time on the picket line.

It was obvious that Pole-Carew was not going to back down, but the stand-off continued for many more weeks, well into 1979, by which time the mob outside the gates had become just another familiar sight to be seen in Nottingham city centre. They were beginning to look silly, because there are few things more obviously pointless than a picket continuing a dispute that everyone else can see just can't be won, and anyway by now most of them were not proper pickets at all, but hangers-on who probably had no idea what it was that they were hoping to achieve by standing outside in the street day after day with the rain running down their necks.

I can't remember the day when the last of the pickets disappeared, though there clearly must have been one. There was certainly no rejoicing in the office, no party to celebrate a battle well won (as far as I was concerned it was a battle between the union and Christopher Pole-Carew, not me, so I had no sense that I had won or lost, and therefore no reason to make merry) and we just got on with our jobs, just as we had throughout the whole unhappy episode.

The shadow of the dispute hung over us for years, and some people were not prepared to forgive and forget. Many trades unionists and Labour politicians refused to speak to our reporters, and were deeply unpleasant when they were asked to do so, and even in the relative sanctuary of the Features Department, where talking to politicians had never been a key feature of our jobs, I occasionally experienced vitriol from some PR person who happened to be a paid-up member of the NUJ.

11

NOBODY WOULD CALL ME a religious man. My idea of a supreme being, if there is one, is that the echoes of everyone who has ever lived come together in an amorphous spiritual mass which might, just might, have some influence on how the world behaves today; and I believe the only form of life after death comes when the way we have lived our lives continues to impinge upon the people we have met along the way, working out, like ripples in a pond, from our wives and children all the way out to the people we bumped into in the bus queue. So what happened to me in Leominster Priory, the magnificent church in which Tricia and I had been married five years before, was all the more remarkable.

The easy rationalisation is that the strike had left me more punch-drunk and emotionally drained than I knew, so I was ripe to be overwhelmed by the quiet majesty of the place, but whatever the explanation the fact is that when I went into that church one day, while on a visit with the children to see their grandparents, I felt as if a comforting arm had been put around my shoulder with an unspeaking voice telling me: 'You don't know it yet, but you'll be needing this.'

We returned home to the news that my Dad had been diagnosed with terminal lung cancer. The shock of it was immense, even though he had been rather under the weather for some time and had got worryingly out of breath while walking back to the car the last time I had gone with him to a Bristol City match, but he was only 59 and the idea that he could die so young seemed absurd. I responded to the news in the way I usually respond to any crisis – by going for a walk – and I spent more than an hour wandering around Bottesford, criss-crossing the village from one side to the other and back again, trying to absorb what was soon to happen.

Richard Harris

It was dark and it was raining and anyone who met me would not have known that I was crying.

Dad had been a smoker for most of his adult life (in those days nobody had even suggested it might be anything other than good for you) and although he had given up in his 40s by then it was too late. After growing up in the lung-clogging smog of pre-war Birmingham, and coming from a family whose menfolk seemed to have a predisposition to lung cancer (his father had died from it in only his early sixties) he probably never stood a chance.

Whether he knew he was dying was impossible to tell, for we never spoke to him about it, but he wasn't a fool and was probably pretending not to know just to make it easier for us in the same way that we were pretending not to know, and telling him that yes, of course, he would get better, just so that it would be easier for him.

We went to see him as often as we could, to the bungalow on the outskirts of Weston that he and Mum had bought for the retirement he would not live to see, and as we left at the end of our last visit he was sitting crying in his armchair, probably knowing that he would not be seeing us again. On that visit he asked me, without admitting that he knew the inevitability of his condition, how Mum was coping. That was the only thing that worried him, he said, apart from the fact that since he had started taking all his bloody pills he had become impotent.

Dad died much sooner than any of us expected, on the afternoon of Friday April 20 1979, in the Bristol Royal Infirmary, from a blood clot on his lung. He was 17 days short of the joint birthday upon which at 60, he would have been precisely twice as old as me.

The next day I had to do the hardest thing I have ever had to do. My Gran – Dad's mother – was 78 years old and had lived in a bungalow in Banwell, a village a few miles from Weston, since leaving Birmingham following the death of my grandfather. She knew that my Dad was seriously ill but, like the rest of us, had no idea he was likely to die as soon as he did. So when I arrived knocking on her door that Saturday morning (she didn't notice my sister going next door to tell Mrs Pardy the news and ask her to sit with Gran after we had left) she was delighted.

'Richard!' she said, smiling broadly. 'What a nice surprise. I didn't know you were coming down this weekend.' Then she noticed the look on my face. 'What's wrong?'

I shepherded into her bedroom (she was still in her dressing gown) and sat her on her bed, desperately trying to think of a kind way of telling my favourite old lady that her only child was dead.

I put my arm around her.

'I'm sorry, Gran, it's not a nice surprise at all. I'm afraid there's no easy way of saying this. Dad's died.'

She looked at me puzzled, and when she grasped what I had said the look of horror spread across her face as if in slow motion. I put my other arm around her and pressed her face against my chest because I couldn't bear to hear her sobbing.

'Why?' she said. 'I could have given him 19 of my years. Why him and not me?'

It might have been Dad's death that unsettled me at work, or just the feeling that I had been doing the same job in the same place for long enough and I needed a change. Whatever it was, it wasn't long before I started scanning the *UK Press Gazette* for advertisements of vacancies elsewhere. My search for a job should have been reasonably easy since all I wanted was a new challenge in some place other than Nottingham, but not being fussy about what I wanted to do, or where I wanted to do it, was really no help at all. I had an unsuccessful interview (the first one I had ever failed!) for the features editor's job at the highly regarded Shropshire Star in Telford, but after that there was nothing at all that excited my interest, so to stop my career drifting away within the cosy confines of the *Evening Post* Features Department, I wrote a vague but optimistic letter to Westminster Press – owners of a huge number of local and regional newspapers all over the country – offering myself to them in much the same way as I had once offered myself to the *Western Daily Press*. My ambition, such as it was, was to become a features editor, since that was the only role for which my years at Nottingham had equipped me, so the last thing I was expecting was a letter from Nicholas Herbert, the group's editorial director, apologising for the fact that at the moment Westminster Press did not have any vacancies for editors.

Since, notwithstanding the lack of available editorships, he invited me for an interview, I went to meet him in London, and got on well enough with him to express my surprise that he thought I might be ready to be considered for the top job on one of his newspapers. But I had reckoned without the reputation of the *Evening Post* – in particular the way it had confronted the challenge of new technology – and how marketable it made anyone who was working there. It is difficult to exaggerate the position the *Post* held in the newspaper industry at that time, and most proprietors, it seemed, by now realised that the sort of technology pioneered at Nottingham would sooner or later sweep the industry, so it made sense for them to try to appoint people like me who had some, albeit limited, mastery of it.

'How about Chief Sub on the *Evening Advertiser*?' he suggested. 'That's available if you want it.'

I was hugely flattered by his keenness to find me a place in his Westminster Press empire, and the *Evening Advertiser* certainly had its attractions. It was a reasonable sized paper, though much smaller than either the *Evening Post* or the *Western Daily Press*, and even though it had the misfortune to be based in Swindon, a thoroughly unattractive town, it was only 40 miles from Bristol and therefore within very easy reach of my beloved Somerset. The only problem was the job itself; I could not believe that the two weeks I had spent being a news sub (and a very unsuccessful one at that) in Bristol were enough to equip me for one of the most specialised and demanding jobs on any newspaper. Would that fortnight's experience be enough for me to lord it over a group of seasoned news subs, most of whom would no doubt have been doing the job for donkeys' years and would quite justifiably look upon me as an underqualified young upstart who should by rights have a seat at the bottom of their table, not at the top of it? No, of course not, so I turned him down.

There were several reasons why, as months progressed, I realised that maybe leaving the *Evening Post* was not as essential a career move as I had thought. The first was that the sober old Features Department was rather suddenly transformed into a much livelier, more interesting and younger place. To cope with the still increasing workload several more staff were taken on, and this time they weren't old and timeworn like Bill Tomlinson and Harold Mount, but young, eager and – mostly – female. Among them was May Jeffrey, a shapely Glaswegian with a penchant for tight T-shirts and dirty jokes (or, at least, they were dirty compared with anything the Features Department had known before) who joined to help in the production of the supplements, and, better still, Janet, who gave up working from home and came to work in the office, albeit only part-time, as a feature writer.

All this didn't happen overnight, of course, and the new recruits did not all join at once, but it happened quickly enough for poor Wilf Berry not to know what had hit him, so that more than ever he just kept his head down over his desk in the corner and, though still nominally features editor, left someone else to run what had once been his department.

That someone, naturally, was Ian Scott. Though he tried hard, Ian still had little idea how to handle people without causing them offence. Although I had come to admire him for his energy and technical ability, I could not say the same about his man management skills. One day he shared with me his management philosophy. 'You have to be a bastard,' he told me, and I disregarded it immediately, preferring instead to follow some advice my Dad had once given me – 'Don't shit on people on your way up and they won't shit on you on your way down' – and made a vow that in the unlikely event of my ever being in such a position I would always try to treat people with decency and politeness.

The uprisings against Ian in the office were frequent and heated and even when he tried to display his human side he usually got it wrong. On one occasion, for example, he stood in the middle of the room and proudly announced that his wife was pregnant. Peter Frater, our newly appointed motoring correspondent, replied 'Just tell us who did it and we'll get him for you', which caused great mirth among the rest of us but left Ian no option but to try to save face by turning on his heel and walking out, with neither his dignity nor his sense of humour intact.

Ian decided that with so many people working in a now-busy department we needed proper job descriptions and he entered into this task with supreme gusto, as he did with everything he turned his attentions to. But, as so often, he managed to cause great displeasure to the more conservative members of the staff, for whom job descriptions were just an example of the gobbledegook to be found in some management handbook. Bill Tomlinson could see no point in it at all, since he had never had a job description in all the 50 years he had been in journalism, and Wilf went into an almost tearful sulk when, with it being spelled out in writing for the first time, he had finally to accept the fact that he had in effect been demoted and was indeed answerable to Ian. I, on the other hand, was pleased to have my duties spelled out (it made me sound rather important, I thought) and I was even more pleased to see – in words that proved yet again that journalists do not always write what they intend, especially when double entendres are concerned – that among the lovely May's tasks was 'to provide relief for Richard'.

Ian did eventually become more popular – or less unpopular, anyway – and it was not just because he had responsibility for the *Post*'s travel supplement. Such a role meant it was he who received offers of free press trips . . . and he who had the responsibility of sharing them out among the staff. It was thanks to him that in the late summer of 1979 I flew off for a few days in Gibraltar. They put me up in a modern hotel in the main street, as guest of the Gibraltar Tourist Board, and told me that – apart from a day-trip across the sea to Africa – the highlight of my visit would be the Miss Gibraltar beauty contest, being held the next night, for which I was invited to be one of the judges.

I had been chosen, they told me, because they had scoured the list of visitors arriving at the airport and I, being a journalist, was just about the most interesting one they could find. So I and two students (being the second and third most interesting people to have flown in that week) were whisked by taxi to St Michael's Cave – a huge natural cavern under the Rock, turned into a rather impressive concert hall – and asked to take our places on the stage, where we would be joined, after they had completed the cabaret, by Tony Hatch and Jackie Trent (an enormously successful husband-and-wife songwriting/singing duo, who between them were responsible for a string of hits throughout the '60s and '70s).

There was just one problem with the Miss Gibraltar competition. Gibraltar, being only a very small place, had very few young women to choose from (the previous year only three girls had entered) so the dozen who lined up on the catwalk that night included several who would have been rejected even from the qualifying heats of Miss Weston-super-Mare (I know, because I once judged that too).

Of the 12 there were maybe four who would not quite have disgraced any other small town's beauty pageant, but only one who had the sort of looks that would not be totally out of place in the Miss World competition, for which she would be sent to London later in the year. Our decision could have been made in an instant, because when it came to voting for the winner all five of us judges had her at the top of our very short shortlists, but for the sake of the many no-hopers we pretended to give our discussions considerably more time than they needed before proclaiming the winner: Miss Gibraltar 1979 was Audrey Lopez, a sharp-featured brunette with sparkling eyes and a self deprecating sense of humour. A couple of months later I watched the Miss World finals on TV from London and was not in the least surprised when Audrey was knocked out in the first round.

I had still not put out of my mind all thought of leaving the Evening *Post*, but in the meantime I had other things to think about. Tricia was pregnant again, which we were both delighted about even though it presented us with a major problem. With our house already proving too small for a family with two growing children, we had to search still harder for somewhere that would be big enough to cope with three – a search which had just as depressing a result as before. The houses that might have been suitable, we could not afford; and the houses we could afford were not the sort we wanted to live in.

The solution came unexpectedly, from just up the road. Our friends Peter and Sheila Murphy told us they had decided to move with their three boys back to Ireland, and would be putting their house – a big detached one, four doors away from ours, right at the end of Toll Bar Avenue – up for sale, and the price they would be asking was just about within our budget. It was not exactly the country cottage we had dreamed of, but it was a good deal better than any other alternative, so we reached an informal agreement that, when they came to sell, we would buy.

It was Peter I turned to when our new baby looked like dying.

William Hugh was born in Grantham hospital in the small hours of the morning of Monday June 16 1980 and it was immediately obvious that something was very wrong. I had witnessed enough births (well, two anyway) to know what to expect, and this was not it. He was grey and almost lifeless and bathed in far too much blood. The midwife, making a very poor attempt to remain calm, hurried over to the wall and pressed a red panic button that I had hardly noticed before and almost immediately a doctor and another nurse arrived. They wrapped William up and handed him to Tricia for a cuddle, but there was no time for the joyous celebration that had accompanied the births of his brother and sister, and within minutes they took him away again to be further examined by another doctor.

They quite simply had no idea what was wrong with him, but it was clearly serious and when I returned home to tell Antony and Juliet that they had a new brother I was convinced he was going to die. I managed to phone my mother, but having told her the bad news just could not face doing it all over again . . . so I asked Antony to phone Tricia's.

It sounds like cowardice, I know, and so it probably was. But making that one phone call had taken out of me what little emotional strength the morning's events had left me with and I knew that Antony, at five years old, was at that moment better equipped to do it than I was at 31. 'Hello Granny, we've got a little brother but he's very poorly,' he told her matter-of-factly.

That afternoon, encouraged by the hospital, I took Antony and Juliet in to see their brother, for what I was convinced would be the first and last time. They were fitted with plastic shoes and little surgeon's gowns, which though small were still far too big for them, and dressed like that – with the hems hitched up untidily into their waistbands and their long sleeves rolled several times up over their arms – they were escorted in to see him. He was lying in an incubator with an ominous tube into his head and they had to stand on tiptoe to peer inside.

I had worried that they might be traumatised by the experience, but I should have had no such fears. 'It's all right Daddy,' said Antony when we got home. 'If he dies we'll just have to get another one.'

By the time I returned to the hospital things were a little clearer, though not much. There was something wrong with William's blood count, so he had had a huge transfusion in an attempt to stabilise it. For a while that seemed to have done the trick, but soon his blood count was falling again, so he needed another transfusion. And another. We gazed at him constantly, looking and praying for any sign that his cheeks were maybe just a little pinker, that he seemed to be just a little more lively, but they still did not know what was causing the problem and I was convinced that there was something wrong with his little body that made it impossible for him to produce the quality of blood he needed to survive.

That evening at home I was able to put on a brave face long enough to put Antony and Juliet to bed, but there was nothing brave about me as I prepared for a long evening downstairs alone. Less than 24 hours earlier I had been sick with excitement at the prospect of our baby's birth; now I was sick with worry about his dying. Then, in the greatest act of kindness I had experienced from anyone since Alexis Stacey sat at the desk next to mine after Philip died, Peter Murphy arrived. Uninvited, and with a bottle or two, he stayed with me for hours, talking or just sitting in silence well into the night, and doing everything that a brawny Irishman could that did not involve actually holding my hand or mopping up my tears.

Next day there was talk of transferring William to the Queen's Medical Centre – a huge and very well equipped new hospital in Nottingham – where he would receive care unequalled anywhere in Britain. His blood count was still falling (though maybe not quite as fast) and still nobody knew what was causing it. But just as the final arrangements were being made to move him he seemed a little better, and the doctors decided to give him more time. 'He's going to be all right, I just know it,' Tricia said when I went to visit her and found him at her breast. 'He wouldn't be feeding as well as he is if he wasn't going to survive. He's a fighter.'

She was right, of course. Once his blood count had stabilised – which in fact took only a couple of days, though it seemed forever – he maintained a healthy colour and became far too lively to be contained any longer in his incubator, which at any rate was designed for a baby much smaller than he was.

Nobody ever told us what had been wrong with him, probably because it would have reflected badly on the hospital, but we reckoned it was that nobody had noticed that his umbilical cord had ruptured in the early stages of his birth, so that by the time he was born he was almost empty of blood. The transfusions had merely been needed to fill him up, in the same way that a car needs petrol after it has run dry.

We didn't feel like recriminations, though. Not when, at just four days old, he came home and our family was complete.

Soon after William was born Peter Murphy came back to our house full of apology. He and Sheila had changed their minds and would not be returning to Ireland after all. Or, to put it another way, their house was no longer for sale and we were back to square one . . . but with the added problem that we now had three children, not just two, and for the foreseeable future would all have to fit into a house that hardly had room for us.

The solution – in one of those happy accidents that seem to have been a feature of my life – came that very evening. By the time Peter had left, Tricia and I were too disappointed to think about cooking, so we decided to have fish and chips for our supper. Our take-away from the Bottesford chippy came wrapped in several pages of the previous week's Grantham Journal, a newspaper which we were no longer bothering to buy because we had only ever read it for the estate agents' adverts and, with our purchase of the Murphys' house almost finalised, there seemed to be no further need.

The page facing me as I unwrapped my fish supper contained the pictures of dozens of houses for sale, each just as hopeless as those that had gone before – except for one. Field Cottage was a whitewashed semi detached property in Normanton, a hamlet just a mile north of Bottesford, and in every respect looked the house we had been dreaming of. It was old and quaint and when we saw it we fell in love with it instantly.

Not even the fact that it was next to a goat farm, which we worried – wrongly, as it turned out – might get a bit smelly in the summer, could put us off. With views over open fields and a lovely garden, and despite the road which ran right past the front windows, it was a little piece of rural heaven, especially to us who had spent eight years on a modern open-plan housing estate. And we could afford it!

Field Cottage had only three bedrooms, so was not really very much bigger than 9 Toll Bar Avenue, but it somehow felt much more spacious, and anyway there was potential for a fourth over an extended kitchen when we could afford it.

Having already worked out our finances to buy the Murphys' house, we knew precisely how much money we had and where it would be coming from, so the purchase was straightforward even if the selling of 9 Toll Bar Avenue, which took almost another year, was not. We moved in just before Christmas and were met by Anne Cox, the tiny ruddy faced goat farmer from next door, who welcomed us with 'I'll say hello and I'll say goodbye at the same time because I'll probably never speak to you again' (in fact Anne, who revelled in a reputation for being unfriendly, became one of several good friends we made in that little village).

12

MOVING HOUSE HELPED to cure my restlessness at work, but it was still a little while before I realised that my immediate future more sensibly lay in Nottingham. With the new more lively Features Department, journalism had become more fun again, and anyway, thanks to Ian Scott and the travel features he needed for his glossy holiday magazine, we now had the considerable bonus of fairly regular free trips abroad.

After my visit to Gibraltar I was soon off again – to Jersey in the Channel Islands. And it was a trip that changed my life.

Six of us went, all journalists from newspapers and magazines in the East Midlands, and among the excursions the local tourist office arranged for us was one to a vast underground hospital built by the Germans – or, rather, by the prisoners they had brought there from every corner of conquered Europe during the Second World War. The tunnels, hewn and blasted out of the rock by hundreds of forced labourers who toiled like slaves underground, were originally intended as barracks to house enough German soldiers to turn the island into an impregnable fortress, never to be defeated, but in the weeks leading up to D-Day, as the Allied invasion loomed, that plan was altered, and the tunnels became instead a huge underground hospital, where casualties from the expected battles would be treated. In fact the anticipated invasion never happened, the hospital was never needed and the Channel Islands' occupying forces surrendered peacefully in May 1945, a day after the rest of Europe.

The underground hospital was left unused, and unchanged, after the war, as a monument to the hundreds of men who had suffered such unimaginable hardship and brutality at the hands of their captors and when I went into it on that warm sunny day it was the coldest, scariest, most chilling place I had ever been in. We walked around it mostly in silence, awe-struck by the ghosts that seemed to lurk in the shadows from nearly 40 years before.

And on the way out we walked through the brightly lit souvenir shop where for the price of a pint I could have bought a wind-up clockwork goose-stepping German soldier to march across the floor of my cosy cottage when I got home. It was the tackiest thing I had ever seen, a gratuitous insult to the men who had so harshly suffered there and when I got back I devoted my travel feature on Jersey not to that lovely island's gentle climate and beautiful beaches (which is what my hosts had wanted) but to the grossest example of insensitivity and bad taste that I had ever had the misfortune to experience.

It was many months before I came to experience the repercussions.

Psychologists would no doubt enjoy trying to explain why I am the way I am – why I don't have any close male friends; why I can sometimes be, in many people's eyes, distant, cautious and hard to get to know; why the idea of a 'night out with the boys', so much enjoyed by so many men, holds no appeal for me at all; and why almost all the important people in my life have been women. I'll save them the trouble and offer my own explanation.

It would be too easy to say that it's all just because of my innate shyness or the fact that I'd had my fill of male company by the time I left school at 18 (though both are probably at least partly true). I believe it's rather more complicated than that – that after Philip's death I built a protective barrier around myself so that I would never be so badly hurt again. I had friends, it is true, but I kept them at arm's length so that they never became close ones, because deep down I was worried that they might be snatched from me just as Philip had been. Occasionally, since, people have come close to breaching that barrier, and some – all women – have even climbed over the top of it . . . but probably only because they have been able to use some sexual chemistry (unspoken or otherwise) as added ammunition to help them do so. Even then it has taken them a while to achieve it, and even Tricia took time to break down my wall before I admitted I liked her, let alone fell in love with her.

Which brings us on to the one person who, astonishingly, frighteningly, defied all that.

Ambra Edwards was a copywriter for a small London advertising agency, and in 1981 she was given the job of accompanying a group of journalists – me included – to Mauritius, whose tourist board her firm worked for.

She exploded into my life like a firework and, once we had got our initial spiky meeting out of the way, did what no one else had done before (or has ever done since), as if making up for all the people I had never previously allowed to breach my barricades.

We met at Heathrow airport and by the time she arrived with our tickets after a problem at the airline desk she was so late I and the other journalists had resigned ourselves to the fact that there had been some sort of mix-up and we would not be going on the trip after all. Ambra bounced towards the knot of worried journalists gathered at the check-in desk with an engaging jollity and encouraging smile and was met by me (I had elected myself as the group's unofficial spokesman) complaining vigorously about the anxiety her tardiness had caused us all. I was, I think, thoroughly and unforgivably unpleasant.

That night, we were all invited to try our luck in our hotel's casino, but Ambra and I gave away the free gaming chips we had been given and spent several hours lying on our backs on a paradise beach in the Indian Ocean instead, watching the stars shooting across the southern sky and wondering if it was true we had only just met. We were strangers yet we had known each other all our lives. We talked and laughed and sometimes just lay in silence, and both were aware, I think, that we had chanced upon something very special.

It was more than just the chemistry, which fizzed between us for all to see; an empathy I had not experienced so instantaneously with anyone before (and haven't since), an extraordinary compatibility which allowed us to enjoy a deep and immediate pleasure in each other's company.

It was also, for a man with a wife and three small children, frankly pretty scary.

I returned home in a state of wretched confusion. The sensible thing, I knew then and know now, would have been to try to forget all about Ambra, to put the seismic affect she had had on me down to experience and get on with my life, which was already more than good enough. But I was in no mood to do the sensible thing. Even after just four days she had become too valuable to be thrown away as if I had never met her, and I agonised over how to keep her in my life without ruining everything else that was important to me. There was, of course, no answer and on several evenings I sat miserably on the floor beside Antony's bed, asking him what I should do; but he was only seven – and asleep, anyway – so was no more able to come up with a solution than I was.

If I had not been married – or if I had been married, but unhappily – the answer would have been simple. I would have thrown in my job in

Nottingham, found another one in London, and seen where my relationship with Ambra might have taken me.

Ambra, I know, was plagued by feelings similar to mine. She called me her 'shadow of a love', which I understood and appreciated, and I much later admitted to her that I had loved her almost since the time we met, which I regretted (the telling, not the loving) because it made even more complicated an already complicated relationship. So-called 'experts' would no doubt have advised Tricia to put up with none of it, to threaten me and to give me ultimatums, and to tell me I had to choose between Ambra and her, but she was far too level headed for such a gross, though understandable, over-reaction. Having justified confidence in the strength of our marriage, she simply carried on more or less as normal, confident that the storm would pass, while I sorted myself out.

Of course the storm did pass and I did sort myself out and – after causing much pain to them both – in the end managed to achieve what for a long time had seemed impossible: Keeping Tricia as a loving wife and Ambra as a friend. There have been many times over the years when I have wondered whether our friendship was worth all the hurt but today, nearly three decades on, with my marriage happily intact and Ambra still a loved and loving friend, I believe it was. Whether she, or indeed Tricia, would agree is, of course, debatable.

What I am sure of, though – and I am well aware of how selfish this sounds – is that her presence in my life has added immeasurably to it. Not just the fun and the laughter and our shared sense of the absurd (we revelled in the tackiest of Mauritius gift shops and their bizarre choice of souvenirs nearly all of which – table lamps, bread baskets, alarm clocks and teapots – somehow contrived to be in the shape of the dodo, the extinct bird for which the island is famous) but the sometimes contrary view she has on the world and the way she made me question many of the values which I had held for years without ever bothering to doubt them.

One way or another trips abroad seemed to have a habit of having profound affects on me. And the three weeks I spent in Peru were no different. I was chosen to go there to check whether South America would be a good destination for members of the *Post*'s readers' holiday club (it wouldn't, I decided, because such a journey into the high Andes to see Macchu Picchu and the ancient Inca sites around it would have been far too strenuous for the pensioners who made up a typical Signpost trip).

Apart from Mauritius, where we were able to turn a blind eye to the local poverty by confining ourselves to our shamelessly luxurious hotels, it was my first experience of a Third World country and it shook me to the roots. Lima, the capital, was a noisy, dirty, bustling city which at first frightened me and then made me fall in love with it, and it was there that I belatedly discovered my social conscience. As I walked through its heaving streets – with my valuables safely locked away in a hotel safe – I was plagued by the guilt that comes from having far too many riches (not just money, but health and opportunity too) in a country in which most of the population have none.

A small boy selling matches on the steps of the cathedral gave me an expert guided tour of the interior and in return I presented him with a few coins which, to me, were nothing more than a nuisance jangling in my pocket, but to him would have amounted to what his father, if he had one, might have earned in a week. And on the next day I went on a tour of the city's sights, during which our bus pulled into a specially prepared lay-by so that we could all pile off and enjoy the 'photo opportunity' presented to us by a hideous hillside shanty town where whole families – possibly including the little boy from the cathedral – lived in cardboard boxes, plywood sheds or, if they were among the lucky ones, rough houses built of old bricks and rusting scrap corrugated iron.

I'm not sure what horrified me more – the fact that thousands of people were living there in such conditions, or that those in charge of the country's tourist trade expected people like me to want to take a bus trip to take photographs of it.

I returned home, I believe, radically changed and that Christmas, as we gathered round the fire in our comfortable little cottage, opening far too many presents and eating far too much food, I simply could not settle. I felt restless and guilty and useless . . . and what I really wanted to do was to fly out once again to Peru to find my little boy on the steps of the cathedral in Lima and give him the sort of Christmas I knew he would never have.

What I experienced in Lima has affected my life – and, I like to think, my approach to newspapers and what goes into them – ever since.

With Ian Scott's influence becoming more pronounced, more features pages had to be filled, which meant that someone had to write them. I, being bored by subbing other people's copy and keen to have a go at more writing myself, was happy to lend a hand whenever I could. It felt somehow appropriate that one of the first articles to appear under my name was on the death penalty (which maybe showed that my old English teacher at Walton Lodge had been right when, faced with what I had written on the subject at the age of 11, he told me 'You should be a journalist').

Richard Harris

Even though it had been abolished in Britain in 1969, the death penalty was frequently in the news in those days, with regular opinion polls telling us that the vast majority of people wanted it reintroduced and with MPs courting popularity by trying to get it debated once again in Parliament. My views had not changed since childhood and when someone was needed to argue against it, in response to a piece by the fervently pro-hanging woman's editor Daphne Oxland, I was happy to oblige. This is what I wrote:

I REMEMBER as a kid having a struggle to eat my cornflakes because I knew that at that very moment a man was being dangled on the end of a rope in the name of justice.

We'd have the radio on for the news over breakfast, and the announcer's brief statement that a man was being hanged in some faraway jail seemed to me, a small child in the warmth of my own home, inexcusably barbaric.

So if anyone ever asks me how I feel about capital punishment – and I don't see why they shouldn't since they seem to be asking everybody else these days – I have only to think back to when I was eight.

And I will tell them quickly and concisely that I can't see how a country can claim to be civilised if it still has to resort to such barbarity.

While I've never claimed to be religious, I'll accept that most of the Ten Commandments are pretty sensible rules to live by and Thou Shalt Not Kill is as good as any.

And I'm sorry but I can't respect anyone who tries to amend that to satisfy his own conscience – 'Thou shalt not kill unless thou art doing it in the name of the law, in which case it's all right.'

I know there are fearsome arguments in favour of bringing back the rope – rising crime, thugs' disregard for innocent life, the ever-growing threat of terrorism – just as there are equally strong ones against it.

But it's not the arguments one way or the other that have convinced me; it's not the dread of terrorist reprisals, or of IRA men being made martyrs, or even the fear of hanging the wrong man, although that takes a lot of answering.

If the decision were to be made simply on the strength of these arguments, I would have to admit that I'd changed my mind.

Quite honestly, I sometimes wish I could change my mind. For I do believe that, if hanging were brought back, it might be a deterrent against the sort of violence that could leave the likes of you and me lying dying in the gutter.

I wish I could change my mind but I can't.

Because – although it seems an inadequately simple thing in the face of so many arguments so well expressed – deep down in my guts, I feel that the death penalty is wrong. Nothing more nor less than that.

Many times I have been asked: 'Yes, but what if it were your wife or your child who'd been murdered? You'd soon change your tune then, wouldn't you?'

And, yes, of course I would.

I'd probably be first in the line, trying to string the killer up before the police reached him.

But surely it can't be right to let our attitude to capital punishment be decided by how we might feel at a time like that?

Would we really want such an important issue to be decided by anyone so emotionally disturbed?

It surely cannot be that breaking the neck of a murderer is the only way we have of fighting back against the killers.

I agree that they are not punished severely enough, I agree that most of them should never be released from prison, and I agree that our whole system of punishment needs an overhaul.

But hanging? It's wrong. And it's not just a little bit wrong. It is so wrong that society must have the courage to do what is right – and to pay whatever price is necessary to do so.

COURTESY OF THE NOTTINGHAM POST

I doubt that it had the impact of the school essay that ended with my dramatic 'Aaaagh!' as the condemned man fell through the trapdoor and had his neck broken, but I was pleased to be given the opportunity to put my views – views that I have held so strongly all my life – before a potential readership of more than 300,000 people. And indeed, as I stumbled into my new role of feature writer rather than features sub, it was the prospect of having my work read by so many that made the job so stimulating.

Suddenly all the old excitement of being a journalist – of doing the sort of things and meeting the sort of people that only a journalist can do and meet – was back. While we on the *Evening Post* recognised that we were a regional paper, not a national one, we could see no reason why that should confine our thinking, so many was the time I found myself working in some far-off part of the country. And if that part of the country happened to be London, so much the better; it meant I could meet Ambra (often in some dark and dingy wine bar which made a suitable backdrop for the emotional turmoil of our relationship).

When a movie was made of D H Lawrence's novel Lady Chatterley's Lover, for example, I was sent to London (purely on the strength of Lawrence having been born in Eastwood, just up the road from Nottingham) to interview the star – Sylvia Kristel, a beautiful Dutch actress who had made her name in the Emmanuelle soft-porn films, and who was now hoping her new role would help her be accepted as a serious actress. Sylvia was witty, highly intelligent and very good company and probably the sexiest woman I have ever met, but I'm not sure that I was at my journalistic best interviewing her over lunch in a posh London restaurant when I had only just watched her rolling so splendidly naked in the fields with Mellors the gamekeeper.

Sylvia Kristel – probably the sexiest woman I have ever met

When someone wrote that the great thing about Britain was the freedom to do what you liked without anyone telling you that you shouldn't, I was sent to Nottingham's huge Old Market Square, to sit for two hours beside the stone lions and fountains beneath a sombrero and a stripey blanket, just to find out if it was true (it was, and the only person who came anywhere near me to disturb my siesta was a young woman who lifted the rim of my hat far enough to look into my eyes and tell me 'Yeah man, that's cool' before staggering away to sleep off the drugs she was so obviously high on).

When we heard that 19-year-old Pilin Leon, a brown-eyed doctor's daughter from Venezuela and the reigning Miss World, was coming to Nottingham as part of a nationwide promotional tour, I was sent to Leicester to accompany her in her car on the last leg of her journey, unaware that she had been learning English for only three days and was therefore a bit short in the art of conversation. We travelled together in her limousine, in silence, and passed the time by smiling frequently at each other as she clutched her crown in a little basket on her lap ('she takes it with her everywhere,' I wrote, 'as elderly ladies take their chihuahuas').

When the Eurovision Song Contest was held in Harrogate, I was sent there for the rehearsals and arrived just in time to see the workmen high up on the scaffolding fixing the golden Os to the sign above the stage that read EUR VISI N S NG C NTEST. I spent a happy day there, enjoying the daftness of the occasion and rubbing shoulders with people for whom this would be the most exciting weekend of their lives, and came away writing in the *Post* that I had spotted the certain winner (a gentle love song by a boy-girl duo from Austria), not foreseeing that overnight they would ruin both the song and their chances by giving it a thumping beat and singing it twice as fast as they had when I'd heard it.

My job was always interesting, and often exciting, and, with Christmas approaching, life enhancing too. I deputised for Father Christmas in his grotto on the first floor of the Nottingham Co-op, and – though 'the elastic of the whiskers was threatening to slice through my ears and I was fairly certain that the thick red suit was going to stew me alive' – had one of the most rewarding days of my working life. 'I saw maybe 100 children,' I wrote afterwards. 'They bounced on my knee, kissed me, laughed with me, confided in me and poked at me to see how fat I was after all the mince pies they'd left out for me last year. Sometimes they screamed at me (though usually they stopped once I showed them the bag of chocolate they'd be getting) and quite often they just stared, mouths open, because now they knew for sure that there really was a Father Christmas.' It restored my faith in children and in Christmas.

13

ALTHOUGH I WAS NOW ENJOYING work more than I had done for some time, I still felt I would need to leave Nottingham before very long if I was not to stagnate. I was still on Westminster Press's mailing list, and was briefly tempted by the vacant editorship of the *Wiltshire Times*, the group's weekly paper in Trowbridge. But all thoughts of moving ended – at least temporarily – with the news that Bill Snaith was retiring. Only a fool leaves a newspaper when there's a new editor in the offing, I thought, because you never know how he might change things for the better and how he might breathe new life into your flagging career. Best to wait a while, I thought. There would be time enough to move once the new man had arrived and proved himself to be not to my liking. Until then I would give him the benefit of the doubt, whoever he might be.

It was fairly obvious that the new editor would be an outside appointment. There was nobody already on the staff who was of the calibre to step up to such a job, and though it was widely known that Ian Scott had applied for it we were confident that, if they didn't know already, the board of directors would soon find out enough about his abrasive style of man management to rule him out at an early stage. We guessed that the *Evening Post* was an important enough newspaper for its editorship to attract some of the industry's big names and the smart money was on either Colin Brannigan, the high profile former editor of the *Sheffield Star*, or one of the up and coming younger editors of other evening papers of the East Midlands, such as the *Derby Telegraph* or *Leicester Mercury*.

Nobody was expecting our new boss to be a bloke called Barrie Williams, who had worked at the *Post* a few years before – writing On The Square, just as I had done – before going off to rise very quickly to become editor of the Kent *Evening Post*. His appointment took everybody by surprise, and left those who had once worked with him in the Features Department scratching their heads, because most of them could barely remember him, and those who could had seen nothing in him that had marked him out as a potential editor.

Those of us who hoped for a major revolution as soon as Barrie took over in early 1982 were disappointed. For many weeks it was no more than the subtlest of changes – perhaps just people working a little harder, or more flamboyantly, to catch the eye of the new editor – but after a while it became clear that he had a very different idea of what his job was about. Those who had met him described an energetic, friendly man, perhaps with a touch of arrogance, who once he had settled in intended to get fully involved in the day-to-day business of producing a newspaper. Gone was the old Bill Snaith approach that we had grown used to, in which the editor spent most of his day shut in his office doing who-knew-what behind a closed door and only rarely venturing out (and always in his jacket) to talk to the hoi polloi in the newsroom, and in its place would be the new style of a shirt-sleeved editor who wanted to be visible, approachable and, most of all, a journalist.

I watched all this with interest and some frustration from my out-of-the-way desk in the Features Department, knowing that in there we would be the last to be hit by whatever storms were coming, and though I confess I came to enjoy the discomfiture so obviously being felt by some of the more reactionary senior staff in the newsroom – not least Bill Ivory, who clearly considered the new editor's hands-on approach to be an unwelcome intrusion into his role of news editor – I longed to be able to play some part in the exciting goings-on elsewhere. For six weeks I watched, and for six weeks I had no reason to speak to – or indeed go anywhere near – the new editor. I had put my plans for a move away from Nottingham on hold just so I could give the new man a chance but, while others were getting to know him and forging a useful working relationship with him, I was stuck in the Features Department where he didn't even know I existed!

That changed when Ian Scott went on holiday and Wilf Berry was at the last minute either too busy or too timid to stand in for him at the afternoon editorial conference, where the heads of department met with the editor to discuss the next day's paper. Being (unofficially) third in line, it fell to me to deputise for the deputy. As I entered the conference room I saw that everyone else was already there, gathered around the large oak table, with Barrie (or the man I took to be Barrie, since I had hardly seen him until then) at the head. I had no option but to walk up and introduce myself to him, shake him by the hand and inwardly curse him for making me look such a fool in front of the entire senior journalistic team.

The next day he called me into his office.

'I'm sorry about yesterday, mate,' he said. 'I'm afraid I just haven't had time yet to get round to meeting everybody and the newsroom had to come first. I'll get around to Features soon, honest.'

I'm not sure which was the bigger surprise – an editor apologising to me or an editor calling me 'mate'.

I discovered that Barrie was just a few years older than me, with eyes that managed to be both piercing and laughing at the same time. He seemed friendly, though I had no doubt there must be a tough side to him too, and his obvious excitement about his job was engaging, and his enthusiasm for journalism refreshing after the sometimes stultifying atmosphere of the Features Department.

He was an easy man to talk to and when he came to ask me about my ambitions I did not feel the need to be anything other than honest. I told him that I had been looking for a move, but only because I wanted to be accepted as Features editor at the *Post*, since that was in effect the job I was doing anyway, but realised there was little chance of that since it would mean an intolerable demotion for Wilf, who was a good man and a friend.

'Is that all?' he asked, as if it somehow wasn't enough. 'Features editor?'

'Well,' I said, casting around frantically for something that might suggest that I was part of the thrusting bright new generation waiting for him to give us a chance. 'Well . . . I suppose I wouldn't mind being news editor.'

He raised an eyebrow and I left his office cursing for making a fool of myself. I'd had my opportunity to make a good impression on the new editor but succeeded only in making myself look a total prat by coming up with some ridiculous, damn fool idea for which I was not in the least bit qualified.

It was almost a year before Barrie called me into his office again.

'You once told me you that if you couldn't become features editor you wouldn't mind being news editor,' he said.

'That's true,' I nodded, feeling all the old foolishness return.

'Well, do you want to?'

'Want to what?'

'Be my news editor.'

It was then that I discovered I need not have worried about opportunities passing me by while I was stuck in the backwater of the Features Department. Barrie had been aware of me all the time. In fact he had first noticed me even before he arrived in Nottingham, when he was being sent copies of everything the *Post* published in the months between his being appointed and his taking over as editor, and had had me earmarked for possible promotion ever since.

'I liked what you wrote about the clockwork German soldiers,' he told me. 'That's the sort of stuff I want. A bit of emotion.'

Being plucked out of Features to be given what is possibly the second most important job on any newspaper was almost unheard of, and the fact that Barrie even thought of it illustrates how determined he was to do things his own way. He had been observing me for a year, reading what I wrote and watching the way I conducted myself, and had decided that I was the man for the job and to hell with anyone who thought I had been away from news reporting for too long.

I asked for time to think about it (in truth there was nothing to think about, but it was such an unexpected proposition I wanted to clear my head and talk it over with Tricia before accepting it). The next day I told Barrie that I was his man. The only problem was that Bill Ivory, whose job I was taking, knew nothing about it.

I was sworn to secrecy and the only person with whom I was allowed to discuss my promotion was Ian Scott, whom Barrie had made his deputy editor and who naturally was in on the secret. Ian was very pleased for me, no doubt believing – rightly – that the way he had taken me under his wing in the Features Department had a lot to do with my new situation. Barrie wanted time to persuade Bill to become Assistant Editor (nominally a more senior position, but one far away from the day-to-day exhilaration of running a department of more than 30 reporters), and he needed also to give me a crash course in what he expected of his news editor. It would all take at least six months, probably more, he said, and in the meantime I was to get on with my normal job and not tell a soul.

I had very little idea what the job waiting for me was likely to involve, but the better I got to know Barrie (not least over the frequent carvery lunches we had together in the posh Royal Hotel opposite the office) the happier and more confident about it I became. As an editor he was every bit as inspirational as Eric Price – but without the bad language – and his idea of what a newspaper like the *Post* should be was much the same as mine: A paper with a heart, a conscience and a sense of humour, a paper that fought for the downtrodden and battled against injustice, a paper that entertained just as much as it informed and, perhaps most of all, a paper about people. Like me, he believed that journalism was a great job and that anyone who didn't enjoy it wasn't doing it right, and that people worked better if they were encouraged and felt their efforts were appreciated by the management.

In the meantime Barrie's changes were beginning to be felt throughout the newspaper, even in the Features Department. The news was to be more punchy, with the paper developing a more campaigning style; features were to become more personal, and there were to be a range of by-lined columns, with the best writers being promoted as 'personalities'. I was flattered to be chosen to be one of them.

Having to write a column every week imposed a different kind of discipline upon me compared with anything I had been used to. It was one thing to be sent out on an assignment, knowing roughly what it was likely to involve, and how I was likely to write it when I got back to the office . . . but quite another to be faced with filling a hole on the page every week with a thousand words on a subject that existed only in my own head. Five of us had been selected, one for every weekday, and I was given Wednesdays – a slot I filled, with breaks only for holidays, for the next seven years.

I soon realised that the idea of writing a column was a good deal more attractive than actually doing it. I enjoyed the opportunity to have something published under my name every week, and possibly read by enough people to fill four Wembley stadiums; I enjoyed the recognition it gave me, and the people coming up to me in the pub or in the street as if they knew me; and I even enjoyed having to walk past the larger than life-size photograph of myself displayed in the office window on my way to work. But I discovered that the actual writing of the column – or, rather, not so much the writing, more the deciding what to write about week after week – was quite difficult. More often than not I fell back onto writing about the only other thing about which I was anything like an expert – my family. It won me the not altogether welcome nickname of 'Homely Harris' among some of my workmates, but more remarkably it struck a chord with the readers.

Here, for no particular reason other than that it is fairly typical, is an example:

THE question the whole village wants answered, it seems, is this: Is it really my Auntie Vi who does the judging at the local fancy dress competition . . . and, if it isn't, how else do I account for the fact that one of my kids has walked off with a prize now for three years running?

There have been rumblings of discontent, I'm told.

The subject has been raised in high places (well, someone did mention it in passing at a meeting of the Bottesford and District Pre-School Playgroup Committee) and I fancy people are beginning to eye me in a manner tending towards suspicion.

Well, I'll let you into a secret – and no, it's got nothing to do with my Auntie Vi. While I don't deny my family's apparent domination of the fancy dress department, I can't claim that it has much to do with anything other than pure luck.

Indeed, if there ever has been a less deserving winner than our Antony over these past three years then I've yet to meet him.

(My two other children would no doubt agree with this, since they too have been entering the same competition for years and have yet to get a sniff of even a Highly Commended).

You see, our success in this most keenly contested of competitions owes much to the fact that, in our family, we never quite get round to doing things.

While other doting parents work feverishly into the night, sewing sequins onto tiny fairies' frocks and fluffing up the pompom buttons on the junior clowns' outfits, we just tell our offspring to go to bed and we'll think about it in the morning.

And so it is that, come The Big Day, when all the other kids in the village have had seventeen dress rehearsals in front of full-length mirrors and several admiring relatives, ours still haven't a clue what they're going to wear.

Three hours before the might of the village's 12s-and-unders are due to be parading as three Supermen, four Draculas, a host of ballerinas and a couple of somethings which might be strangulated slugs but are more probably ETs, the cry goes up: "Daddy, what AM I going to wear?"

Well . . .what can you do in three hours except hope that you can come up with something ingenious enough to stop your kids making complete fools of themselves in costumes which have very obviously been run up at the last minute?

And so it is that two years ago we sent young Antony, then six, into the arena laden under the weight of a pair of walking boots, a full-size

Richard Harris

backpack, a big map and a load of flowers that we'd hastily made from red crepe paper left over from the previous Christmas.

The result? "First prize goes to Antony Harris as the rambling rose."

And last year . . . he staggered to the show carrying a dead branch that we'd hacked off the apple tree at the bottom of the garden and hung with old boots and shoes.

Again – "First prize to the Shoe Tree."

This year, confident in the knowledge that the judges seemed to like this kind of visual pun, we sent young Ant into the fray wearing an Egyptian head-dress and an old sheet, and carrying a milk crate.

"Second prize to the Milk Sheik."

Second? What did they mean, only second? I tell all those doubters in the village that if my Auntie Vi had really been there she'd have had no hesitation at all and given us first prize.

COURTESY OF THE NOTTINGHAM POST

For some reason articles such as this proved rather popular, and I came to be disappointed if I did not get at least three or four letters a week from readers telling me how much they had enjoyed them. Chief among these letter-writers was a mysterious woman called Dolores M Behrman, who wrote to me often, signing herself every time as 'Your Number One Fanny'. I had no idea who Dolores was, except that she was one of those people who seem to derive satisfaction from having their views published regularly on their local papers' letters pages. I guessed that she was old, and probably lonely, and knew from the style of her letters that she was also well educated and keenly interested in the world. I had been writing my column for several years before I met her.

I was walking back to the office after a lunchtime stroll around the city centre when a strange little woman, dressed all in black, leapt up at me from the pavement, grabbed me round the neck and planted an over-moist kiss upon my cheek. 'What the . . .?' I shouted as I shoved her away, probably more roughly than she deserved. 'Richard, dear – it's me, Dolores!' she said. 'I've met you at last.'

My work did not always result in such happy consequences. I had never been close to Tricia's sister Ann, and as the years went by our relationship became increasingly strained, not least because she and her husband David, a vicar, seemed to look upon us as a 'Golden Couple' who had it all – happiness (which was true), money (which was true, but only when set alongside the meagre earnings of the clergy – and then only when ignoring the fact that they didn't have to pay for the spacious five-bedroom vicarage they lived in) and a life totally untouched by problems (which was true only because Tricia and I chose to cope in our own private way with the various crises in our lives – the Somerset plane crash, my three months off work so early in our marriage, my father's premature death, the strikes, William's traumatic birth, my meeting Ambra . . .) The fact is that Ann and David have always made rather heavy weather of life and it is only alongside them that Tricia and I have seemed to be a couple blessed by especially good fortune.

I did, though, have enormous sympathy for them when their third son was born. Stephen suffers from Down's Syndrome, the disability which, above all others, Ann feared, and the news was broken to her in hospital in the most unfeeling way. Ann and David were, quite understandably, shattered and – also understandably – thought themselves so unable to cope that they considered giving Stephen up for adoption. I put my thoughts into my column and it met with a hugely positive response – except from Ann and David, 150 miles away in Herefordshire, to whom Tricia sent a copy, feeling it would help them know how well we understood and sympathised with them. I had letters from people thanking me for what I had written, including one from the local chairman of the MIND mental health charity, who applauded me for having the courage to tackle a subject he had never seen before in a newspaper and for encapsulating in a few hundred words the agony felt by any family in such circumstances. Ann and David, though, have never forgiven me. They accused me of poking my nose into their personal business, of not understanding the trauma they had been going through and of 'making money' out of their family tragedy. In hindsight I wish we had not tried to express our sympathy by sending them a copy of what I had written, though the positive response from everyone else meant that I could never regret writing it. And I wish that they had read the whole of my column, and not, apparently, just the start of it, because then they would have seen that I finished by condemning not them, but myself.

Here is what I wrote:

I HAD WALKED past the poster countless times before on my way home from work. It was a huge thing showing a little mentally handicapped girl, her big smile adorned with the beard, moustache and Dracula's teeth scribbled by the passing yobboes.

I'd never even noticed it before, but this time I couldn't take my eyes off it. 'Twenty children born today will always have a cross to bear,' it said.

I'd had a bad day and I wanted to grab people by the shoulders and make them notice it for the first time, as I was doing.

I'd tell them about my own three healthy children, about my two lovely nieces and three smashing nephews. And I'd tell them about Stephen, my latest nephew, who'd been born that day.

For our Stephen, like the little girl in that poster, would also have his own cross to bear. He has Down's syndrome, and for him life will forever be a struggle.

He's got two lively, laughing brothers – as normal as any kids can be – and for the past few months his mum had been telling everybody that, yes, of course she'd like a girl to complete her family but she didn't really mind what her new baby was as long as it was all right.

It's the sort of thing every parent says when a baby's on the way.

We say it so often and so easily we don't always stop to wonder what we would do if the unthinkable happened and one of those 20 handicapped babies born every day turned out to be ours.

I, for one, certainly have little idea how I would react.

So I'll just tell you this.

When Stephen was born his mother couldn't bear to touch him; she didn't want to hold him or cuddle him or even look at him as he lay in his hospital cot.

I admit I condemned her for it at the time.

Since when, I wanted to know, has any mother had the right to deprive a baby – especially a handicapped one, whose needs are greater – of the warmth and love it craves?

I was still busy condemning her when I discovered the reason she was turning her back on her child – she was frightened that she might love him too much, that if she once cuddled him she would never be able to give him up.

And since half of her told her that it would be best if Stephen were adopted, if he went to a home where he could be given all the care he needed and not just most of it, she didn't dare so much as hold him in her arms.

And, yes, I confess I condemned her for that too.

Since when, I wondered, did any parents have the right to give a child away because he looked like becoming too big a burden on their family?

Since when did they have the right to send their baby back because he didn't quite come up to their specifications?

Where would it end?

With parents getting a child adopted because he was crippled? Because he was deaf? Because he was a boy and they wanted a girl?

I'll tell you where it ended. It ended with Stephen's parents realising that their immediate reaction, understandable though it was following the shock and pain of his birth, was one that they could never live with for long.

It ended with Stephen going home last week, to start life with his mum and his dad and his brothers in a home which once again is full of fun and laughter.

And it ended with me feeling as guilty as hell for daring to criticise a family whose world and emotions had, for just a few days, been turned upside down.

COURTESY OF THE NOTTINGHAM POST

I always left writing my column till the very last minute (like many journalists, I work best when the deadline is fast approaching) and one week found myself sitting at my keyboard with nothing written . . . and nothing in my head either. I cast my mind back to the previous evening, when Juliet told me she had heard on the radio that the Americans had launched an attack on Col Gaddafi's Libya, and in desperation I started writing, much as a composer might start running his fingers over a few chords on the piano, hoping that a tune might emerge. It took me about 15 minutes and this was the result:

DON'T WORRY about being scared. You're only nine years old, and Colonel Gaddafi and President Reagan between them have scared people much older and much braver than you.

To tell you the truth, I was pretty scared myself.

When I turned on the radio that morning and heard the sound of the American planes dive-bombing Tripoli, I wasn't sure that I wasn't listening to the beginnings of the Third World War.

Yes, of course I was scared.

But I'm your Dad and I wasn't supposed to show it.

I was scared but I tried to hide it, just as you did, until I realised that you were putting on a big act just like me.

You see, I found the atlas on the sofa (you never do put things away when you've finished with them, do you?). It was open on the page which showed the map of Libya, so it didn't take much for me to guess that you'd been sitting there, working out how far away Libya was from our house and trying to find out if Colonel Gaddafi had any planes that could fly that far.

So I came upstairs and sat on your bed in the dark, and for an hour we talked about Gaddafi and Reagan, and bombs and missiles, and death and mutilation and a whole lot of other things that fathers don't much like talking about with their daughters.

We talked about good men and bad men and I tried to explain that there is really no such thing, just an awful lot of men who are some sort of mixture of the two.

But I don't suppose you understood, because you're used to a story-book world where people are all-good or all-bad and where you can be sure that, whatever happens along the way, the goodies will beat the baddies in the end.

We talked for a long time there in the dark, trying to put the world to rights, and I tried hard to make you laugh, but the only way I could find was to say we'd invite Colonel Gaddafi to dinner and give him some of Mum's runny semolina because that was a weapon more fearsome than anything Ronald Reagan could throw at him. But you knew as well as I did that really it was nothing to laugh about.

Not when we'd sat there – you with your eyes full of tears – talking about the children, not very much different from you, who'd been killed in their beds, not so very different from yours.

So I can't ask you to forget about it now or to pretend that it's never been.

But I ask myself what difference it has made, to you and to me, so many miles away from the war.

Well, it's meant that we had a good chat (which is never a bad thing between a man and his daughter).

It's meant that you know a little bit more about world affairs and about some of the other worries that grown-ups like me keep trying to forget about.

And most of all it's meant that I'll never forgive President Reagan and Colonel Gaddafi for bringing an end to the innocence of your childhood and for filling your head with thoughts of bombs and suffering instead of ice skating and kittens.

COURTESY OF THE NOTTINGHAM POST

I really have no idea where that came from, but I confess that as I sat re-reading it at my computer I was surprised by how good it was. The result, when it was published next day, was extraordinary. When the phone on my desk rang it was Barrie. 'Brilliant, mate,' he said. 'I read it and then I read it again.' And then Jean Davey, a sweet and jolly lady and one of my fellow columnists, phoned. 'That was lovely, dear,' she said. 'I've got tears in my eyes.' Even David Teague, the high-powered marketing director, and a man I had only ever met briefly in passing, rang to congratulate me. And at lunchtime Bill Ivory sought me out in the canteen to tell me how moved he had been. It continued through the afternoon as more people around the office – people not easy to impress, and usually very sparing with praise of any sort – rang me after finding their way to the bottom corner of Page Four of that day's paper, and the next day a pile of letters from readers was waiting for me on my desk when I arrived for work. It had somehow managed to strike just the right note at just the right time and, when judged by the response of people reading it anyway, was the most effective thing I have ever written.

We were managing to keep my impending promotion a secret. Although word had got out that Bill Ivory was fairly soon to be given a new role, no one had any idea who was going to take his place. Various names were being rumoured, and I was surprised to find that mine was among them – and even more taken aback when I heard that Tony Donnelly, the chief reporter and the best hard news journalist I have ever known, was saying that of all the people on the list I was the only one he would be prepared to work with.

Barrie was still not ready though . . . and anyway he had other things on his mind. One of the continuing ramifications of the NUJ strike was that some of the more die-hard local Labour politicians were still refusing to have anything to do with us – and they did not come any more trenchant than David Bookbinder, the controversial and buccaneering leader of Derbyshire County Council, who banned the *Post* and all other T Bailey Forman publications from every school, library and council-run old folks' home in Derbyshire.

With Barrie successfully convincing the socialist burghers of Nottingham that there was a new dawn breaking at the *Evening Post* (not least with some pretty anti-Tory leader columns), he found Bookbinder's conduct across the county boundary unfair, dictatorial and undemocratic and said so in the *Post*'s comment column.

At the same time word starting coming to the news desk that Bookbinder was maybe not all he claimed to be, that there were perhaps secrets from his past which might bring about his downfall. Such allegations were not unusual against any politician, but against someone like Bookbinder, with all the enemies he must have made in his controversial career, they were inevitable.

Barrie called me into his office.

'I've got a job for you,' he said.

For the next six weeks I – features sub, columnist and news editor-in-waiting – worked in Derbyshire, trying to find if there was any truth in the rumours we had been hearing. I met most of Bookbinder's political adversaries (including several Labour councillors who simply couldn't stomach his way of doing things), I met former council officials who had taken early retirement just to be rid of him, I met former friends who were his friends no longer and I met people who didn't really know him at all but knew plenty of his reputation. I met them in pubs, cafes, offices, hotels, their homes and, sometimes, in lay-bys where we talked sotto voce in my car as if we were spies. There was no doubt that David Bookbinder was deeply unpopular among many of the people with whom he needed to work most closely, but I found that for every one who despised him there was at least one other who thought he was a fine man and a born leader, who was misunderstood only because of his strong principles and deeply held political convictions. It is perhaps a sign of my limited skill as an investigative reporter that in searching for the skeletons in David Bookbinder's cupboard I found none – all I found was that his chief executive (a man who apparently liked to spend his evenings wearing leather motorcycling gear and dancing on pub tables) was suspected of having used his influence to install a girlfriend in a council house many months before her place on the waiting list merited.

After yet another day of achieving very little I called in at Derby city market, where Bookbinder had, of all things, a doughnut stall. He was not there, but I bought a bag of his doughnuts just so I could be the first one ever to claim for such a thing on *Evening Post* expenses and returned to the office to share my haul with my friends in the Features Department. I was still brushing the sugar from my fingers, when the phone on my desk rang.

'Richard Harris?'

'Yes,'

'It's David Bookbinder. Did you enjoy the doughnuts?'

As I tried to suck the last remnants of his doughnuts from between my teeth he gave me a list of almost all the people I had met in the previous six weeks, and told me where I had met them, and for how long.

'If you wanted to find out about me,' he said very charmingly, 'why didn't you come and see me? I'd have told you everything.'

14

BARRIE HAD ONE RESERVATION about me: He thought I wasn't ambitious enough. 'Where's the fire in your belly?' he demanded on numerous occasions. I told him I was ambitious but just didn't show it, but knew deep down that he was right – that alongside him the fire in my belly amounted to nothing more than a weakly flickering candle. Barrie was a proud working class lad who had only ever wanted to be a journalist, who left school at 16 with just that one thought in his head and whose every move since had been made with the single-minded aim of progressing as far as he could in his profession. How could I tell him that in fact I'd always hankered after being a sailor and that I'd only drifted into journalism because, after giving up my dream of going to sea, it seemed a rather better alternative than a career shovelling horse shit on a mushroom farm?

I would tell him that I was indeed ambitious, but that my ambitions were maybe just a little wider than his. I wanted to do well as a journalist, certainly (and seemed to be doing all right so far, belly-fire or no) but I also wanted to succeed as a husband and as a father and as someone who had a life outside work. He would smile sadly and shake his head and repeat 'No fire in your belly, that's the trouble with you!' but I did on one occasion, over one of our many carvery lunches, get him to concede that maybe he would not have been driven to get as far as he had in his career if he and his wife Pauline had had children.

Quite why we got on so well, and how, despite the huge differences in our backgrounds, our thoughts were so well in tune, is something of a mystery. But get on we did, and as the time approached for me to become news editor I was as certain as he seemed to be that we would make a very good team.

Richard Harris

My promotion had still not been announced, but the big day was clearly getting nearer so I made it my business to get to know Bill Ivory and pick up any tips on how the job should be done. Even an old-style news editor, I reckoned, and one whose example I had no intention of following, would have at least a few hints to help me over what was certain to be a difficult initiation into the job.

I had already discovered that Bill was a more complicated character than I had appreciated. He had a reputation for being an arrogant tyrant and a womaniser, all of which, I gathered, was well deserved, and he dwelt too much in the past, and boasted too much about his RAF service and his early days as a journalist (though he strangely never talked about the night he got himself blind drunk at some civic function and was accidentally locked inside Nottingham's finely marbled Council House after falling down the stairs into a cubby hole) but I found that underneath all the bombast and posturing there lurked a strangely insecure man whose position in the hierarchy of the office – and probably in the world in general – was of huge importance to him. In the circumstances it was a great credit to him that he never treated me, the upstart who by then he knew was being given his job, with anything other than courtesy and respect.

I persuaded him to take me out for lunch – to the Royal Hotel carvery, where else? – and prepared to soak up his 30 years' experience. There seemed to be no hard feelings and Bill appeared genuinely excited about his new role, even if no one else understood exactly what it involved. If he felt that he was being pushed aside to make way for me, he didn't show it. To him, his promotion happened first, and mine followed along behind it, not the other way round. Barrie had clearly done his job well, and I wasn't going to spoil it by telling Bill that I'd known about it for considerably longer than he had.

I asked him about his wife (whom I knew was suffering from motor neurone disease, a hideous and incurable affliction which progressively wastes the victim's muscles until it causes death, and whose care bestowed upon him the burden of what amounted to another full-time job when he got home in the evenings); and I asked about his son, William 'Billy' Junior, who was embarking on a career which would soon bring him enormous success and critical acclaim as a TV playwright.

But despite the small talk (and, yes, I did take the opportunity to tease him about the way he had doubted my 170 words a minute shorthand when we had first met ten years before) we both knew why we were there. I told him I was looking forward to being news editor, but would appreciate any advice he could give me about how the job should be done (I trusted myself to be able to pick out the useful bits and discard the rest), and he leaned forward with the look of a man ready to impart all the wisdom he had acquired over a long and busy life. 'You will,' he said, chewing on a large piece of horseradishy beef, 'be able to fuck every woman in the office.'

I returned to the office and walked quietly past the newsroom – the kingdom that would soon be mine – diverting my eyes to take in the people working there. That night I returned home to Tricia and told her not to worry, I had counted no more than six nubile young reporters with whom I probably wouldn't mind following Bill's advice.

My lunch with Bill had not gone unnoticed. Duncan Elliott, a sub who prided himself on doing as little work as possible while also knowing everything that was going on in the editorial department – and who was not very often wrong – had spotted us crossing the road towards the Royal Hotel as he walked to the pub for his regular three or four lunchtime pints. Knowing that I would not normally choose to have a cosy lunch with Bill, he put two and two together and announced to everyone willing to listen to him that I would, without doubt and with absolute certainty, be the new news editor.

I eventually became news editor, just as Duncan predicted, on September 19 1983. 'I look forward to your influence and contribution – both of which I am confident will prove to be successful,' Barrie wrote in a memo in which he confirmed my salary as £13,500 a year. Another, more unexpected, note came from Christopher Pole-Carew: 'I see we have a new news editor. Very many congratulations, I hope you are pleased. I am delighted for you and wish you well.'

There is nowhere on a newspaper that is more exciting than the news desk. And there is nobody who has more direct influence over what appears in a newspaper than the news editor. It is he who decides which stories should be covered and how, who chooses which reporters should do which jobs and who decides whether the finished result is what he and his newspaper want. Even an editor like Barrie, who got more involved in the day-to-day content of the paper than most, often has little idea of what – apart from the most major of stories – is on the news schedule until it is almost too late. It was a role I revelled in.

We had a staff of more than 20 reporters, ranging in age and experience from those just out of college (by now most young journalists were taken not straight from school as both I and Barrie had been, but from a journalists' college after graduating from university) to a couple of long-serving hacks who had just a few years left before retirement.

With me on the news desk I had Neil Maxwell, a former news sub a few years younger than me, who had been promoted at the same time to be my deputy; a couple of experienced reporters elevated to assistant news editors; a chief reporter and a secretary. We were (I like to think) a hard-working, competent and happy team, although only Tony Donnelly, the chief reporter, was someone I would have called a friend. Tony was an exceptional reporter, with both the technical and personal skills to tackle any kind of story. He was a chameleon-like character, able to adapt himself to the requirements of any situation – talking on the phone to an old lady who had just returned from a nightmare holiday in which her coach had crashed, her luggage been lost and her hotel burned down, for example, he would be as sympathetic and charming as a favourite grandson; talking to a crooked businessman suspected of employing staff on wages fit for slaves, he would be tough and uncompromising, refusing to put up with even a hint of bullying or prevarication. He could turn out a complicated news story – immaculately, precisely and with every comma in its right place – in a matter of minutes . . . even when his eyes were glazed and his speech was slurred from too much drink, which, sadly, was often.

Neil I was never quite so sure of. He was keen and efficient and seemed to enjoy the job, but he had an immature side to him that I found infuriating (once, when I was appearing as a studio guest on a local radio phone-in programme, he called under an assumed name and a silly accent to ask questions about newspaper ethics which he hoped I would find difficult to answer – something I considered to be both puerile and unprofessional). He was also excitable and prone to rashness, which probably made him a very good foil for my more thoughtful, laid-back approach.

Someone once described me and Neil as being like a swan and a duck sharing the same pond – I was the swan, gliding apparently effortlessly through the water, with my feet paddling vigorously but unseen beneath it, and he was the duck, skittering about this way and that and making a lot of fuss with its splashing and quacking, but probably achieving rather less.

I soon discovered that the days on which there were major fires, motorway pile-ups, stabbings and riots were the easy ones. The real test of a news desk comes on the days when, on the face of it, there is nothing happening. It is then that a news editor earns his money, using his contacts and his experience – but most of all his news sense – either to pluck stories out of nowhere or to turn run-of-the mill downpage news into something fit for the front. On such days it was the tricks I had learned in Burnham and Yeovil that came to my aid.

Our first major story came after six weeks. Sixteen-year-old girls going missing from their homes were not unusual; they can do so for a variety of reasons – illicit nights with their boyfriends, rows with their parents or just something simple like missing the last bus home, for example. But when Colette Aram did it, it was immediately worrying because there was nothing about her or her family to suggest that her failing to return to their home in Keyworth, a large village a few miles south of Nottingham, could be anything other than ominous. The police asked for our help in trying to find her and we sent Tony to talk to her parents and get a photograph of her. He returned, typed out his predictably good copy just in time for the first edition's front page . . . and then got a call from one of his contacts in the police (Tony's police contacts were legendary, so good that he often knew what they were doing almost before they knew it themselves). Colette had been found naked in a ditch, raped and murdered. Tony, calmly and soberly re-wrote his copy, turned the quotes he had got from Colette's mother from the present to the past tense ('She was a lovely girl' rather than 'She is a lovely girl') and still made it in time for the first edition deadline.

The paper was being printed by the time Tony received the next urgent call from the police: Colette's body had indeed been found but her parents had not been told yet and there was no guarantee that they would be at any time soon. Now some journalists and some newspapers would not care about telling a mother and father that their daughter had been found brutally murdered, but I did and I knew Barrie would. Somehow we had to buy enough time for the police to break the news to Colette's mum and dad so that they did not see it first on a billboard outside their local newsagent's. Our problem was that Keyworth was one of the first villages on the run of the first delivery van – and that van was just about to leave. Unless we did something quickly it would be only a matter of minutes before the Arams' newsagent was taking delivery of a newspaper with a front page headline shouting 'Girl, 16, found murdered' above a photograph of a smiling Colette.

It was at such times that I was proud to work for the *Post*. Barrie was in a meeting so I took it upon myself (overstepping my authority, I have no doubt) to run downstairs to the circulation director's office and hastily explain the problem. On other newspapers they would probably have had to call a meeting, insisting that someone more senior than I was involved, before discussing all the options and, half an hour after it was too late, making a decision. But not at Nottingham. Don Gray, the circulation boss, gave it hardly a moment's thought. 'Don't worry, we'll divert the van,' he said as he picked up his phone to give instructions that the driver be radioed and told to do his delivery drop in reverse order.

'It's no problem,' he told me as I thanked him.

'Really?' I asked, relieved and surprised in equal measure.

He gave me a hard stare which told me what I already knew – that it was actually a very big problem. 'But it's not impossible,' he said, 'and I don't want to be the one who tells the parents what's happened to that poor girl any more than you do.'

Colette's murder sparked a huge police investigation and made history by being the first case featured on the BBC's Crimewatch TV programme, but even so it was more than 26 years before the man who killed her was caught. And even then it was only by chance. A man called Jean-Paul Hutchinson – born six years after Colette died – gave police a routine DNA sample after being arrested for a relatively minor motoring offence. That showed a near identical match with the DNA the murderer had left on Colette's body, so it was clear that the killer must have been one of his very close relatives. The trail inevitably led to his father, Paul Hutchinson, a 51-year-old who, at the time of her death, had been living in Keyworth, just a few streets away from Colette, while working, by grisly coincidence, as a part-time *Evening Post* street vendor. In January 2010 he was jailed for life after pleading guilty to her murder, but just ten months later managed to kill himself in his cell at Nottingham prison.

The trouble with being a journalist is that when anything happens you want to be there with a notebook and pencil, reporting on it. You hear about a train crash and you want to be there scrambling through the fields to get to it; you hear about a violent criminal holed up inside a house and you want to be there with the armed policemen hiding behind the dustbins outside; you hear about a fishing boat that's gone missing off the coast and you want to be there on the pier, eyes straining for its return. And the trouble with being a news editor is that you are expected to sit in the office while you send out some other journalist to cover all these stories that you'd love to be covering yourself.

At the *Post* we had more reporters than most newspapers of our size, but there were still not enough to do all the things we wanted to do, so whenever I got the chance I liked to remind myself and anyone else who cared to notice that I was a journalist first and a news editor second. There was never any harm, I reckoned, in proving to any of the reporters who might have doubted it that I could roll up my sleeves and turn out a decent news story at least as well as they could.

This, I gathered, made me a rather different character from Bill Ivory. He had, for example, always insisted on a reporter accompanying him to Citizen of the Month ceremonies, at which he presented awards to people who had distinguished themselves by catching burglars, rescuing old ladies from fires or jumping into canals to save drowning children. That seemed to me to be a total waste of a reporter's time when he would have been perfectly capable of doing the job himself, so when my turn came I armed myself with a notebook and pen and left the reporter behind.

In the spring of 1984 I wasn't left with much choice. That was when 187,000 of Britain's miners pushed the *Evening Post* newsroom to its very limits by going on strike. The Nottinghamshire coalfield was one of the biggest and most important in Britain, but its miners had always been among the industry's most moderate. So when Arthur Scargill, the uncompromising leader of the National Union of Mineworkers, accused Margaret Thatcher's government of plotting to destroy the coalmining industry and – without first holding a ballot among his members – called for an all-out strike to fight the National Coal Board's plans to close 20 pits, it was inevitable that our county would be the main battleground between those who supported the strike and those who didn't. Most miners in Nottinghamshire didn't and went on working. The result was anarchy and the worst violence ever seen in a British industrial dispute (and let's be honest, a fantastic opportunity for a local paper to increase its sales by aligning itself firmly behind the majority of its readers).

The ugly scenes we had witnessed outside the *Post* a few years earlier were nothing compared with what went on in the Nottinghamshire mining villages. Thousands of striking miners and their supporters were bussed in from other parts of the country, gathering as a terrifying rowdy army outside the colliery gates. And when the local 'scab' miners arrived for work the flying pickets surged forward in a frenzy of fists, sticks and baseball bats, beating on their cars (and later, when it was clear that a humble car was no protection against the mob, on the specially hired coaches with their metal grilles to stop the windows being smashed) as hundreds of police in riot gear fought to keep them under control.

The scenes were the same at pits all over Nottinghamshire, with more and more pickets arriving, and becoming more and more violent, as the local miners made it more and more clear that they were not going to be intimidated. And into it all, in the early hours of every morning in the early days of the dispute, we sent our reporters – or as many of them as we could without leaving ourselves unable to cover the other essential day-to-day business of a local paper.

The striking miners had several enemies: The working Nottinghamshire men most of all, of course, but also the police, the National Coal Board, the government and the media – not least the Nottingham *Evening Post*, which not only was supporting the local strike-breakers and their breakaway union (the Union of Democratic Mineworkers), but also, in case anyone had forgotten, was the paper that, according to trade union legend anyway, had its own history of anti-union activities and employing blackleg labour, which meant anyone working for it deserved a good kicking. I told our reporters to wear their oldest clothes, to look as much like pickets and as little like reporters as they could, to not even think of getting out their notebooks to record what they were seeing and, if by some chance they were unmasked as journalists, to say that they worked for the *Sun*, the *Guardian*, the *Daily Mirror* or any other newspaper they liked as long as it wasn't the *Post*. The last thing I wanted was for one of our reporters to be identified as such, and be beaten up by a rampant mob.

I believed that if ever there was a need for a general to lead his troops from the front, it was then. If I expected some petite young girl reporter fresh out of college to get up at four in the morning so she could put herself at risk of being beaten up by a gang of angry Welsh miners then, I reckoned, I had to show I was willing to do it myself. I told my colleagues on the news desk that they – we – would be joining the rota of reporters to be sent into the battleground.

They all agreed it was something we simply had to do. And anyway, they wanted a taste of the action just as much as I did! All except one, that is.

Neil Maxwell argued heatedly that his place was on the news desk, that he would be of more use controlling things from the office than getting up in the early hours to witness what was going on at the gates of some coal mine 20 or so miles away in a village most of us had never heard of. And anyway, he reminded us, he was leaving. Neil had handed in his notice and was just working out his time before moving to a better job on a bigger newspaper and felt he therefore did not really have to do anything he didn't want to do. I told him that, like it or not, he would be part of the rota just like the rest of us and would be expected to take his turn at the pit gates. And the next day he went off sick. And his wife, a formidable young woman called Ellen, phoned me to tell me that Neil was too ill to come to work so wouldn't be able to go out to cover the picket lines, not for the foreseeable future, and wasn't that a pity.

We sacked him. Barrie agreed with me that, at a time when everyone was working almost around the clock – and sometimes in great danger – I could not afford to have a deputy who was (or appeared to be) unwilling to play his part. I have no idea whether Neil was really ill, or just pretending to be, but I knew for certain that his attitude, and his wife's, could destroy the team spirit we would need to get us through the crisis. So with Barrie's backing I went round to his house in the smart Park area of the city, handed him his cards and told him not to bother to come back to work out his notice. At six o'clock the next morning, dressed in jeans and a baggy sweater, I stood at the back of the seething mob outside the pit gates at Ollerton, the colliery where a couple of days earlier a picket had died beneath the wheels of a car, with my hands shoved into the pockets of an old donkey jacket so that nobody would notice that they were far too soft and clean to be the hands of a miner.

The strike lasted almost a year, and collapsed only when more than half of the miners gave up and returned to work. By then it had cost the nation £3 billion, more than 5,000 pickets had appeared in court for offences of violence and 14 people were dead. Still, Margaret Thatcher greeted it as an almost personal victory, and only much later, with Britain's once-proud coal industry reduced from 190,000 people working in 170 pits to fewer than 5,000 working in 20, was it proved that Arthur Scargill had been right all along. It was the end of an industry that had once been the backbone of industrial Britain.

We replaced Neil with Bob Turner, a man a little older than I, who came to us from the *Daily Mail*. He was at first sight everything I distrusted about national newspaper reporters – rather too full of himself, too quick to cut corners, too dismissive of what I considered to be common decency and too patronising towards those of us who had chosen to pursue careers on what people with his background tended to look upon as 'lesser' newspapers in the provinces. And yet as Barrie and I interviewed him for the job I sensed that here was a man I would enjoy working with.

Bob and I gelled immediately – each bringing out the other's strengths and compensating for his weaknesses – and the months we ran the newsdesk together remain the most rewarding of my career. I quickly found that his brashness was largely an act, as if he thought that was what national newspaper reporters were expected to be like, and that underneath it his values were very similar to mine. He was excited by newspapers, just as I was, and by the never knowing what the next day would bring. He found people fascinating, just as I did, and believed the most interesting news stories were those that involved the so-called ordinary man or woman in the street because, as we both knew, there was usually nothing ordinary about them. Although we were very different personalities we worked well together, with him adding a rather harder and more robust side to my nature just as I brought out a more sensitive and thoughtful side to his. Only occasionally did I have to remind him that he wasn't still working for the *Daily Mail* – and that getting a story through bullying, subterfuge and dishonesty wasn't our style – or point out that, while national paper reporters could afford to upset the communities they visited because they were unlikely ever to have to work in them again, provincial newspapers could not afford to alienate the very people whose help they would be needing again on some other story before very long. But if I was able to introduce a touch of caution to his work, he in turn managed to add a bit of toughness to mine and I know that I was all the better for it.

I was conscious that the two of us – with Bill Greenhough, the chief photographer who followed Barrie from Kent, and Tony Donnelly, who still reigned supreme as chief reporter – made a successful, if unlikely, combination and I had no worries about whether we were doing a good job. I just knew it, and I knew that Barrie knew it too. We were all working – and helping each other to work – at the very peak of our abilities; a classic case of a team being much more than the sum of its individual parts. It was an extraordinarily satisfying feeling, and an exceptionally fulfilling phase of my life, and when I met Bob many years later I was pleased to hear that he remembered those days just as fondly as I did.

The great joy of being news editor – and indeed the joy of being a journalist of almost any sort – is that you never know what is going to happen next. You think you have your day neatly planned out, but then something happens that makes you have to throw out all those plans and start again. Never did that apply more, or more often, than in the case of Graham Neale, a disc jockey with Radio Trent, Nottingham's independent radio station. Neale was a high profile local 'personality' who enjoyed a huge following thanks to his prime time rock show, and he and his girlfriend Lynn Goldingay – a beautiful 24-year-old he had met in the brief time she had worked on the station's reception desk – were looked upon as something of a local golden couple, moving easily in showbiz circles and numbering numerous rock stars among their friends.

So when in March 1985 Lynn went missing it was big news. Tony Donnelly went to see Neale at the home he and Lynn shared and produced an excellent 'heartbroken DJ begs his lover to come back to him' story, complete with a picture of him gazing wistfully at a framed photograph of the missing woman whom, he said, he had last seen catching a bus to work. For several days – with the encouragement of the police – we ran follow-up stories, all featuring an increasingly tearful Neale begging people to let him know if they heard anything of her whereabouts. And then we discovered why the police were so keen for us to keep the story in the headlines: They suspected him of killing her and wanted to see if he said anything to us that did not tally with what he had said to them.

In the end Neale was unable to continue the charade. He broke down under questioning (by the police, not by Tony), admitted what he had done and led them to a small wood beside a patch of waste ground near a power station where he had hidden her body. With his initial arrest, his being charged with murder and his first appearance in court, it was, by any standards, a major local story even if, because of the legal restraints imposed as soon as a suspect is arrested, we were able to report it in only the flimsiest detail. Tony set about gathering background information for the full story which we would be able to publish only when (and, from what we had discovered by then, it seemed to be a case of when, not if) Neale was convicted.

Tony's investigations showed that in fact by the time of her death Neale and Lynn had separated, and she was in a new relationship with a man she had fallen for at the accountants' office to which she had moved after leaving Radio Trent. Even so, it seemed, they were still good friends, and – with her new lover's blessing – she had gone with Neale to a concert by the singer Paul Young, one of their many mutual celebrity friends. Afterwards they went back to the house they had shared and, in the bedroom, had a row, which ended with her taunting him about his sexual prowess. Neale flew into a violent rage, picked up a hammer he had left in the bedroom after some minor DIY chore, and in a blind fury beat her over the head with it, stopping only when he realised he had killed her.

None of this, we knew, could be published until Neale had been found guilty – and it never would be if, by some quirky decision of the jury, he was acquitted – but Tony had done a great job and we knew that, when the time came, we had a story which would increase the sales of the *Post* by several thousand.

Nobody could have foreseen that the next terrible twist would come with Duncan McCracken, Lynn Goldingay's new boyfriend, being found dead in his car, in the street where she had worked. There was a plastic pipe leading to the exhaust and, beside him on the passenger seat, an album of photographs and a note explaining that he blamed himself for her death because he had encouraged her to go to the gig with Neale.

The McCracken family were keen to talk to us, as many families are in such circumstances (though in this case we had to be careful not to publish any of their comments which might have prejudiced Neale's trial before a jury). For them it was a helpful way of keeping his memory alive . . . and for us it was a very effective way of obeying the legal limitations but also keeping the story fresh while waiting for the court case.

But the court case never took place. The story, which was already so full of tragedy, came to a wretched conclusion on June 6 1985 when Neale was found hanged in his cell in Lincoln prison. It seemed he could live with one death on his conscience but not two.

I had much more confidence in Bob Turner than I'd had in Neil Maxwell and I had no doubt that he was well capable of running the newsdesk in my absence . . . and he had to prove it on the many occasions when, at Barrie's behest, I was not there.

Barrie seemed reluctant to let me give up writing. Even though he admitted that being news editor was job enough for any man, he wanted me not just to continue writing my regular Wednesday column but also – capitalising on what he saw as my popularity with the readers – to start an occasional series called the Harris Interview, in which I met a wide variety of public figures, ranging from politicians to pop stars, and from top authors to international film stars. I had no argument with this. It allowed me to indulge my ego by getting my name and picture in the paper at least once a week, it gave me the opportunity to meet some fascinating (and, mostly, likeable) people and it took me, just occasionally, away from the furnace that was the news desk.

So it was that in the Theatre Royal at Lincoln I met Omar Sharif, the Egyptian actor and heart-throb who had starred in Doctor Zhivago and Lawrence of Arabia – a charming, polite and old-style gentleman

The Accidental Editor

who, on hearing that Tricia was waiting for me outside, insisted I fetch her in so he could say hello to her too; in a posh London restaurant I met Mary Whitehouse, the founder of the National Viewers and Listeners' Association, a self important organisation dedicated to keeping anything remotely saucy off our TV screens, whom I really rather liked although I disagreed with almost everything she said; on a boat on the Thames I met Harry Secombe, a lovely, gentle and thoughtful man whom nobody would have guessed had invented a new style of comedy as one of The Goons had it not been for his startling habit of punctuating his conversation with a series of high pitched giggles; in her dressing room at a London theatre I met Su Pollard, a hyperactive Nottingham-born actress and star of several popular TV series, whose way of answering my questions was to poke and prod me as if she were a little girl and I were her favourite Teddy bear; in an office at the House of Commons I met Edwina Currie, whom I found worryingly sexy for a Tory cabinet minister (a view shared, it seemed, by Prime Minister John Major, who, it was revealed much later, was having an affair with her at the time). In the bar of the Theatre Royal in Nottingham, just opposite the *Evening Post* office, I met Jeffrey Archer, the bumptious but surprisingly engaging Tory party chairman and millionaire novelist, who years later would be sent to prison for perjury after telling lies in court in an attempt to defend himself against a newspaper's accusations that he had been spotted passing money to a prostitute outside a railway station. I got on very well with him – liked him, even – and not just because, after discovering that we both came from Weston-super-Mare, he insisted on conducting the whole interview in a mock Somerset accent, much to the chagrin of his sober suited lady personal assistant, who made it very clear that she found something distasteful about a journalist addressing her master as 'My Lover' (which, in case you wonder, is a routine form of greeting between men in Somerset).

Over lunch in a smart London restaurant I interviewed Russell Grant, the unapologetically camp astrologer who compiled the *Post*'s daily horoscope and had become a national celebrity through his regular appearances on breakfast television. We were shown to a table in the shadows at the back which, he said, was the one he always used because he liked to be inconspicuous – and he didn't mind when I pointed out that this was a bit rich coming from a man who had just walked through a crowded restaurant wearing a purple jacket, pink shirt, yellow scarf and bright green trousers! Russell was great fun (it was more of a friendly chat than an interview) and our lunch extended well into the afternoon, with

Richard Harris

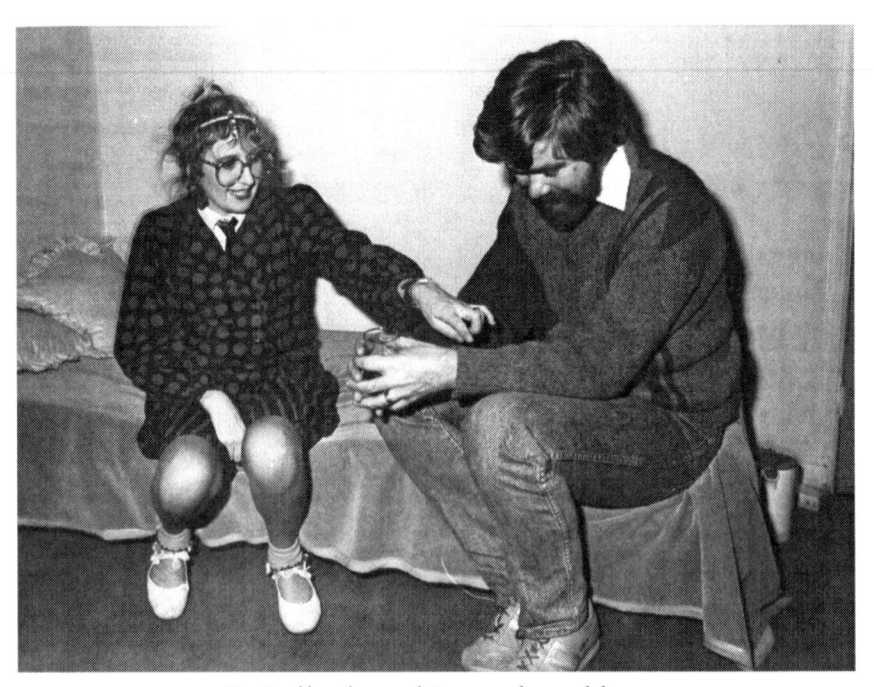

Su Pollard – poking and prodding
COURTESY OF THE NOTTINGHAM POST

him insisting on giving me an off-the-cuff astrological forecast based on when I had been born – the day, the date and the time – and where. He was clearly surprised. 'That's an unusual combination for a journalist,' he said, as he told me how at the moment of my birth Taurus had been moving into Saturn, with Pluto crossing the Andromeda galaxy in parallel with the sun (or some such nonsense). 'You're different, not like most journalists.'

I told him that he was not the first person to say such a thing, but that the last one – blonde and beautiful and with big blue eyes – was considerably better looking even than him. He looked puzzled for a moment, then laughed when I told him how I did not find him quite as attractive as Sissel.

Barbara Cartland – reputed to be the world's most prolific author (she turned out 723 romantic novels, at the rate of one a fortnight) and surely the weirdest – invited me into her stately home just north of London, where we sat at opposite sides of a huge oak table sipping tea from antique bone china cups and eating cucumber sandwiches with the crusts cut off. She was, though well into her 80s, just as eccentric as I had hoped, with enormous false eyelashes and wearing so much pink chiffon that it billowed up around her like the dry ice drifts around the bass guitarist at a rock concert. She spoke for many minutes at a time without drawing breath or pausing for what might have been appropriate punctuation. She politely deflected any questions about her step grand-daughter, Princess Diana, and cleverly returned our conversation to the safer subject of the billion books she had sold in 36 different languages, and threw in just for good measure how she had invented the glider as a way of getting troops to the battlefields in World War II. She signed a book – *Love At The Helm* – and told me to take it home to Tricia, who, she was certain, would enjoy it. It remains on our bookshelves, unopened.

I expected to find I had much more in common with John Denver, a country singer who was at that time one of the most popular American performers in this country. But I was wrong. Although I liked many of his songs (he wrote such hits as *Leaving On A Jet Plane*, *Take Me Home Country Roads* and *Annie's Song*) I found, when I met him at a London press launch to promote his latest record in May 1986, that he was an over-earnest man, lacking any discernible sense of humour and obsessed with his twin dreams of saving the environment and becoming the first civilian to travel in space. The beautiful, sensitive songs that he wrote seemed totally at odds with the withdrawn and detached man with whom I tried and failed to build up any rapport and I returned to Nottingham thinking that I might have got a more interesting interview if I had spent my time ignoring him and talking to the photograph that adorned the cover of his new record. It was, though, the prelude to one of the most memorable days of my working life.

A week after interviewing him I chanced to be home early from work and saw he was a guest on the Terry Wogan chat show, which was one of the most popular television programmes of that time. I was happy to see that cutting through Denver's reserve posed just as big a problem to Wogan as it had to me, but I paid particular attention when he started talking about his love of running, and of how, given half a chance, he would have loved to join in Bob Geldof's 'Race Against Time' – a worldwide series of more or less simultaneous sponsored runs to raise awareness of poverty and hardship in Africa. Denver said he thought it was a great idea to get so many people running at the same time but regretted he would not be able to take part because he would be on tour at the time.

The next day I rang his agent pointing out that on the evening of the 'Race Against Time' John Denver would be playing at Nottingham's Royal Concert Hall, and how about it if the *Evening Post* organised a run specially for him? The message soon came back that Denver would be delighted, as long as we could fix it during the couple of hours he would have available between completing his sound checks in the concert hall and going back to his hotel for the nap he always liked to have before a show.

Quite what it all had to do with being news editor of a major evening newspaper, and why nobody else on the staff could do it, I don't know, but Barrie was very supportive and anyway it was my idea and I was reluctant to let go of it.

There was no time to organise a major event from scratch, but fortunately a local committee had already started planning a small run to be held in the park next to the National Water Sports Centre at Holme Pierrepont, across the River Trent a couple of miles outside Nottingham, and, once I had assured them that if the *Post* got involved we could promise them the attendance of one of the world's top singers, they were only too happy to allow us to muscle in on their event.

The only problem was how to get Denver to the park and back again in the short time he had to spare, for although we had no idea how many people might turn up we could be sure that even a couple of hundred would result in the traffic chaos for which Holme Pierrepont was notorious. If, as I hoped, the thought of running alongside John Denver might attract a turn-out to be measured in thousands rather than hundreds, there was a real danger that he would spend his precious nap time sitting in a car in a five-mile traffic jam.

It was the police who came to our aid. I knew the head of the Nottingham river police reasonably well, and he readily agreed to put his motor launch at our disposal. 'It will make a change to use it for something other than fishing dead bodies out of the Trent,' he told me. Our plan was to by-pass the queues of traffic by whisking (if a boat with a top speed of ten knots can be said to whisk) Denver up the river to a jetty beside the park, from where a reporter in a car would drive him the half mile to the podium from which – just as people all over the world were doing the same thing – he would fire the gun to start the run.

When the day came we still had no clue how many people might turn up, and I had a sleepless night beforehand worrying whether after all our planning we would arrive at the park to find just a handful of small children and a couple of dogs clustered around the hastily erected scaffolding dais from which Denver was to declare the run in progress. When I passed the entrance to the Water Sports Centre on my way into Nottingham to pick him up from the theatre there was no sign of anything happening at all, and I wondered how best to prepare him for what could turn out to be one of the smallest audiences of his career.

He and his girlfriend (he'd long since separated from the wife who had inspired *Annie's Song*) were waiting for me, dressed in immaculate matching tracksuits, at the stage door and piled into the back of my sparkling clean Ford Sierra, which I had taken through a car wash that morning in honour of the occasion. A quick drive through the city centre took us to the river police headquarters, where the launch was lying, engine throbbing expectantly, and ready to be cast off. Everything was going like clockwork and I began, at last, to relax.

And then, as I followed Denver and his girlfriend to the boat, I saw that they both had very obvious damp patches on their bottoms, almost as if they had wet themselves, but more probably that they had been sitting in a puddle. A puddle on the rear seat of my car! Only then did I realise that one of the children must have left a back window slightly open, so when I took the car for its morning wash a gallon or two of soapy water had squirted in all over the seat. Suddenly I found myself liking John Denver a whole lot more, for there he was, an international star on his way to meet (we hoped) hundreds of adoring fans, looking for all the world as if he had an uncontrollable bladder problem. And he did not utter a word of complaint.

Our voyage up the Trent took precisely the 23 minutes we had planned (yes, the police and I had tested it in a dummy run three days before) and the reporter was waiting for us in the car as we pulled into the jetty alongside the park. But still we did not know how many people had bothered to turn out, because the starting point – and indeed the whole course of the run – was hidden out of sight, on the far side of a small hill.

'We really have no idea how many people will be here,' I told Denver, attempting at the very last minute to stop him building his expectations too high.

I need not have bothered. As our car crested the top of the hill we saw for the first time what was on the other side – a bustling sea of excited people, most in running clothes, a few in fancy dress and somewhere among them, one (Juliet, who had damaged her leg a few days previously) in a wheelchair, about to be pushed around the course at terrifying speed by Antony.

Precisely as planned, Denver arrived at the start just in time to fire the starter's gun, and more than 10,000 people began jogging around the Holme Pierrepont Water Sports Centre, just as millions of other people

Richard Harris

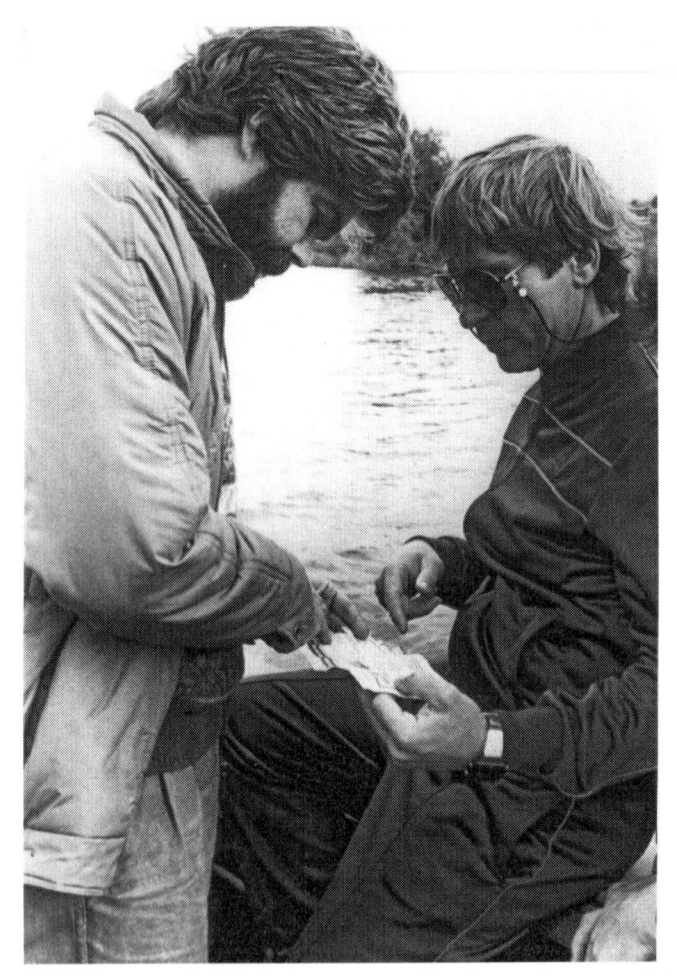

John Denver – one of the most memorable days of my working life
COURTESY OF THE NOTTINGHAM POST

were jogging around other places in all corners of the world. Denver and his girlfriend joined them for one lap, signing autographs as he went, before running back to the car, ready to make the journey back down the river to the city. As he reached the police boat Denver turned and looked at me, smiled and said simply: 'Well done.'

Tricia and I were in the audience for his concert that evening, and Denver took the opportunity to talk about how much he had enjoyed his day, and how indebted he was to me for organising it for him. For one ghastly moment I thought he was going to ask me to stand up and take a bow, and I sank deep into my seat in an embarrassed pretence that I was not there until a few chords on his guitar told me he was about to start his next song and it was safe to surface again.

I still enjoy John Denver's music – and the memory of that day – and, though I can't say I warmed to him as a man, I was saddened when 11 years later he died when the private plane he was piloting crashed into the sea off the Californian coast.

When Barrie received a letter from Michael Hammond, the chief executive of Nottingham City Council, complaining about some perceived unfairness or bias in our reporting, his response was typically forthright: 'Dear Michael, Bollocks, Yours sincerely . . .' That's the image he liked to cultivate – blunt, unpredictable and a world away from any of the editors who had gone before him at the *Post*.

His method of recruiting staff was just as unorthodox. Bright young reporters would arrive for their interviews, have a half-hour chat with Barrie and me over a coffee (with him lolling back comfortably in his chair, often with his feet up on his desk) and then be invited to accompany me on a tour of the building. Almost always, as I led them away from the editor's office towards the newsroom, the candidate would pause and ask me: 'What time is my interview?'

'That was it,' I'd tell them. 'You've had it.'

Barrie believed, quite rightly, that it was a person's character that mattered, and that the books that all the applicants clutched, containing the cuttings of their best stories, amounted to nothing at all because even the worst reporter can be made to look good by a clever sub editor, just as a good one can be made to look second rate by a newspaper which puts blandness before flair and imagination. So much more could be gleaned from a friendly chat over a coffee than could ever be obtained from a formal interview with its predictable questions for which the candidate had no doubt been preparing for days beforehand.

One of the questions Barrie always asked, in his deceptively congenial style, was 'What will you do if we don't give you a job?' The only answer he accepted was 'If you don't give me a job today I'll keep on pestering you until you do' and anyone who made the mistake of replying that they would probably apply somewhere else, stay where they were or take up teaching/accountancy/taxi driving instead was immediately discounted. 'I only want people who would give their right arm to work here,' he'd explain.

Other people were rejected for more unlikely reasons. One poor lad had been sitting opposite me for many minutes before I realised what was so unusual about him – he had no ears. His hair was carefully trimmed in a way which would have left his ears neatly exposed if he had had some, but he didn't, and the sides of his head were entirely flat and devoid of anything resembling any sort of auditory apparatus. He seemed to be able to hear perfectly well, though, and there was much to be said for the cheery confidence with which he took such an abnormality into the world.

I would have been happy to offer him a job, but Barrie was not so sure. 'He'll have nothing to hang his glasses on when he gets older,' he said later without a hint of a smile, and I never knew whether or not he was joking.

On another occasion Barrie was keen to offer a job to a young woman who appeared to have an impressive pedigree, and it was my turn to be unconvinced. 'There was something about her,' I told him. 'I just didn't like the look of her.'

'What do you mean you didn't like the look of her? You don't have to sleep with them, you know!'

'That's not what Bill Ivory told me,' I said, enjoying the satisfying look of puzzlement that crossed his brow.

Neither of us would have given a job to a reporter called Colin Meakin, but it was too late because he had been working for the *Post* for years. Colin was a journalist quite unlike any other I've met. He was big, untidy and smelled dreadful (he had two suits, a blue one and a brown one, both decorated with white dried-out sweat patches under the armpits) yet somehow just about everyone in the office loved him. He had few social skills, thinking nothing of sitting at his desk picking his nose, belching and farting – equally enthusiastically and often all at the same time – and, though keen, made far more mistakes than any other reporter (he was incapable of spelling someone's name the same way throughout a story, for example, so that a Mr Rogers might indeed be Mr Rogers, or just as likely Roger, Rodgers and Rogres). And yet within the confines of the newsroom he was almost universally popular, not least perhaps because of the way he remained so cheerfully unfazed by the affect his appalling personal habits had on the rest of us. He was like the pongy old dog that a family loves even though it craps on the carpet and takes chunks out of the favourite armchair.

Outside the office things were different. We had to think very carefully about which assignments we could send him on (jobs in the open air were always the best bet) and had to avoid anything, such as a court, where accuracy was not just advisable, but a legal imperative. But when a posh lady, a member of Nottinghamshire's moneyed county set, rang demanding to see a reporter on a matter of some urgency I had no choice. Colin was the only reporter in the newsroom at the time, so it was him or no one, and the lady had already made it clear that 'no one' was not a response she would accept. And anyway, I confess, she annoyed me with her patronising attitude to both me and my newspaper, so I considered a visit from Colin to be the least she deserved. He had not even had time to return to the office after visiting her before she rang again. 'When I asked to see a reporter,' she said, in her gloriously haughty tones, 'I did not expect you to send that thing!' Every word she said – especially the 'thing' that she spat out with much more vitriol than was strictly necessary – was no doubt true (he looked a mess, he stank and, worst of all, he had dared to call her 'Love') but he was one of ours and if anyone was going to call him a 'stinking tramp' it was going to be me, not her, so I sprang to his defence with no heed to the fact that I was defending the indefensible.

The problem, though I could hardly tell her, was that Colin had been tolerated at the *Post* for many years, and he had been a stinking tramp throughout. He had deserved to be sacked in his first week – in fact he should not have been given the job in the first place – but since he wasn't, and Bill Snaith and Bill Ivory had put up with him apparently without complaint ever since, we could hardly sack him now. He would claim unfair dismissal, and quite rightly so, on the grounds that he was no more offensive now than he had been all along, and he would tell the industrial tribunal that if the newish editor and his even newer news editor didn't like it the fault was theirs not his.

He was a willing worker, though, and was as desperate to please as a puppy, and when he came to tell me he had an exclusive – a really good exclusive – his eyes were shining with excitement. He was right, it was a good one. The only question was whether he was the man to tackle it.

Colin had met a retired policeman who was convinced he was being conned by a salesman working for a company which fixed stone cladding to the external walls of houses, thus making them – or so they claimed – more attractive and more durable. The deal was that if the ex-PC, Peter Oldfield, agreed to spend a few thousand pounds on the stuff, the firm fitting it would use his house as a show home and use it to attract more customers. And for every customer persuaded to buy stone cladding as a result of seeing it on his house, Oldfield would get a substantial payment, which if all went well would soon cover the cost of his original investment.

It seemed a good deal, especially since the salesman assured him that his would be the only such show house in the area... until Oldfield discovered that a family just round the corner had been sold stone cladding on precisely the same basis.

Oldfield asked the salesman back on the pretext that he was about to agree to the deal, but he also invited Colin and the near-neighbour to hide behind a full-length curtain in the living room to witness the meeting as it progressed.

'Let's go through the arrangement one more time, can we?' said Oldfield.

'Of course,' said the salesman.

'I buy the stone cladding from you, you fit it and then this house becomes a show house, yes?'

'Yes.'

'And then I get commission on every sale you make to people who like what they see here?'

'Yes.'

'And I should do all right because there will be no other show house like mine for miles around?'

'That's right. The nearest one will be 20 miles away.'

'Really – 20 miles?'

'No closer than that, no.'

'That's a promise?'

'I give you my word,' said the salesman.

'In that case there are a couple of people I'd like you to meet.' Oldfield said. 'Behind that curtain. First there's Mr Donohue from around the corner. I think you already know him. He's the one you made the same promises to last week.'

'Ah,' said the salesman.

'And then there's Mr Meakin. He's a reporter from the *Evening Post*.'

'Oh.'

'And we have tape recorded this whole conversation.'

'Oh my god.'

The salesman knew when he was beaten and even went as far as admitting he was a conman – and he used that very word. But he insisted it was only because that was how his employers expected him to behave. He grudgingly signed a statement to that affect, which Colin took away with him along with the tape from Mr Oldfield's cassette recorder.

I told Colin I was impressed. He was right. It was a good story, he had handled it well so far and it would have been dreadfully unfair now to take it off him and give it to some other more reliable reporter. Instead I assured him he would be allowed to see it through, and told him to get the tape professionally copied so we could keep the original in the office while he went to confront the directors of the business.

The next day Colin, with another reporter to act as a witness, called unannounced at the company's headquarters, with a portable tape recorder in his hand and the copy of the vital tape in his pocket. He got past the receptionist and into the office of the managing director who sat startled, so I was told later, behind a desk several sizes too big for him.

'I don't want you to say anything – yet,' Colin said in a masterful tone. 'I just want you to listen to this tape and when you've heard it I'll be asking you some questions. All right, me duck?'

'All right,' said the MD.

Colin inserted the cassette into the tape recorder, and pressed the Play button.

And the managing director's office was filled with a sound which we later established was the first track of 'Barry Manilow's Greatest Hits'.

I had been so confident that nothing could possibly go wrong that I had given Colin's investigation a big build-up at that afternoon's editorial conference. We were going to use it – and use it big – the next day. So it was down to me to break the news to Barrie that all had not gone according to plan.

'What's occurred?' he asked as I arrived grim-faced at his office door.

I explained, and in some detail.

'The bloody useless idiot,' he said, beating his head on his desk in theatrical fashion. 'I hope you gave him a right good bollocking.'

'I tried to,' I confessed, 'but I laughed.'

Barrie looked horrified. Here was his news editor, the man supposed to uphold discipline and maintain standards in the newsroom, and he couldn't even keep a straight face when his newspaper was made to look ridiculous. 'Send him in here – I won't bloody laugh,' he glowered. 'He's less use than a ruddy chocolate teapot. I've had enough. This is the final straw. He's sacked.'

I returned to the newsroom and shouted over to Colin that the editor wanted to see him, but gave him no clue what lay in store. When he returned a few minutes later Colin seemed – for a man newly unemployed – surprisingly chirpy. I poked my head round Barrie's door.

'Well?' I asked.

'Well what?'

'Did you sack him or just give him a right good bollocking?'

'Neither,' he snapped.

I raised an eyebrow, wanting more.

'I tried to,' he said. 'But I laughed too. Now go and find me something else for tomorrow's front page, for God's sake.'

Barrie had warned me he would be a hard taskmaster, and so he was. But he was also quick to give credit for a job well done and, though he was always demanding more and better news stories, and frequently made his displeasure known if he didn't get them, underneath it all I knew there was a mutual respect. I was confident that he appreciated my efforts, and that he was usually pleased with the results, and I took the occasional bollockings he gave me to be just a necessary charade that an editor had to play with his news editor – the anger and exasperation from his side of the desk usually being just as much an act as the air of injured innocence I adopted on mine. I, like almost everyone on the staff, would have jumped through burning hoops for him . . . except on some rare occasions when we would not have helped him to his feet even if he had fallen down in the street in the path of a fast approaching juggernaut (it was only later that I learned that his unusual brusqueness on these occasions was brought about by some shenanigans that were troubling him in the boardroom).

Having been a news editor himself, he understood the pressure I was sometimes under, and encouraged me to deal with it in the most enlightened of manners. 'You need time to think – and you can't hope to do that on a busy news desk,' he would often tell me, 'so I'll understand if you just bugger off somewhere for some peace and quiet.' And so it was that, with my boss's encouragement, I would often find myself being paid to go for a walk around the city – or, if I had some bigger problem to mull over, even to drive to one of Nottinghamshire's fine country parks for a stroll in the sunshine.

Christopher Pole-Carew (so much reviled by people who did not know him) was even more understanding. He demanded hard work and high standards from his middle managers, and could be brutal with them if they failed him, but he balanced the equation by being unusually supportive of them when things got tough. 'I know what Barrie's like and how hard he makes you work, and don't think I don't appreciate it,' he told me once. 'So if you get to feeling you need some extra time off, take it – a few days, a week, whatever you need – and don't waste time feeling guilty about it.'

I found it an extraordinarily encouraging thing for a managing director to say to one of his staff, and his saying it was enough; as far as I know, nobody ever took him up on the offer.

The higher I got in the organisation the more I was aware that it was Pole-Carew's example and management style that resulted in its employees feeling happy and secure in their work. There was never any doubt that he was the boss, and that he would take whatever drastic action was needed to make the firm successful. But equally he was a man who took the time to find out what people's jobs involved (he spent many evenings working beside the men on the presses, for example, so he could better understand the problems they faced) and there was no doubt that if you were loyal and worked hard he appreciated your efforts and made sure you were rewarded accordingly.

So when one evening I was phoned at home by the reporter on the late shift the news he gave me came as a bombshell.

'What's the least likely thing that could have happened tonight?' he asked me.

'I haven't a clue! The Royal Concert Hall's been burned down? Nottingham Forest have gone bust? The Lord Mayor's been arrested for streaking across the Old Market Square . . . ?

'More unlikely than all three put together. PC has been sacked! His filing cabinet has been locked up in chains and he's been escorted off the premises by a security man.'

Even allowing for the fact that his excited report probably contained a bit of journalistic exaggeration (we never did established the truth about the chains on the filing cabinet, although years later I discovered even that part was true) the rest turned out to be pretty accurate. The man who had done so much to make the *Evening Post* the most admired newspaper in the country was gone, suddenly and dramatically – the victim, it seemed, of his increasing disillusion with the Forman Hardy family and their reluctance to seize the opportunities offered by the future as keenly as he wanted to.

In truth, the stress of being news editor was never as great as I had expected, probably because the pressure of the job was balanced by the sheer enjoyment I got from it. Only occasionally did the strain get to me – and always it was because of some unexpected staffing problem, not because of the need to find news to fill the paper every day.

When, for example, we found we had a thief in the office (the woman's editor was having things taken from her room in great quantities) we called in the police and with their help set up a hidden surveillance camera. The culprit, we discovered, was not one of the night-time cleaners, as we expected, but a male reporter who was caught quite clearly on film, sneaking into the room late at night and helping himself to all sorts of expensive cosmetics and fashion clothing. The police, having invested so much time and equipment into catching whoever was responsible, insisted on prosecuting him, even though we did not want them to, and he felt – probably wrongly – that he had to resign.

On another occasion I returned to my desk to find a letter, carefully sealed in a brown envelope, from one of our senior reporters. 'Dear Richard,' he wrote, 'Please don't blame yourself, but by the time you read this it will be too late.' Jon had just suffered the break-up of his romance with another journalist, and decided that such a trauma – combined, no doubt, with the alcoholism which frequently saw him arrive in the office stinking of drink and with a bottle of vodka sticking out of his pocket – was more than he could stand. He planned to kill himself. It was what I imagined a typical suicide note to be, full of reassurance that he knew what he was doing and that he just wanted to tell me it was nothing that I had done or said, and it was clearly intended to be taken seriously.

We still had a newspaper to get out, but I and as many reporters as could be spared immediately stopped work to search for him. His ex-girlfriend rushed back to her flat to see if he was there, and his friends ran to some of the pubs and drinking dens they knew he favoured. I allocated myself the main city cemetery, simply on the grounds that I knew him well enough to know that he would, even in that torrid emotional state, appreciate the prospect of his death being recorded under the headline 'MAN FOUND DEAD IN GRAVEYARD'. I searched among the tombstones, looked up into the old elm trees and even peered into an unfilled grave in case he was curled up in the bottom of it, but – just like all the other searchers – eventually had to return to the office with only failure to report. It was several hours before we discovered he had checked himself into the Accident and Emergency Department of the Queen's Medical Centre, having taken a nowhere-near-fatal overdose of barbiturates.

It was on days like that that I donned my tin helmet. This had been supplied by Kenneth Alan Taylor, director of the Nottingham Playhouse, and one of a few good contacts I regularly had lunch with (it was he who gave me a taste for a good bottle of Chablis) and upon whom I could always rely to provide me with off-beat news stories when we most needed them.

I had learned that Kenneth had served his National Service in the Army with Ray Moore, a disc jockey who had a cult breakfast time programme on BBC Radio 2. He was desperate to meet his old friend again after a period of many years and asked me if I could fix it for him.

I did, and invited Ray and his wife Alma ('management', as he referred to her on the radio) to join me and Tricia, and Kenneth and his wife Judith, one Saturday for lunch in a city centre restaurant. We had enormous fun there, and probably drank far too much, before returning to the office late in the afternoon for the obligatory photograph, in which Kenneth (the ex private) cowered under the World War II soldier's helmet he had found in his theatre's props cupboard while a fierce-looking Ray (the sergeant) hit him over the head with a clenched fist.

Afterwards the two old friends wandered off giggling, for more reminiscing and no doubt more drinking . . . leaving the helmet on my desk, where it remained as a bizarre badge of office which I wore to protect myself whenever danger threatened me – bollockings from Barrie, complaints from angry readers, moans from under-achieving reporters – in a childish but rather satisfying parody of the way that a squaddie might have used it to protect himself in the trenches many years before.

15

IT HAS OFTEN SURPRISED ME that our marriage survived – not because of anything that either of us did, or didn't do, but simply because Tricia and I were so young and inexperienced in life when we knelt beside each other in Leominster Priory on that day in 1973. Many young couples, who no doubt initially loved each other no less than Tricia and I did, find that as they grow older they change in ways that make them no longer compatible. We were lucky that although we changed – and I reckon we were in our early thirties by the time we had developed into something like the people we are today – we changed in similar directions, so that we always wanted the same as each other, although what we wanted by then was not necessarily what we had wanted to begin with.

Tricia had become the young woman she had always shown signs of becoming – someone for whom the glass is always half full, and never half empty, someone who always searches out the best in people and someone who has an almost unlimited capacity for love. A radio programme once suggested we should try to come up with a single noun that best encapsulated our partner's qualities, and she, after a little thought, settled upon 'rock' for me; I had no hesitation at all in choosing 'love' as her word, because she is overflowing with it – whether for me, her children, her friends, her home, or for the world and every bird and animal and beautiful thing within it. She is, quite simply, the most loving person I have ever met and I have never thought of myself as anything other than lucky to be her husband.

By the time I was promoted to news editor, she had a job of her own which used her personal qualities to the full. Pat Poyser, Antony and Juliet's headmaster at Bottesford Primary School had invited her (probably breaking all the rules that said he should advertise every vacancy) to take on the job of caring for John Harris, a boy who was returning to school with learning difficulties after suffering a brain tumour. It was difficult, frustrating and worrying work, and something for which as a nursery nurse she was not really qualified, and it placed on her the extra emotional burden of putting William into the care of two friends who took it in turns to be childminders, but Tricia took to it in the way anyone who knew her would have expected – with enormous patience, compassion and understanding – and she stayed with John us he progressed through that school and well into the next. It was no surprise either that he made remarkable progress or that he and his grateful parents stayed in touch with her for many years afterwards.

She somehow found time also to continue immersing herself in her family and, more than ever, in our garden (evening classes at a local college gave her a much deserved horticultural qualification) which became such a perfect oasis of colour and tranquillity we even opened it to the public to raise money for the local playgroup. And she found yet more to do with her time when – after much persuasion – the Coxes next door agreed to sell us part of one of their fields that ran across the end of our garden. That gave us another third of an acre in which we planted trees, dug a pond and built a wooden summerhouse, but more importantly introduced Tricia to the joy of keeping poultry (a couple of the Coxes' ducks were included in the deal), which has stayed with her ever since.

It was an idyllic place for a family with three young children to live – an almost old fashioned way of life, with country walks, birdwatching, growing our own vegetables in the garden and collecting fresh eggs from the ducks and chickens in our own field. I know the sun did not always shine there – in fact that part of the country could be gloomier, colder and windier than any other I have known – but looking back on it now, it seems to have.

The children took it for granted that their antics would very often end up in my Wednesday column in the *Evening Post*, which must sometimes have been embarrassing for them, but they also began to enjoy some of the perks which came with my job – not least the free holidays (a luxurious seaside cottage in Pembrokeshire, a cabin cruiser on the Norfolk Broads and a narrowboat on the Llangollen canal, for example, were all provided on the understanding that I would write a half page feature for our travel supplement) and tickets for the local theatres. Antony, in particular, being the eldest, often came with me when I had to review a show at the newly opened Royal Concert Hall, and he and Juliet and William got used to seeing shows at the Theatre Royal or Playhouse which were beyond the experience of most children of their age. Juliet – having been inspired to take up ice skating by local Nottingham heroes Torvill and Dean – came with me to London to see the first night of the world tour they embarked upon after turning professional following their gold medal success at the Olympic Games, and she and the rest of us saw the same show four more times (and handed a birthday bouquet to Jane Torvill) when they brought it home to Nottingham.

And all three children also enjoyed the November 5 fireworks shows the *Post* staged at Meadow Lane, home of Notts County Football Club – and, because even then they shared my love of a good cock-up, they enjoyed the first one most of all, when all the spectacular rockets exploded out of sight in the sky because nobody had considered that the overhanging roof of the old grandstand would mean that anything happening more than 100ft above the ground would be invisible to the audience.

Antony, Juliet and William got used to being in the paper – here they are helping the Evening Post find out if a family of five could survive on a week's dole money
COURTESY OF THE NOTTINGHAM POST

Being treated as VIP guests at the first nights of the pantomimes (the Theatre Royal's were always bigger, glitzier and more full of 'celebrity' performers, while those at the Playhouse, where my friend Kenneth Alan

Taylor was acknowledged to be one of the best 'dames' in the country, were more traditional and, in many ways, more fun) became second nature to them, and they thought nothing of mingling with the stars at the opening night party after the show. Though still only very young (William first went hobnobbing with the famous when he was about four) they took it all in their stride and never failed to behave impeccably. They remained unfazed by whatever excitements my career threw at them – seeing Kylie Minogue in the foyer of the Birmingham hotel where I had gone for a conference, being greeted on first name terms by the dickey-bowed director of a major theatre, rubbing shoulders and scoffing sausage rolls with some famous comedian after a show . . . They probably thought that all children lived like that!

It was the best job I'd ever had but it came to an end when Bill Ivory retired and Barrie offered me promotion to fill the vacancy as assistant editor. I was not fool enough to turn down the opportunity – to be third from the top of arguably Britain's best provincial newspaper was beyond the wildest of the dreams I'd had when I walked as little more than a schoolboy into the archaic offices of the *Weston Mercury* not so many years before – but it was with much regret and considerable misgivings that I accepted it. For one thing being news editor was everything I had ever wanted from a job and I knew I would miss the excitement of being at the very heart of the paper's most dynamic department, and for another neither I nor anyone else understood exactly what being Barrie's assistant editor involved. Certainly nobody knew how Bill had spent his time (which suited him, coming as he was towards the end of his career, but was no good to me in my mid 30s) and I had no wish to be eased into some indefinable role as far removed from the daily action as he had appeared to be.

What convinced me was the confidence I had in Barrie – and the knowledge that he had a high enough regard for me not to want to shunt me into the sidings. He explained that I would, in effect, be his deputy in all editorial matters. He couldn't give me the title of deputy editor because Ian Scott already had it and my promotion was not intended to result in a demotion for him, but the idea was that Ian and I would work as a team, as equals – with Ian in charge of the things he was good at (budgets and administration, for example) while I would be doing what I was best at (coming up with ideas, making sure all stories were developed to their full potential and acting as a link between the other journalists and the editor). And – most important of all – when Barrie was away I would take the editor's role as far as the content of the newspaper was concerned, which meant everything from chairing the afternoon editorial conference to choosing the front page splash and deciding what line the paper's daily leader column should take.

It meant I was no longer involved just in news, but in every aspect of the editorial department's work – news, features, sport, pictures and production – which gave me an unparalleled opportunity to have some influence over the whole newspaper, not just part of it (though to some people, no doubt, it meant that I was no more than a busybody who was free to interfere in anything into which I wanted to poke my unwelcome nose).

I discovered – rather to my surprise – that people who had previously been my equals, and in some cases my superiors, now seemed to be happy to regard me as their boss. It's a strange thing that with responsibility comes confidence, and with confidence comes authority – or so it did when applied to me, anyway – so that I found I grew into my new role even though I had had no formal training for it.

I even managed to overcome my dread of standing up and speaking in public. As news editor I had been expected to give the occasional talk (my first was to Sherwood and District Toc H, an organisation dedicated to helping the disadvantaged, of which, in Nottingham, there were many, and it was followed by a wide variety of social and community groups, mostly comprising elderly women in knitted hats) and that role increased upon my promotion, so that as assistant editor I was giving up to three such speeches a week.

My talk always started the same: 'I am a journalist. I'm telling you that right at the start, to give you the chance to walk out now if you wish. I know that a survey has shown that journalists are among the most despised people in the country – with only traffic wardens and estate agents below them in the public's esteem – so I will quite understand if some of you would rather not stay here in the same room with me.' It always got a bit of a laugh – except once, when my audience greeted it with a self conscious shuffling in their chairs and a few embarrassed coughs (I learned afterwards that there were several estate agents, though thankfully no traffic wardens, among the Newark and District Round Table) – and set the flavour of what was to follow, which was an outline of some of the ethical difficulties faced by the modern newspaperman lightened by a few humorous anecdotes and an explanation of why the *Evening Post* was by far and away the best newspaper in the country (it probably wasn't – quite

– but I felt obliged to present something of a marketing message on behalf of my employers).

Tricia was finding that being married to the assistant editor of the *Post* carried certain duties too, and she often accompanied me to some official function or other (invitations to me usually included one to her as well – Nottingham was very enlightened in that respect). This was a role encouraged by Barrie, who was very fond of her and clearly considered her to be both an ideal consort and a very good influence on me, just as Pauline had always been for him.

He even forgave her – no, more than that, he actually admired her – when, at a Guild of Editors Conference at a swanky hotel in the North-East, she, politely but firmly, told some of the most influential people in the British newspaper industry that she would not eat the veal being presented for the official gala dinner since there was no doubt it had been produced under appallingly cruel conditions in which the animals had been denied proper food or even daylight during their sad harsh lives. She was so passionate and so persuasive that all eight people on our table told the waitress they'd really rather have an omelette.

One of the unexpected pleasures of my new job was working with people from the marketing department, whose relationship with journalists was traditionally one of mutual suspicion, if not actual dislike. The worst sort of marketing people (and there are plenty of them!) look upon editorial as the necessary evil that fills the spaces between the advertisements, and upon journalists as nothing more than a drain on the company's resources, and the idea that a marketing department might try to promote and sell the paper on the strength of the editorial it contained was just about unheard of. It was almost entirely thanks to Barrie's healthy working relationship with David Teague, the marketing director, and Don Gray, the newspaper sales director, that at the *Post* such antediluvian attitudes had at last begun to change.

Part of my new role was to build on the progress that had already been made and act as an intermediary between our two departments, using their marketing skills to promote the best of the editorial content and arranging, when appropriate, for their work to be supported by editorial.

Such close contact with the marketing department was highly unusual for a journalist and it opened my eyes to a different way of looking at both the newspaper and the people working for it. I could never get used to their calling the *Post* the 'product' any more than they could understand what they saw as my weirdly irreverent view of the world, but we developed a rapport in which my tolerance of their obsession with profits was matched by their amused acceptance of what they saw as the maverick ways of the journalists who worked on the floor above.

I even joined David Teague and his senior team on several of their trips abroad – marketing people arrange their conferences in such places as Paris, Copenhagen and Brussels while editors have theirs in Birmingham, Telford and Newcastle-upon-Tyne – and through them I learned more about the marketing of newspapers than most journalists ever get the chance to.

But while I came to understand them better, my working so closely with them confirmed that there was indeed a fundamental difference in our philosophies. Marketing people are altogether more disciplined and respectful than journalists – too disciplined and respectful, in my opinion – and are happiest being part of a well-ordered machine and working under the sort of strict rules that would be an anathema to us.

Such differences manifested themselves most obviously on the streets of whichever European city we found ourselves. They, in their smart dark suits and subservient smiles, would be happy to follow their boss wherever he went, fawning on his every word and laughing dutifully at his jokes, while I, in my inquisitive and often faintly anarchic way, would prefer to give them the slip and wander off on my own for a quick beer in a pavement café before heading off to see for myself what lurked around the next corner.

While it was interesting working in this strange new world, it was always good to get back to what I enjoyed best, among people who found nothing remarkable in my perverse outlook on life. Best of all were the days when I had the chance to play at being editor, even though, while I regularly stood in for Barrie when he was away, it was only rarely that I was called upon to make any real management decisions and assume full control of the paper.

One such occasion started only because he had gone to a football match. It was on the afternoon of Saturday April 15 1989 and, after spending the morning in the office overseeing that day's *Post*, I was at home in the garden, weeding and listening out for reports of the Bristol City match on the radio. There was no word of what was happening at Ashton Gate though, and when instead news started coming in of crowd trouble at the FA Cup semi final between Nottingham Forest and Liverpool, I listened with some interest because I knew that we would be covering the match at the Hillsborough stadium in Sheffield in some detail in our next paper, on the Monday. I also knew that Barrie was there, so if the mighty Forest lost it would at least give me, a supporter of humble Bristol City, something to tease him about the next time I saw him.

It soon became clear though that whatever was happening in Sheffield would be no cause for teasing. The news flashes on the radio were becoming more insistent, more anxious, and it was obvious that this was rather more than just another bout of the violence that scarred the image of British football at that time. There was real fear in the voices coming from the little transistor radio at my feet. Men who had gone to report on a football match were finding that what they were commentating on instead looked like becoming a tragedy – and a real tragedy at that, not the sort so often described by sports journalists when the opposition's centre forward slots in an undeserved winning goal three minutes into injury time.

In the middle of it all, I knew, were thousands of people from Nottingham – our readers – and in the middle of them all was Barrie. I dropped everything. Almost literally. I had time to ring the circulation manager before I left home, and within half an hour we were talking in my office. I was still in my grubby gardening clothes with the soil between my fingers.

As the minutes passed the Press Association – the national news agency which at that time of a Saturday afternoon should have been doing no more than sending us details of all the goals as they went in – started reporting on people being badly hurt. Of fans lying motionless on the pitch, surrounded by St John Ambulance volunteers. Of others who looked almost dead, but surely could not be, not at a football match. And then of some being laid out on the pitch with coats over their faces.

For once I really was the editor, with full responsibility for whatever we were going to decide to do. We had no more than a skeleton staff on duty – a late news reporter for the *Post*, and a handful of sports subs ready to produce the *Football Post*, the tabloid sports paper that we published within minutes of the final whistle every Saturday during the football season – which was more than enough to turn out a newspaper containing the football results. But producing a paper covering what was turning into one of Britain's major human tragedies was something else entirely.

But I knew we had no choice. I have never been scared of making big decisions (it's the little ones like which pub we should go to, or which tie I should wear that cause me to hesitate), and anyway on an afternoon like that the decisions made themselves. With the support of the production and circulation managers we decided to turn the *Football Post* into a special edition containing as much news as we could get of the dreadful events happening at Hillsborough. Our sports reporter, who had expected to be writing on a cup semi final, was suddenly pressed into reporting on the biggest unfolding news story in the world, and instead of sending out football scores the Press Association was filling the wires with grim descriptions and photographs of people dying terrible deaths, trampled underfoot or trapped behind the unyielding wire fences which the football authorities had deemed to be a good idea to control football hooligans and keep rival fans apart.

The skeleton staff rose to the occasion magnificently, relishing the opportunity to get involved in a real newspaper for a change, and almost the only thing I had to do was make sure we hit the deadlines set by the production department – and decide on how far we could go in portraying the carnage without upsetting our readers with unnecessarily graphic details of the slaughter. Some of the photographs that landed on my desk that afternoon were so gruesome and so distressing there was no question of any newspaper ever using them. Others were so bland they failed totally to give any idea of the scale of the disaster, and were just as easily rejected. It was those in the middle – the dozens of pictures that were shocking without being gory, showing anguish rather than of agony – that caused me the most difficulty. We had a duty to cover the horror of Hillsborough in all its dreadfulness, but we equally had a duty not to sicken our readers with photographs that were too harrowing and explicit. My solution was to use pictures of people suffering, but not near death, and one of those I rejected was the one that eventually became the almost iconic image of the disaster – of four teenaged girls clawing at the wire with their faces pinched and distorted by the mesh (it was many days before it was discovered that those girls, apparently on the verge of death, had in fact survived).

Ninety-six people died and more than 200 were badly hurt that afternoon, in what turned out to be the worst sporting disaster in Britain's history. A public inquiry later established that, with more than 2,000 Liverpool supporters still outside the ground at kick-off time, the police decided to open a gate to let them into what was already an over-full stand. As the fans rushed in those already there were pushed forward and crushed against the grotesquely-named 'safety fence', and continued to be so for at least five minutes before people elsewhere in the stadium realised what they were seeing.

Throughout the afternoon I was confident that Barrie – who I knew would be sitting in the grandstand, well away from the trouble – would phone as soon as he could (this was in the days before mobile phones) and issue brisk instructions on how we should be approaching the job. I like to think that the fact that he didn't showed that he was confident that the people running his newspaper in his absence would be up to the job.

I still had time to enjoy some unlikely perks of my position. A trip to Berlin with a group of senior provincial journalists as guests of the British Army, for example, saw me flying in a helicopter over the Berlin Wall shortly before that fantastically exciting night when the oppressed population rose up at last and knocked it down, and taking part in a rifle shooting competition against some of the officers entrusted with the defence of our nation. I won the competition handsomely – which was satisfying, even though the fact that I did it while not wearing my glasses caused me to ask questions about the quality of the modern soldier.

When I made the mistake of writing in my Wednesday column that, as a child, I had always longed to be the one called up on stage in a pantomime, Kenneth Alan Taylor phoned me and told me everything was set and a seat was reserved for me at the next Tuesday's matinee performance, from which I would be invited to go onto the stage for a bit of tomfoolery with a man dressed as a piano.

He would not listen when I told him that he was at least 30 years too late, and that in fact I'd never wanted to do any such thing, and had said I had only because it was a way of finding something to write about that week, so I made my debut at the Nottingham Playhouse on the allotted afternoon, being taken up onto the stage and made to look a complete idiot alongside a couple of children who were much more relaxed about the whole business than I was, even though they quite clearly could not understand what a big bearded bloke in a suit was doing making a prat of himself in exchange for a goodybag containing a carton of orange juice, a cardboard policeman's helmet and a bag of fruit bonbons.

And when I wrote about my love of 1960s pop music (a subject which remains the only one upon which I am anything like an expert) the programme controller of GEM-AM, the local golden oldie radio station, invited me to present an hour-long show one afternoon – a task I approached with considerable enthusiasm until I discovered at a rehearsal just how difficult it is to talk reasonably sensibly into a microphone at the same time as cueing up a record on a turntable and making sure you don't over-run into the various segments allocated for the news, the weather forecast and the travel update.

Richard Harris

A bit of tomfoolery with a man dressed as a piano
COURTESY OF THE NOTTINGHAM POST

I was allowed to indulge myself and play whichever records I chose, and after many hours deliberating I came up with a list which included songs that I'd always loved (*Walk On By* by Leroy Van Dyke, *You're The One* by The Vogues, *If You Go Away* by Dusty Springfield and *Every Time We Say Goodbye* by Ella Fitzgerald), two that had good anecdotes I could attach to them (*You're A Lady* by Peter Skellern and *Back Home Again* by John Denver) and, just for the sake of having something rather more mainstream, *The Last Time* by the Rolling Stones and *California Girls* by The Beach Boys.

There was no way I could have been mistaken for a professional broadcaster and goodness knows what my 'listeners' made of it all, but for me it was great fun and just one more thing I would never have had the chance of doing if I had been in any other job.

16

BEING SO CLOSE TO THE TOP JOB on a newspaper like the *Post* inevitably made me think about becoming an editor myself. I seemed to be able to cope with most that the job involved – though I was very well aware that being a stand-in editor under Barrie was a good deal easier than having to shoulder all the responsibility myself – and other people seemed to think I would be up to it even if I had no great desire to make their ambitions for me come true ('No fire in my belly,' as Barrie would say).

There was no escaping the fact that while part of me felt it would be much easier and safer to stick with doing a job I was good at among people who appreciated me, another part of me knew I would never forgive myself if I did not at least try to take the final step. It is, after all, a strange person who, being so near the top of a mountain, decides not to take the last few paces to the summit to look at the view on the other side.

Barrie happened to be on holiday when I applied to Cumbrian Newspapers in Carlisle, who were advertising for an editor to take charge of the weekly *Cumberland News* and its sister paper the *Evening News & Star*. I knew a little of the company (Neil Maxwell's father had been its managing director some years previously) but next to nothing about Carlisle except that it was a city we had often passed by on our way to holidays in Scotland.

Even when I sent off my letter of application I did not really know that I wanted the job, but I knew that if nothing else I might be able to use it as a levering tool to get a pay rise from Barrie when he returned.

As soon as he got back from his holiday I told him I had applied for an editorship, and he had no doubt.

'Carlisle?' he asked simply.

'Yes,' I told him.

'You'll get it.'

I learned then that a recent party of visitors to the *Post* (we had a lot of such people, all wanting to discover the secret of our success) had included the managing director of Cumbrian Newspapers, and he had been so impressed by what he had seen that he'd taken Barrie aside and asked him, only half jokingly, what he had to do to entice his deputy to join him in Cumbria.

I was therefore not surprised when I received a reply inviting me to Carlisle for an interview; indeed thanks to what Barrie had told me, I already had the feeling that the job was mine to lose.

I was interviewed by the managing director Robin Burgess, a huge florid faced man a couple of years younger than me, and by Peter Simpson, the production director, who seemed altogether sharper and shrewder and, I guessed, was the streetwise power behind the organisation.

I did well, I know – probably because at that stage I really didn't care whether I was given the job or not – and answered all their questions calmly, confidently and politely and was called back for a second interview, this time with Burgess, his board chairman, a gentleman farmer called Joe Harris, and another director, Richard Winfrey, who was also a director of East Midlands Allied Press in Peterborough.

I'm not sure what I expected, but I knew something of the many difficult hoops Barrie had had to jump through before being appointed editor of the *Post*, so I had prepared myself for rather more than the 'What would you do you if you found the local MP was having an affair with his secretary?' line of questioning which dominated much of the interview. They spent a little time quizzing me on my politics, said they wanted their newspapers to be 'slightly right of centre' and told me they expected the tabloid *Evening News & Star* to be 'lively but not necessarily salacious', whatever that meant. They asked me about the state of my marriage, wanted to know if Tricia was willing to fulfil the role of 'editor's wife' and were somehow impressed that we had just come back from a holiday in which we – complete with three children – had spent a fortnight backpacking around France on public transport.

The next thing I knew Tricia and I were being invited back to Carlisle to rubber-stamp my appointment after a lunch with Burgess and his wife Alex – and, bizarrely, a couple of non newspaper people who were staying with them for the weekend – in a posh local country house hotel.

This was the strangest encounter of them all. I joked with Tricia that they just wanted to check that she knew which hands to hold her knife and fork in and didn't swear, pick her nose or show too much of a taste for the wine. She sat next to Robin Burgess and charmed him, and perfectly played the part of a wife who was devoted to her husband's career but who was also not afraid to show that she had a mind of her own (in fact, she was just herself – but emphasised the bits of her character, and her relationship with me and my job, that she knew would best please my prospective boss).

I sat next to the female half of the Burgesses' houseguests – a lady so much like Ambra that I hit it off with her immediately, feeling that I already knew her, so that when Burgess glanced at us from his seat at the head of the table and saw us chatting busily and laughing I could almost hear him thinking: 'We've made the right choice – this man is a real social animal who can get along with anyone' (which, of course, was far from the truth).

He offered me not much more money than I was earning in Nottingham, and a basic Ford Granada which was considerably downmarket from the top-of-the-range model I had at the *Post*, but there was really no question of my turning the offer down by then. My career had suddenly developed a momentum of its own and it would have been no easier to stop it than it would have been to leap from a moving roller coaster.

It would be silly to suggest that I had no doubts about the prospect of moving to Carlisle. I had been supremely happy working at the *Post*, after all, and my time there had coincided with the best years of my life, my marriage and the birth of my children. My decision to take the Carlisle editorship was, perhaps, more a step that I felt I had to take, than something I desperately wanted to do.

When I told Barrie I had been offered the job he made only the mildest attempt to persuade me not to go, telling me that if I stayed he would recommend me as his successor if ever he left, which I took as a great compliment but a worthless one. I knew he had no plans to move from Nottingham, where he was doing so well and was so happy, and also that if he did ever leave his opinion of me would probably not count for much in the board's search for a new editor. And anyway, while I had some confidence in my ability, I knew I was not of the calibre to take over the reins of a major newspaper like the *Post* – at least not until I had learned the job on some much smaller newspaper, just as Barrie had done when he moved to Kent.

I wrote to Robin Burgess and accepted the job, telling him I would be free to leave the *Post* just before Christmas in 1989 and therefore could start at Cumbrian Newspapers in the first week of January 1990.

The next time I met Robin was a month or so later at a hotel on the shores of Derwentwater in the Lake District. Even though I was still an employee of the *Post* he had cheekily summoned me to a weekend management meeting where, he said, I would be able to meet my future colleagues and play a part in the 'forward planning' (I was too polite to ask what other sort of planning there might be) of his company.

My new colleagues seemed a good bunch and I got on well with them – so well that I was no longer on my best behaviour by the time the sharp-suited management consultant divided us into teams of three to draw up a Mission Statement (yes, I'm sure it just had to have capital letters) which would guide the company through its next couple of decades. I had no more experience of mission statements than I had of management consultants and so struggled to take it all very seriously. At Nottingham we had no need for mission statements because we all understood that our 'mission' was simply to work as well as we could, produce the best newspaper that we could and by our efforts allow the company to prosper and thrive in the future just as well as it had in the past. Such an attitude would have been no good to Robin Burgess. He wanted something much more. So, in the safety of the little room into which I and my two new 'colleagues' were ushered, giggling like schoolboys and with tears streaming from our eyes, we decided to give it to him: 'Cumbrian Newspapers will never be content just to be the best newspaper company in Cumbria, nor even in the North of England, nor indeed even in Britain. It must forever push forward and progress until it is recognised as the finest, most successful and most profitable news and publishing organisation in the whole wide world.'

It was absurd and very childish but, we thought, very funny, and later, when the leader of our group was asked to stand in front of a flip chart and present our statement to the others it became even funnier, with him delivering it in the style of a Shakespearean actor, declaiming it with far more dignity than it deserved and rising to a flamboyant crescendo as he came to the end. After a couple of seconds of stunned silence, which the rest of us struggled not to disturb with our stifled sniggering, Robin Burgess clapped his hands together in delight. 'That gentlemen,' he beamed, 'is just the sort of attitude we want.'

I returned to the saner world of the *Post* after that weekend with just a hint of wondering what I had let myself in for.

Apart from satisfying the demands of my career there was no good reason to uproot the family. All five of us had been very happy in both Bottesford and Normanton, the children were doing well at school and had many friends and interests, and Tricia and I were content living in the cottage of our dreams. If we were to move anywhere, we had always thought, it would be somewhere further south, closer to our families and the few friends we still had from our early days. None of us would have guessed that when I came to leave the *Evening Post* it would be for a newspaper so far north that it would be just eight miles from the Scottish border.

But moving we were . . . and we had to find a house. My new contract of employment stipulated that I had to live within 15 miles of Carlisle (which ruled out a cottage in the Lake District, even if we could have afforded one) and we found ourselves drawn to the area east of the city – not least because, on one of our exploratory visits, we were deterred by the hostile silence that greeted our arrival in a pub in the village of Abbeytown, a few miles west.

It was on a Sunday morning that we first set eyes on Woody Glen, only the third house that we had looked at, but one which had caught our eye when it was advertised in the first *Cumberland News* Robin Burgess had sent me when I applied for the job three months before. It was a traditional Cumbrian longhouse, a long sandstone four-bedroomed single-storey cottage (to call it a bungalow would give the wrong impression) set up on a grass bank overlooking the single road that runs past The How, a tiny hamlet attached to the not-very-much-bigger village of How Mill. It had been on the market with a singular lack of success for many months and quite why nobody else had wanted it remains something of a mystery. It had a delightful and quirky interior, great views to the north over Scotland, a garden that was already beautiful and had the potential to be more so, and about five acres of woodland reaching over a hill and down to a tumbling stream on the other side. But it was none of those things that made us fall in love with it. It was the feeling of the place, the sense that it somehow picked us up in its arms and hugged us as we walked through the door, that made all five of us fall instantly under its spell. We offered the owners' asking price on the spot.

In December 1989 I took my leave of Nottingham with the last of my Wednesday columns:

Richard Harris

THIS week, of all weeks, I wanted to come up with something special. Something profound. Something, perhaps, a shade entertaining. Something good enough for you to remember me by. For after seven years and more than 300 of these columns, this is the last time I will be filling this corner of Page Four.

I wanted to go out with, if not a bang, something a little bit more than a whimper. But I'm not sure I can find the words.

I will miss writing here on Wednesdays and I will miss you as well. I shall miss the people who have taken the trouble to send me letters over the years – a few in always welcome support, but most or them in abject disagreement with what I have written here.

I shall miss the lady who once sent a copy of my column to Colonel Gadaffi because she thought (wrongly, I have no doubt) that it might make him mend his ways.

I shall miss the people of Wollaton who, the week after I wrote about my favourite hymns, sang one of them especially for me when I went to visit them.

I shall miss the lady who, after I wrote lamenting the lack of a proper Nottingham song, sat down and recorded one with her cassette machine plugged in next to her home organ.

I shall miss the elderly lady who recognised me in a restaurant and passed me a note . . . and I shall miss the other lady who spotted me in the street and told me in excited tones 'I know you, you're Emrys Bryson' (the Post's highly respected theatre critic who has a column here on Tuesdays).

I shall miss them and I thank them, because they have all helped to make up a rich mosaic of a memory for me to take away as a souvenir.

As I scuttle up the motorway in search of a new life in the North, I know too that I will start to miss this city which for 17 years has been such an important part of my life.

I don't suppose I will miss Nottingham for itself, not for its glassy office blocks or its traffic or its noise, anyway. But I shall miss it because, like a new overcoat which is stiff when first you wear it, it has become more comfortable as the years have passed by.

I shall miss the blunt humour of its inhabitants and the welcome they give even to people who, like I was when I arrived, are outsiders.

I shall miss the things for which it is famous (the pretty girls, the buskers, the theatres and the beer). And I shall miss the things for which it is less so (the funny fountains, the flowers and the fat old tramp who sits on the bench in Trinity Square looking like a worn-out Father Christmas).

Most of all, I shall miss the people who were once strangers and are now friends.

Yes, I'll miss Nottingham. And when I'm no longer a part of it, I know there will be a bit or me which will wish I were still.

COURTESY OF THE NOTTINGHAM POST

The *Post* said goodbye to me and Tricia with a lavish dinner at a local hotel, hosted by Barrie and with guests including some of my friends from my days in Features, a few from marketing and all the heads of the editorial departments. Barrie made a kind speech, thanking me for my support, praising my talents and wishing me luck . . . and read out loud my article about Juliet and Col Gadaffi (something I found excruciatingly embarrassing, though also hugely gratifying when some of his audience nodded in agreement when he said it was one of the most moving pieces of writing any of his newspapers had ever published). I returned the favour by thanking everyone for their friendship and encouragement, and expressed my very real gratitude to Barrie for having had the courage to pluck me out of what could have been a dead-end job in Features, and spoiled it all by telling him that it seemed I hadn't needed 'fire in my belly' after all, since unknown to him I'd been ambitious all along, but for more things than he had ever been ambitious for himself (which was a cheap shot against someone to whom I owed so much and one that I regretted almost as soon as I'd said it).

At the end of the evening Barrie took Tricia aside and, betraying more emotion than many people would have thought him capable of, told her gently: 'Look after him.'

17

WHEN WE MOVED IN THREE DAYS before Christmas a bottle of champagne was waiting for us on the doorstep, a present from Robin Burgess to welcome us to our new life. It was the first of many touching welcomes, all of which I was happy to take as a sign that moving to Cumbria was the right thing to do.

Later, as I walked down the steps through the Woody Glen garden to meet the removal van, I was greeted by a round and smiling lady who came out of the little cottage opposite. 'Welcome to The How,' she said, cheerily. I returned to the house confident that people's warnings about the probable unfriendliness of the Cumbrian locals were misplaced. 'It's going to be OK,' I told Tricia. 'The natives are friendly.'

That greeting from Nancy Kennedy, as local and as friendly as anyone could be, was typical of our reception in Cumbria. On that first evening, knowing we had to show we were willing to make the effort to win the friendship of the community and be accepted into it, I walked up to the Vic, the little pub at the far end of the village. As I entered the handful of men inside fell silent, looked me up and down, nodded a greeting and separated so I could reach the bar. It was so unlike the hostile atmosphere we had encountered not long before in Abbeytown! I asked for a pint and, in a voice loud enough to be heard by everyone else, began to introduce myself to the landlord. Des Spencer, the elderly man who, with a bit of help from his daughters and their husbands, ran the pub to augment his pension, smiled and held up his hand to silence me. 'It's all right,' he said. 'We know who you are. It's good to see you.'

It was soon obvious that Des and all the others knew rather more than just who I was. He knew what job I had come to do, who I was married to, how many children we had, where we had moved from, what jobs we had been doing there, what sort of cars we drove and, almost certainly, what I was earning and how much we had paid for the house. In different circumstances, and in a different place, I might have felt threatened by their nosiness, intimidated by their unashamed interest in almost every aspect of our lives, but I was more than willing to accept a little lack of privacy if that was the alternative to the chilling indifference many people had warned us to expect.

We celebrated that Christmas in a home still cluttered with half-unpacked packing cases and pieces of furniture which had not yet found their rightful places around the house. My mother came to stay (she always had stayed with us on alternate Christmases ever since Dad died, and we saw no reason to upset that pattern just because we had been in the house for only three days) and spent a large part of Christmas Day helping to put up fox-proof fences around the sheds that we had brought – whole, and still full of ducks and chickens – from our field at Normanton.

It was only after New Year, when I began my new job and the children started at their new schools, that the full enormity of what we had done hit me. The move had been all my doing – Tricia had supported me because she understood that my career made it necessary, but Antony, Juliet and William had come because they were too young to have any option, and the fact that they now found ourselves in a world in which they were strangers, 200 miles from their friends and everything that they knew, was all my doing.

The changes the children were facing, of course, were every bit as great as mine. We had plucked them out of schools in which they had been doing well, and were happy, and placed them instead into a totally alien environment where they were known by neither their teachers nor their fellow pupils . . . and we really had very little idea whether the schools to which they had moved would be any good. We realised afterwards that parents are supposed to check out the local schools first, and buy a house within the catchment area of the best one, rather than decide on the house – as we had done – and only later find our how good or bad were the schools in the area.

As it turned out we were lucky.

William, at nine years old, was young enough to look upon the whole thing as a big adventure and had too little experience of life to realise just how badly it could go wrong. Hayton primary school, in the next village across the fields from How Mill, where he would go for a year, was reckoned to be among the best in North Cumbria, and he settled in very quickly and very happily, making enough friends to compensate for those he had left behind in Leicestershire.

For Antony and Juliet settling into their new school was always likely to be more difficult, because they were at an age at which any move was fraught with potential problems, both personal and educational. The William Howard School, five miles away in Brampton, had a fine reputation both for the quality of the education it provided and for the standards it insisted on from its pupils, but that was no guarantee that they would be happy there.

Antony, being one year into his GCSEs, had made clear his reluctance to leave Leicestershire (we gave him the biggest bedroom as compensation) yet acclimatised to his new surroundings remarkably quickly and soon found that his new classmates even forgave him for the lack of sporting prowess he had inherited from his father (his cheerful and self effacing personality ensured that even when he ruined a promising move by dropping the ball in a game of rugby, instead of turning on him and blaming him for his incompetence, as they might have done, they would laugh and say 'It's only Antony, what else do you expect?').

Juliet was not so lucky. The teacher who was her head of year had, on hearing that she was joining the school, pinned a note on his notice board, in full view of the pupils, proclaiming 'January 1990 – Juliet Harris – very bright' which was all the excuse some of her new classmates needed to turn against her even before she had started. Juliet managed to keep her unhappiness secret for some time, thinking that Tricia and I had enough to worry about following our move, but eventually she admitted that two girls in particular – Hannah and Cathy – were making her life hell.

It is little consolation that fighting her battle against the other girls' bullying helped mould Juliet into the spirited, determined young woman she is today – or that, as the more mature Catherine, the dreadful 'Cathy' later became one of her best friends.

Even without her unhappy start at her new school, it was Juliet, without doubt, who lost most because of the move. It was she who had the closest friends in Bottesford – Emily, Daniel and Claire, a blind girl for whom she learned Braille so she could write letters to her. As if leaving those friends was not enough, we were also moving her away from the Nottingham ice stadium, where she was becoming a remarkably proficient ice dancer (though she was too tall to harbour many hopes of doing it competitively). The pocket-sized ice rink at Lockerbie was no substitute for the grand arena upon which Torvill and Dean had perfected some of their most famous dances, even though when Juliet made her debut there she was so much better than the rest of the skaters that they all stopped to watch her.

Juliet kept her unhappiness to herself for many months, accepting that, while the move to Cumbria had turned out very badly for her, it seemed to be going well for the rest of us. Only gradually did things improve enough for her to realise that it was going to turn out well for her too.

To an outsider Cumbrian Newspapers would have appeared to be a very similar organisation to T Bailey Forman Ltd, publishers of the *Nottingham Evening Post*. Both were long established local companies, hugely successful financially and run by a member of the family which had run them virtually from the start. In many other respects, though, they could not have been more different.

It was very soon clear that the culture of Cumbrian Newspapers was not like anything I had experienced at Nottingham – or at Bristol or Weston, come to that. Perhaps it was that the very nature of the newspaper industry had changed, and that at the *Evening Post* we had been shielded from it by a management which had been determined to go its own way for so many years; perhaps it was that Carlisle was a much smaller city, with none of the big city confidence of a place like Nottingham; or perhaps it was that Robin Burgess was a very different character from either Christopher Pole-Carew or the Colonel, both of whose roles – as managing director and the successor to the family firm – he was trying to fill.

I liked Robin, but also felt rather sorry for him. He cared passionately about his staff and about his newspapers' good name and worked hard to protect the company's independence in an industry which was becoming increasingly dominated by huge predatory organisations which gobbled up local newspapers like a shark consumes plankton. His problem was that he was following his father, Sir John Burgess, a man who, everybody told me, had been universally liked and respected both within the company and in the greater community outside. Following such a man would have been difficult for any son, but was especially so for Robin who, it was also widely agreed, as yet had little of his father's charisma, charm or easy way of man management.

Sir John had died in 1987 but still, three years later, his influence was felt all around the office and the city, not least among long-serving staff who had so much admired him and who took every opportunity to compare his son with him, usually coming to the harsh conclusion that

Robin – the fourth generation of the Burgess family to be involved with the company (his great grandfather had served as editor in 1867) – had some way to go before he could be spoken of in the same breath.

I gather that Robin has since matured into his role and has developed many of the qualities that made his father so well respected, but in those days he was still every inch a novice in the business, and it showed.

But he was pleasant to me, and encouraging, and clearly looked upon me as the man who held the key to the next stage of his company's development. I'm not sure he ever understood me, though, any more probably than he understood any journalist. As an ex Army officer with a more recent background in newspaper marketing, he struggled to cope with the seemingly anarchic outlook of the typical journalist, which he clearly believed to be a threat to the discipline and good order of the company whose future had been entrusted to him.

He struggled, too, to understand me when I tried to explain that I believed that journalists, for all their apparent rebelliousness, were in fact the lifeblood of any newspaper because they usually felt a greater commitment to their craft than most of the other people who worked for him. Ignoring the fact that I had dreamed of being a journalist only after I had already become one, I told him that, unlike the majority of the other people he employed – the printers, sales reps and advertising salesmen – most journalists had set their hearts on doing the job even before they had left primary school. 'When,' I asked (using a question I had often heard posed by Barrie) 'was the last time a little boy put his hand up in class and told his teacher "I want to be an ad rep when I grow up"?'

That, I told him, is what, in my book, makes journalists different, if not special. Not surprisingly, he neither agreed nor understood.

Robin made it his business to introduce me to the people I should get to know (or the people he thought I should get to know, anyway) and Tricia and I got used to going to his house for Sunday lunch with him and his wife and whichever local bigwigs were next on his list of VIP contacts. This rather worried me, because, although I have no doubt that he did it with the best of motives, I believed it was vital for an editor to be seen to be independent, and not under the control of his managing director. While it was true that I needed to get to know these people, I would have preferred to meet them on my own initiative, not Robin's, so that they saw me as my own man rather than his.

It was interesting though to see who Robin thought were the people important enough to be effected an introduction to his new editor – the local MP, the health authority chairman, managing directors of the biggest local firms and so on. What they did not include were many of the people who actually made Carlisle tick – the people on the next rung down in society's pecking order, such as trades unionists, community leaders and councillors or even vicars, police officers, headteachers and sportsmen.

Those were the sort of people I made it a priority to get to know, and I was dismayed to find that few of them had ever had many dealings with Cumbrian Newspapers before. They might have used the papers' advertising pages occasionally, or met a reporter at some function or other, but there was no sign of the close and supportive relationship between the newspapers and the local community that, after my time in Nottingham, I had been expecting.

And there was no sign either of the editor being expected to play much of a part in the activities of that community. In Nottingham Barrie could have dined out every night if he had accepted all the invitations that came his way, and I could have done nearly as well in my time both as news editor and assistant editor. And, there, our wives were often invited too.

But in my time in Carlisle invitations to any function were few and far between, and those to which Tricia was also invited were even more exceptional. It was a city which, it seemed to me, had no special regard for the newspapers which tried to serve it.

From the start, though, I had bigger, more immediate problems than wondering why the social life of the city was passing me by.

Most noticeable to me – and most worrying – was the fact that the journalists with whom I was to work appeared to be an unhappy, downtrodden bunch who felt as if their efforts were neither appreciated nor properly rewarded. I was aware that I would not get a true feeling for the staff until they had got to know me and stopped being on their best behaviour whenever I appeared, but from the confines of the editor's office I could see precious little sign that they enjoyed their work, and still less that they thought, as I had always thought, that they were lucky to be doing the job they were doing.

I was not encouraged by my first afternoon conferences. The heads of all the editorial departments – the news, sports and features editors, with the chief photographer and chief sub – came into my office to discuss the next day's paper . . . and just sat there in morose silence. There was none of the good natured banter that had energised such meetings in Nottingham, or of the confident swapping of ideas and excitement over good stories which I had come to expect. Just a moody sense that they wanted to be anywhere but where they were. I hoped it was some kind of joke, that they had decided beforehand to play a game with their new editor, to behave like awkward teenagers just to see what I would make of it. But I feared it wasn't. I feared it was simply the way they were. Or the way they had been encouraged to behave in the past.

I was confident that I would be able to change things, just by using a more relaxed management style than perhaps they had been used to under my predecessors, or by encouraging people to use whatever talents they had without fear of failure, by praising them when things went well and, I hoped, by helping them to enjoy their work. By simply behaving as I had behaved in Nottingham, in other words.

I was not so confident that I would be able to overcome the other major problem that confronted me whenever I set foot in the newsroom.

The editorial department was plagued by something I had not even heard of until I arrived in Carlisle – Repetitive Strain Injury (RSI). It was ironic that in Nottingham, where computers had been installed on journalists' desks with very little planning or consultation, not a single person had developed RSI, but in Carlisle, where they had been introduced only after lengthy discussions with the staff and supposedly expert advice from the NUJ and assorted experts in ergonomics, it was rife throughout the whole editorial department.

Two sub editors were so incapacitated they could no longer do their jobs, and had to have other work – far away from a computer keyboard – found for them instead; a reporter was so disabled she could neither type nor write and had to be retrained as a photographer; a copytaker was in such pain she could not type and had to be found a job in the cuttings library; and several other reporters and subs could work only if they took regular lengthy breaks and had their wrists and lower arms supported by medical splints.

It put an enormous strain on what was already a very small department and some members of the management team would no doubt have been happy if we had been able to get rid of the victims on the basis that they were skivers who had taken an easy opportunity to get out of doing the work they were paid to do. But – while there was no doubt that most of the sufferers shared a highly-strung and rather gloomy disposition, which probably made them more susceptible than most to any passing ailment – I was convinced that the problem was not all in their minds no matter how much some people appeared to want it to be. They had nothing to gain from malingering, I thought, except the likely ending of their chosen careers or, for some, a future spent being bored to distraction doing a job which would not have existed had it not had to be invented for them.

Our company doctor John Bone, a local GP who was paid a retainer to care for the newspaper's sick, shared my opinion, spending hours in my office as we attempted to find a solution and doing his best to patch up the injured and try to prevent the 'epidemic' spreading.

My own view was that the reason no one at the *Post* had developed RSI was that they were happy and felt appreciated. At Carlisle, on the other hand, many of the staff, justifiably or not, felt unhappy and undervalued and had therefore become vulnerable. It was a theory which was unproven and untested, but probably as good as any, and it was gratifying many years later to read that many doctors involved in the treatment of RSI had come to the same conclusion.

The firm published two newspapers in Carlisle, the weekly broadsheet *Cumberland News* – which sold 40,000 copies a week and made all the money – and the tabloid *Evening News & Star*, which sold only 30,000 a day and had to be funded by the profits made by its big sister because it could not have survived on its own. I was editor of both, although the West Cumbria edition of the *News & Star* was supplied with copy by reporters answerable not to me, but to the editors of the firm's two weekly papers there – Roy Maddison at the *Whitehaven News* and Terry Kirton at the *Times & Star* in Workington, who were quite understandably keen to keep all their best stories for themselves and to let me have only just enough to keep me from complaining too loudly. I would have done precisely the same thing if I had been in their shoes, but it was, I told Robin, a recipe for chaos.

I was proved right within weeks, when I discovered that, against all of Robin's rules, both Roy and Terry were indeed regularly starving my paper of their best stories so they could use them to good effect in their own. My phone calls of complaint always met with precisely the same response, no matter how often I made them.

Roy – one of the most pompous men I have ever met, but also one who was very good company in a social setting – regularly feigned surprise and promised week after week that it would never happen again. 'Leave it to me, dear boy,' he would bluster every time I phoned him to protest. 'It shouldn't be happening. I had no idea. I'll put a stop to it.' When I made the same complaint to Terry, a straightforward Midlander for whom I had rather greater respect, the answer was a cheery and very understandable 'Piss off!'.

That was not the only way in which I felt some of the company's policies made being editor of the evening paper far more difficult than it should have been.

Another was the relationship between my two newspapers, which might have made perfect sense to people steeped in Cumbrian Newspapers tradition, but to me, an off-comer, some of it seemed little short of ludicrous.

We spent most of the week, for example, trying to convince our readers that the *News & Star* was a different, separate entity from the *Cumberland News*, so if they wanted to keep fully abreast of all that was happening in the locality they should buy both papers not just one of them. Yet on Fridays those arguments came to nought when the company chose not to publish the evening paper in Carlisle because it was thought that to do so would queer the pitch of its more profitable weekly stablemate (it was strange that the same argument did not apply to Whitehaven and Workington, where the *News & Star* continued to be published on the days when the company's weekly papers there went on sale).

That policy, I told Robin, was absurd, since it simply confirmed the popular view that there was really no point buying the daily paper because if people waited until the end of the week all the news would be in the *Cumberland News* anyway. Robin responded to any such argument with a bemused smile and small shake of the head and said that, while I was welcome to come up with suggestions on how the situation could be improved if I liked, I probably would not convince him that things needed changing because they had been done like that for a very long time and they had always seemed to work reasonably well.

He showed no more understanding when he asked me why, when the *Cumberland News* was the more profitable newspaper, most of our reporters liked to say they worked for the *News & Star* (in fact they, like I, worked for both). I explained that it was because journalists, being not greatly interested in how much money a newspaper makes, enjoy the excitement and kudos of working for a daily paper rather than a weekly one. He gave me the uncomprehending smile that was his trademark on such occasions and I only compounded his discomfiture by telling him that I quite understood the reporters' attitude since I felt the same and would not have applied to be editor of the weekly paper if it had not had an albeit loss-making daily to go with it.

It took some getting used to, being called 'The Editor' – and receiving the respect, and in some cases the suspicion, that the title inspires, even though I had not yet had time to do anything to inspire it myself. The power attached to the job surprised me too. In my first week I let it be known that I disliked photographs of cheque presentations, particularly those which featured two local worthies grinning stupidly at either end of a giant laminated cheque. Such photographs, I remarked, demonstrated little except a lack of imagination on the part of the photographer and achieved nothing in a local newspaper except a waste of much valuable space and the granting of a lot of free publicity for the bank whose cheque it was. I was astonished, but rather pleased, to hear that my casual observation had been taken as a blanket ban on such pictures – 'The Editor says he doesn't want any more like that,' people were told – and in all my time in Carlisle no more such photographs were ever published.

Other changes were not so easy to enforce. One of the most surprising things about the Cumbrian Newspapers' workforce was the number of people who had worked there for very many years, if not actually for the whole of their careers. There seemed to be none of the steady turnover of staff that had been a feature of the three other newspapers upon which I had worked and, despite their apparent dissatisfaction, few of even the most junior reporters seemed to have any ambition to move on to bigger and better things.

This resulted in a logjam at the top, with no chance of the brightest young talents being given the promotion their abilities deserved and no opportunity for me to build around me a senior team who understood my ideas. Many new editors bring with them a reliable lieutenant from their previous newspaper, so they are guaranteed at least one person who is in tune with their thinking, but no such thing was possible for me because Robin had told me at an early stage that he wanted none of the blood-spilling that a major reorganisation of the editorial hierarchy would bring.

Anyway I was far from convinced that such a reshuffle would be necessary. I knew myself well enough to know that I would be in danger of rushing into too many impulsive changes, trying to turn the *News & Star* into a Cumbrian version of the *Evening Post* without first establishing whether we had the resources – or Cumbria the appetite – for it, so I was happy to find in Bill Duckworth, my deputy editor, a man far removed from any form of recklessness. Bill was a steady, loyal and likeable man who was approaching sixty, and therefore retirement, and his only failing was that he had never worked anywhere else. He, like so many of my new Cumbrian-born-and-bred team, had little experience of how things were done on other newspapers and therefore no idea of whether they might be done better than they were being done in Carlisle, but that made him a perfect foil for what I knew could be my latent impetuosity.

Astute advice from him and my secretary Alison Sisson, who had worked for at least two editors before me and understood better than anyone how the editorial department worked, probably kept me in check more than either of them ever knew.

Even so, the typical Cumbrian person's laid-back approach to life – what I came to call their *mañana* attitude – drove me to despair. It was no good simply imposing my ideas on the workforce; to make them work I needed people to accept them as an improvement on what had gone before. But even if I managed to persuade them of the sense of some new initiative (which meant overcoming their 'But this is the way we've always done it' objections) I had still to convince them that it should be implemented immediately, not next week, next month or even 'maybe sometime in the next year unless circumstances have changed in which case it might be best if it wasn't done at all'.

No wonder I sometimes resorted to the authority of being editor and simply got on and did it!

My first year in Carlisle coincided with the 175th anniversary of the founding of the *Cumberland News'* forebear, the *Carlisle Patriot*, which in its first edition had carried news from the battlefield at Waterloo. Very few newspapers can trace their roots back so far – even *The Times*, first published in 1788, beat the *Patriot* by only 27 years – so the company naturally set out to mark this remarkable event with a series of special celebrations including a 'family fun day' for the staff, a service in the cathedral and an It's A Knockout competition between its senior executives and Border Television, the local ITV station.

I reckoned the occasion deserved a more lasting reminder than all that so, with the enthusiastic help of a handful of senior journalists, launched an appeal to raise money for the piece of equipment which, we established, was most needed at Carlisle's biggest hospital, the Cumberland Infirmary. The response to the appeal was immediate, with readers and local businesses rallying round by holding collections, coffee mornings, sponsored slims and fund-raising concerts – and me doing my bit by selling 'pick-your-own' Christmas trees from the Woody Glen garden – and within a few months our CHAT Appeal (it stood for the Cumbria Haematology Autoanalyser Target) had raised more than £80,000 to buy a vital piece of blood-testing equipment which, I like to think, went on to save countless lives.

For any small paper in any small city it was an impressive amount of money to have raised. For the *Cumberland News* and Carlisle it was, it seemed to me, truly astonishing, because by then I had come to suspect that Carlisle was just not that sort of place . . .

One of the things that was most obvious about Carlisle was that it was simply not a 'newspaper city' – not in the way that Nottingham had been, anyway. Nottingham was a lively, bustling, go-ahead place which had its lively, bustling go-ahead local paper at its very heart. The *Post* played a central role in the life of the community, and could be no more done without than could be any of the other local institutions – the city council, the chamber of commerce, the theatres, the two league football clubs and so on.

The role of the *Cumberland News* – and the *News & Star*, even more so – seemed to me to be more that of a bystander, watching Carlisle life from the outside rather than being actively involved in it, and one of the things that struck me when I examined the two papers was that they were lacking any sort of personality. I really had no idea what they stood for or what they believed in. And if I as the editor didn't, how could I expect anyone else to?

If I needed proof of the lack of connection between the papers and the community it came with the number of readers' letters we received for publication. In Nottingham the *Post* printed at least a full broadsheet page of letters every day and even then did not manage to publish anything like all the letters it received; in Carlisle the *Cumberland News* and *News & Star* between them might, in a good week, have received little more than a dozen. Even allowing for the fact that Nottingham was a much bigger city and therefore had more potential letter-writers, it was a pathetic response from the readers and a sure sign that Cumbrian people felt no affinity with the papers that purported to serve them.

One of my first decisions, therefore, was to introduce to the *News & Star* a daily leader column, which I usually wrote myself and which I employed whenever possible to try to build a bond between the newspaper and its readers and to bolster Cumbria's opinion of itself by reminding people of the many advantages of living in such a place. It was, I hoped, a small start towards showing our readers that the *News & Star* was a newspaper that cared both for them and for the place in which they lived, and that it would fight on their behalf whenever necessary.

Other changes – grandiosely described as a re-launch for the *News & Star* – amounted to little more than minor tweaking of what the paper was doing already. Headlines were reduced in size, the TV guide given more space and prominence, pictures made bigger and new columns introduced. On the basis that if it had been popular in Nottingham it would probably also be popular in Cumbria, one of the columns I introduced was my own, but once again my expectations fell flat. After more trouble in the Middle East, I took the opportunity to re-run my column on Juliet and Col Gadaffi, hoping that it would achieve something like the response it had in Nottingham. It passed uncommented on – either by readers or by anyone in the office – and attracted not a single letter.

I was aware that no amount of tinkering was likely to have much impact on the sales figures of any newspaper which, being so poorly supported by advertising, sometimes could afford to contain no more than 16 pages. Attracting new readers, I knew, would need something rather more than the sparse publication – or 'leaflet', as I heard it disparagingly referred to by some in the city – we were offering at that time. But that was not a problem we could overcome simply by adding an extra dozen or so pages every day. The number of pages in any newspaper depends on the amount of advertising contained within it (as a rough guide, at least 60% of the space has to be paid for if the paper is to make a profit). And, since advertisers want to reach as many potential customers as possible, the amount of space they buy depends on how many people are going to read it, which depends on the number of copies sold, which depends on value for money, which depends on the number of pages . . . It was a vicious circle of potential failure for which neither I nor anyone else in the management team had the answer.

18

IF I HAD HOPED TO ATTRACT more readers by establishing a new identity for the evening paper (which I confess I had) then I failed. I had underestimated just how many were the changes required to convince readers of a newspaper's new direction . . . and, more importantly, failed to appreciate how hard it would be to ensure that the entire journalistic team stuck to the new guidelines.

The result was that, within a few months of the 're-launch', the *News & Star* did not look very different from the paper it had been before my arrival. I knew then that I should have spent more time building up a reliable team of senior journalists who not only understood what I wanted to achieve but were determined to make sure I got it, and less on the perhaps not-so-urgent business of building contacts and trying to improve my papers' standing in the wider world.

Until I moved to Carlisle I had not realised what a favour Pole-Carew had done us all when, by refusing to re-employ the 28 journalists he had sacked in the 1978 strike, he fell out with the Newspaper Society (an organisation representing all the country's local and provincial newspapers). Thanks to that, and its decision to expel the *Evening Post* from its membership, we had been spared most of the twaddle that emanated from the NS, which at that time was showing what to me was an unwanted zeal for all the latest, most fashionable management ideas.

So I was no more prepared for the relentless enthusiasm with which Robin Burgess seemed to grasp almost every buzzword contained in the Newspaper Society's monthly bulletins than I was for the series of management training days that sprang from it. We were encouraged to embrace each new idea with a fervour that I found difficult to fake. It was a world in which I was expected to 'maximise my potential to incentivise the team to touch base before we all went forward through a programme of blue-sky thinking towards a holistic solution by thinking outside the box' and I could not help being annoyed by the fact that the management consultant taking us on this futile journey was probably being paid more in a day than some of my journalists were earning in a month.

It was a world in which the likes of Total Quality, Customer Care, Creative Teamwork, Time Management, Team Briefings and Annual Appraisals were held to be the answer to all our problems and I have no doubt that Robin Burgess detected that in me he had a member of his senior management team who thought most of it was bollocks.

Total Quality, for example, exhorted us to 'Do the right thing, right the first time, every time' which, in my experience, was something we were all trying to do – even if we sometimes failed – without needing any encouragement from a man in a smart suit, armed with a couple of flip charts and a set of brightly coloured marker pens.

Annual appraisals and team briefings would have had their place in some huge multinational organisation where bosses had little direct contact with their staff, and probably did not even know their names, but I felt that in a small company like Cumbrian Newspapers they should have been unnecessary if line managers were communicating properly with the handful of people under them as they should have been.

And Time Management was an absurdity which took no notice of the fact that we were working in an industry in which the only certainty was that something would happen every day which would throw everything into disarray no matter how we might have been planning to manage our time.

Things came to a head after two more wasted days – this time dedicated to 'Customer Care', in which we were told that everyone was everyone else's customer, and so should be treated accordingly.

'Has anyone any more questions?' the consultant asked at the end of the session.

'Yes, indeed,' I told him. 'Supposing one of my so-called customers is a man who has appeared in court this afternoon for groping a young woman in the park, and I return to my office and find that he has phoned me asking me to keep the report of his case out of tomorrow's paper . . . According to the rules of Customer Care I should go the extra mile' (see how easily I picked up the meaningless jargon!) 'to satisfy his demands, which would mean withholding publication of a story just because the man involved – my customer – doesn't want his neighbours to know what he has been up to. Are you seriously suggesting I should do that?'

The consultant blustered a bit but, I was happy to see, had no answer.

When I met Robin Burgess later in the corridor outside he was plainly furious. 'You were just trying to be awkward!' he spat. 'You were going out of your way to be difficult.'

I told him that, while I was indeed capable of asking a question just to be awkward, on this occasion I felt it was a perfectly legitimate one for an editor – or indeed any journalist – to ask because it struck at the very foundations of our duty to report stories fairly and accurately and without fear or favour to anyone, customer or not.

It was my misfortune that my office lay a few paces off the route from the executive car park to the managing director's office, and it seemed a rare day that Robin failed to take the opportunity of coming in to see me as he arrived for work. I was – foolishly – far too polite to tell him to go away, to leave me in peace to get on with my job at what for any editor of an evening newspaper is the busiest time of day. Instead I dropped hints – an uncharacteristic terseness, maybe, or a failure to look up from whatever work was keeping me at my desk – but they were hints he failed to take.

Usually, in the early days, it was simply to see how I was getting on, to check that I was settling in as well as he hoped, but on one occasion he brought me what he clearly thought was good news. He had been taking soundings, he said, finding out what people thought of me, and he was pleased to tell me that most of the staff had a good opinion of me and regarded me as 'a breath of fresh air'. He could not understand why I was not as pleased as he expected me to be – in fact I was horrified, though tried not to show it, because I could think of few things more likely to undermine the authority of a new editor than a managing director going around talking about him behind his back.

On another occasion, rather later in my Carlisle career, he interrupted an urgent conversation I was having with the production manager Dave Gibson – my closest ally among the senior executives, and one whose relationship with Robin was as awkward as mine – to tell me that neither he nor anyone else he knew understood the headline over a report of a robbery at a local jewellers'.

'What is this word "heist"?' he demanded.

'Heist? It's a pretty common word for an armed robbery,' I told him.

'Well, no one I know has ever heard of it.' He turned to Dave. 'Have you?'

'Yes, of course I have. Like Richard says, it's a pretty common word for an armed robbery.'

I do not say that Robin's way of managing the company was wrong – just that, to me, it was alien. I was not used to a managing director being quite so 'visible', or to one who was so keen to interfere (as I saw it, anyway) in the running of the editorial department. He was perfectly entitled to do as he liked, of course – it was, after all, his company, and running it his way had made it very successful – but my relationship with him was always undermined by the fact that we came from two different, conflicting cultures.

A highlight of his year, for example, came in late December when he, his editors and his other senior executives donned white shirts and black bow ties to serve Christmas dinner to the staff in the canteen. This, he said, helped to break down the gulf between management and staff. I believed – and it was a belief I was happy to see supported by most of the people on the editorial floor – that it did precisely the opposite. 'It was very popular in the Army,' he said when I told him I felt it was patronising and out of place in a modern office, and that almost every one of the company's journalists was embarrassed by it.

It was pure coincidence that the day chosen for my first staff Christmas dinner was the very one on which I had agreed to go out to lunch with Rod Brackley, who had taken up his position as chief executive of Carlisle City Council at almost exactly the same time as I had moved in as editor and who now wanted to celebrate our first mutual year in office with a good meal and a bottle or two of wine.

I passed to Robin my apologies for having to miss the canteen dinner-serving on the grounds that I had a prior engagement with the city's top civil servant. He was furious, convinced, I'm sure, that my 'prior engagement' was one I had just dreamed up to get out of doing something he knew I did not want to do. And a few days later, in the first week of the New Year, he came into my office to tell me brusquely: 'Next year's staff Christmas dinner will be on the Thursday before Christmas. I imagine you don't already have some prior engagement.'

It was then that I recognised that Robin Burgess was never going to be a managing director I would enjoy working for – and, I have always suspected, it was then that he in turn realised that I was not turning out to be the sort of editor he had hoped for.

Our all-too-frequent early morning meetings became more tiresome and more strained as time went on. He reported back to me when the women in the readers' travel department didn't like a story we had published, when his mother felt we were not giving enough space to one of her favourite causes and when the printers reckoned they could do a better job than I was doing myself. 'George thinks your column is rubbish,' he told me after one such visit to the press room (though when I asked him whether George meant the leader column or the column under my own name, he didn't know).

Most annoying of all was the fact that Robin seemed to believe it was his duty to tell me what his chums had thought of the previous day's paper – which stories they liked, which headlines they didn't, which people's names they had spotted as being wrongly spelled, which sentences they believed were ungrammatical and so on. He even told me he hoped I would drop the weekly column by Jane Loughran – in my book the most talented writer on the staff – because nobody he knew liked it. I might have paid more attention if I had thought that his friends were the sort of people we were aiming the paper at, but they weren't, and I often took their disapproval as a good sign because if we were failing to connect with them it might just have been that we were succeeding with the people whom I considered to be our prime target.

I should have known though that it would not be a good idea to call for the sacking of one of Robin's friends.

Ian Carr was a former High Sheriff of Cumbria, a high profile local businessman and, most tellingly in the circumstances, the then chairman of the North Cumbria Health Authority. So when he was caught drink-driving – at a time when the don't-drink-and-drive message was being promoted both by the police and by the nation's health services – it was a very good story. We ran it on the front page, and inside I devoted my leader column to a call for his resignation, or failing that his dismissal, on the grounds that by being caught driving while considerably over the limit he had failed to set the kind of good example expected of a man in his position.

The next morning Robin came into my office to tell me that his pals had agreed we were entitled to publish the story (good of them, I thought!), but they felt we should have used it 'at the bottom of page seven or somewhere' and I certainly had no right to demand that a good man like Carr should lose his job just because he now had a criminal record.

Robin might have thought we should not have taken the stand we did against Cumbrian Newspapers shareholder Giles Mounsey-Heysham, either, but if he did he still allowed him to fight the battle for himself.

Mounsey-Heysham, a wealthy landowner and relative of Robin Burgess by marriage, lived in an impressive mansion on the shores of the Solway Firth. When he launched a controversial plan to build a waste disposal plant on his land a few miles north of Carlisle it was no surprise that an action group was formed to oppose it – or that its members assumed we would not dare to report much about it because of Mounsey-Heysham's connection with our company.

The action group were wrong, of course. For us it was a straightforward decision. It was a very good local news story – the modern day equivalent of the peasants rising up against some perceived wrong being done them by the lord of the manor – and there was no way we were going to allow our treatment of it to be flavoured by the fact that the man involved had a financial stake in our company, so we reported it in great detail.

Week after week the *Cumberland News* was full of the latest news from the battleground, which we reported without ever actually taking sides, and the campaigners, while annoyed that we did not actually support them in their fight, eventually admitted that we were not biased against them either. But what is fairness and impartiality to one person is bias and injustice to another, and Mounsey-Heysham was incensed that our newspaper was – as he saw it – campaigning against him.

He complained bitterly and often, and even reduced himself to counting every line of type that we devoted to the issue, and keeping running totals of 'For', 'Against' and 'Neutral' which proved, he said, how strongly we were supporting the other side.

The more he complained the more determined I became not to be browbeaten away from doing something I knew to be right. No newspaper can be seen to be in the pocket of one of its shareholders and Mounsey-Heysham's role in the company was too well known for me to dare to show him any favour if I wanted our readers to take us seriously ever again. I refused to budge and so did he, so I agreed to meet him at his house to discuss our coverage of the affair, in the hope of settling our differences once and for all. I arrived there with my own set of statistics – a line-by-line count which showed that, according to my news editor's calculations, we had given almost equal space to the two opposing arguments and that our reporting had been just about as impartial as it was possible to get.

It was a wasted exercise. Most of what I deemed to be neutral, factual coverage, Mounsey-Heysham considered biased against him; and what he counted as neutral I reckoned was fiercely in favour of his development. Little wonder that he believed our coverage was slanted against him. And little wonder, either, that, when I left him after a lengthy and often heated argument, he was still incandescent with pent-up fury.

I was rather more cautious when I received a letter from the elderly Earl of Carlisle, enclosing with it a 1,000 word feature on the black grouse – a bird found in exciting profusion, he told us, on his country estate a few miles east of Carlisle. He assured me that I would find the feature both interesting and well written (it was neither) and that I would want to publish it in full and without any amendment in the *Cumberland News*.

In normal circumstances I would have sent it back to him with a polite letter of rejection, but after the Ian Carr and Giles Mounsey-Heysham episodes I had learned that Cumbria's county set were not to be messed with. I also knew that the Earl was reputed to be one of the most irascible men in the area . . . and that there was a very good chance that he was a Cumbrian Newspapers shareholder or, at the very least, one of Robin Burgess's associates.

My letter back to him was a masterpiece of politeness and job preservation. I told him I was fascinated by what he had had to tell us about the black grouse, how I thought it was such a wondrously interesting subject it deserved even more considered treatment than he had given it and that, with his permission, I would ask one of our reporters to contact him so they could between them write a feature looking at the subject in even more detail.

He rang me the next day. 'This man you're sending to see me,' he said. 'Is he any good?'

'Indeed he is,' I told him (I thought it best to keep to myself the fact that the first time I'd noticed David Guide he had been running around the newsroom wearing a leather flying helmet, screaming, and with his arms out-stretched, pretending to be a World War II fighter plane). 'He's one of our most experienced journalists.'

'Is he educated?'

'Yes indeed.'

'Does he know the meaning of good English?'

'Yes, he does.'

'Well,' said the Earl. 'That will make a change because most of your newspaper is bloody rubbish.'

19

ALTHOUGH WORK WAS NOT going as well as I had hoped, I never once regretted making my move from Nottingham. We had found – by pure chance, it's true – a part of the country which suited us well as a family and made us all supremely happy to be living in it.

Tricia, particularly, felt that she belonged in Cumbria. Although she had been born in Bridgnorth while her father was vicar of a parish in Shropshire, her family had its roots in Durham and she always had a greater affinity with The North than with anywhere further south.

She soon made more friends than she had ever had in our time in the East Midlands and – after another mother approached her outside William's school with a cryptic 'Do you walk?' – took up fellwalking with such enthusiasm that it was not long before she had climbed all of the Lake District's Wainwrights (the 214 summits identified by Alfred Wainwright, the doyen of mountain walkers, in the 1950s).

Our huge garden became just another challenge to her, and she set about it with a gusto even greater than that which she had shown at Field Cottage. And, with the greater space our several acres at Woody Glen afforded her, she so expanded her flock of ducks and poultry that at one stage we had more than 100 of them, many of rare breeds that caught her fancy at one of the local auctions.

If I'd had any doubts about taking on the job in Carlisle, they would have vanished at the sight of Tricia finding such happiness and so many friends in her new surroundings. She even eventually decided she had time for a job, and found one without much ado as a relief nursery officer, using her qualities of patience and compassion to look after small children (and, almost equally, their mothers) in the day centres that the county council ran for some of Carlisle's most disadvantaged families.

I too loved Cumbria – its slower pace of life and unspoiled beauty bore more than a hint of the county I had grown up in 30 years before – and felt more at home than I ever had while working in Nottingham. In the East Midlands I had felt like a westcountryman in exile, but in Cumbria I felt I belonged, and for the first time since leaving Yeovil I no longer suffered an almost physical ache whenever the motorway took me across the Avon Bridge, past Bristol and 'home' into Somerset.

With the children growing up, we realised the move had been very good for them too. They were happy and seemed not to miss their old lives whenever they heard reports from their friends in Bottesford. Indeed they agreed that Cumbria offered them a better lifestyle, a superior education and a wider range of interests than they could ever have hoped for had we not moved.

We had, of course, made great efforts to ensure that their lives would be disrupted as little as possible. Juliet, for example, had to continue with her ice skating (I had made a promise to her that she could do so, no matter how far away the nearest ice rink turned out to be) and Antony and William had to be found a piano teacher. Both of these were easier said than done.

Carlisle did not have an ice rink – other than a synthetic one which made a temporary appearance in the city centre at Christmas – and, apart from the small one at Lockerbie, which was too tiny for her to do anything other than the most basic of routines, the nearest were in the North-East. So for many months Juliet and Tricia (and, I am ashamed to say, only occasionally I) made 5am trips to such places as Durham, Sunderland and Whitley Bay – all more than 50 miles away – so she could continue with the sport that had dominated her life for so long.

Sadly, none of the North-East rinks was as good as the one in Nottingham, and none of the instructors as inspiring, so, inevitably, the effort of getting there began to outweigh the rewards she was enjoying from it, and Juliet decided to give it up. It was unfortunate, but at least by then ice skating had served its purpose – it had provided her with an escape while she was having such a hard time at school, and given her time to make new friends and beat the bullies.

In a similar way we encouraged the boys to continue with the piano lessons they had started in Bottesford – even though William was all for giving up. Finding a suitable teacher for two boys who both clearly had great musical talent was more difficult than we expected. The most obvious choice was the church organist in Hayton, a man who had taught most of the children in the area. But people warned us off him in the most oblique manner – 'You might find he's a bit old fashioned' or 'Maybe he's best for beginners' – and it was only much later, after he was sent to prison, that we learned why. He was well known locally as a paedophile, although, to their shame, those who were aware of it had done nothing to alert the authorities and had contented themselves instead with giving cryptic warnings to the parents of any potential pupils. The result was that he was able to go on teaching – and, as it turned out later, claiming new victims – long after we heeded the warnings and sent our boys elsewhere.

We chose a woman called Jo Matthews, who lived 20 miles away on the southern shores of the Solway Firth. Antony, who had already reached Grade 5, was keen to carry on the progress he had made in Bottesford, but William, at Grade 1, was less sure. We persuaded him to try her for one lesson, and told him that if he didn't like her he could give up. At the end of that first Saturday morning lesson both boys walked down her garden path with great grins on their faces. 'She's brilliant,' William said. He never spoke another word about giving up and went on to become a professional musician.

One of the perks of being editor was that I was given a seat in the directors' box at Carlisle United Football Club. It was strange that in 17 years of working in Nottingham – at a time when Nottingham Forest, under the inspiration of their manager Brian Clough, had risen to become the best team in Europe – I had never felt the slightest attachment either to them or to their lowlier cousins, Notts County.

There was, therefore, no sensible explanation why, when for so long I had not bothered to go to watch one of the best teams in the world, I was happy to turn out with no more than 2,000 other die-hard fans on wet Saturday afternoons to watch one of the worst. Yet I had not been in Cumbria for more than a couple of months before I had become an ardent Carlisle United supporter. While my love for Carlisle could never rival my passion for Bristol City, it came a very good second best, and it was only on the rare occasions when my two teams played each other that I was reminded where my true allegiance lay.

I came to know the chairman, the directors and various managers as they came and went with equal lack of success, and through it all the club scraped along at the bottom of the football league, forever threatening to go out of existence, and consistently providing precious little in terms of either excitement or entertainment.

All that changed in the summer of 1992 when I arrived at work to discover that Carlisle United had been bought by a man called Michael Knighton. I had a feeling that this marked something special for Carlisle, the city as well as the club, and immediately faxed to him a letter of welcome, telling him how much I looked forward to being able to work with him to our mutual advantage.

He responded almost immediately and we soon met for lunch in a local hotel – he, flattered by the swift attention of the editor of the local newspapers, and I, excited by the prospect of those papers profiting from whatever success he would be able to bring to a club which had spent too long with none.

It was the beginning of a brief friendship with a character who, within a few years, would become the most reviled man in Carlisle.

Knighton was a charming, charismatic man who spoke eloquently and passionately of his plans for the football club and the better I got to know him the more I realised what a godsend he would be to any local newspaper in whose patch he happened to end up.

He had once harboured hopes of becoming a footballer himself, and had been an apprentice with Coventry City before a nasty leg injury cut short his career and sent him into education instead. He had become a teacher, and later headmaster, at a school in the South of England and, to make a bit of extra money in the school holidays, had started buying and renovating old houses which, in the property boom of the 1980s, he was able to sell on at vast profit. Before long he had made enough money to retire to the Isle of Man – and to start planning his return to football.

He first burst into football's consciousness in August 1989, when, having agreed to pay £10 million for a majority stake in Manchester United, he arrived on the pitch at Old Trafford before a game and – with his portly frame dressed in full kit – juggled a ball on his feet (very skilfully, it has to be said) before scoring a hat-trick in front of the supporters in the Stretford End.

The fans and the media loved it, but his relationship with both soon turned sour, with them questioning whether he in fact had the money to complete his purchase of the world's most famous football club. His deal to take over Manchester United did indeed fall through, and although he spent three years as a director there, he soon began to look for some other club at which he could put into practice his ideas on how the modern football club should be run.

That led him to Carlisle where he found what he described as 'the fundamental absolutes' needed for success in football – a proud tradition, a loyal fan base, a wide catchment area and enough land to allow for future development which, he assured me, would not necessarily be confined to sporting activities (a hotel and a butterfly farm were two of his more fanciful ideas).

He promised – first to me over that lunch together, then to the club's fans when he said it publicly in the *News & Star* – that Carlisle United would be in the Premier League within ten years. I knew enough about football to know it would not be that easy, but that did not matter. Simply having such a flamboyant character, with such outlandish ambitions, at the head of our local football club meant that, for as long as it lasted, we would never be short of stories on the sports pages and – I was fairly confident – on the news pages too.

If, against the odds, he succeeded, my newspapers would benefit enormously from the growing number of people who would want to be kept abreast of the exciting developments at Brunton Park. If, as I reckoned more likely, he failed, we would benefit equally, because people would want to read all about that failure so they could decide who to blame.

He was egotistical and big-headed, and in many ways a ludicrous figure, but I found him enormously good company and very likeable, not least in the way he was willing occasionally to poke fun at his own arrogance while telling me with a grin that he had all the answers to what was wrong with the football industry, not just in Carlisle or even in the UK, but in the world as a whole.

The fans liked him too, and appreciated the dash of showmanship he brought to their long-suffering club. 'Knighton, Knighton, give us a wave,' they sang, as he took his seat in the directors' box before matches, and they cheered as he waved back, grinning broadly from having his ego massaged in such a public arena.

I was determined to cash in on the unique mix Knighton brought us – his arrogance, his intelligence and his popularity with the fans – and offered him the chance to write a column in the *News & Star*. Inevitably, he agreed to the idea on the spot.

His column, which we called Knighton's Day, covered not just football, but sport in general, and it proved to be everything I had hoped – interesting, erudite and often controversial (just like the man himself, really) – and it became very popular. He did not ask for payment and I didn't offer it, knowing that for him having his self esteem polished in such a way would be payment enough. For me, it was especially satisfying not to be paying a penny for such a key feature of the paper's sports pages and I remain, I think, the only person in Carlisle ever to have got something for nothing out of him.

Knighton's running of the football club became an almost instant success. He turned round the team's fortunes on the field, built an impressive new stand, attracted fans in their thousands, achieved an optimism around the place which hadn't been seen in years and provided one of the best running stories any local newspaper could have hoped for. As United won promotion, featured in a Wembley cup final for the first time, and drew crowds four or five times what they had been before, it seemed that maybe his boast of Premier League football within the decade might not have been as daft as it had sounded.

It was only afterwards, after my time as editor, that everything started to go wrong – and all because, I have always believed, he was too successful in those early days. The almost instant success he achieved proved to him, in his own mind, that he did indeed know all the answers, and as a result the decisions he made became increasingly erratic. He came to believe he could do no wrong, but in the end he could do no right, and the football club with which he had promised so much found itself in an even worse position than it had been in on the day he arrived.

He sacked popular managers, appointed inept ones, sold the best players, signed inadequate replacements, and made Carlisle United and himself a laughing stock by telling the world he had seen a flying saucer and – when he came to try to sell the club – finally smashed his crumbling reputation by doing a deal with a 'wealthy Scottish businessman' who very quickly was unmasked as an unemployed waiter from a pizza parlour in Galashiels.

He brought the club to its knees and the fans who had once worshipped him now despised him.

I'm sure it was coincidence that when he eventually came to sell the club it was just five days after I wrote to him, as the ex editor and a former friend, to tell him that, though I remembered the good times he had brought us and therefore did not share the average supporter's view that he was the devil incarnate, it was time for him to go.

There is no hiding place for an editor. All his strengths and weaknesses are exposed, and I had no doubt that mine were being analysed and commented on not just by Robin but by almost everyone else in the office too. It was also a time when I found out a lot about myself – and not all of it was what I expected. I discovered, for example, that, while I had the vision and imagination to see how the newspapers should be improved, I did not have the determination, or maybe even strength of character, to make sure those ideas were carried through.

I found that while most people responded positively to the way my more relaxed management style succeeded in lifting the iron hand which had apparently stifled thought and creativity among the journalists for too long, there were some who took advantage of what they saw as my weakness, by working more casually and with less commitment than they should.

I realised that while I could spot those who had talent, and was able to help them develop it, I did not have the patience to try to help those who had none.

And most surprising of all I found I was no longer excited by my job. I was by nature too much of a journalist and too little of an administrator, so that the interminable round of meetings and management problems took me away from the work that I really wanted to do . . . and that I was good at. In hindsight, what it all added up to was that I had been much better as a deputy editor than I was turning out to be as the editor itself. To use an analogy from the seafaring career upon which I had so nearly embarked, I had been pretty good as a first mate, steering a course when it had been set by the captain, but was not so good at setting that course and being the captain myself. My biggest problem – and I was well aware of it at the time – was that I was too much of a journalist and not enough of a manager to lead the paper in the way Robin wanted.

There were times when I even struggled to remember whose side I was supposed to be on.

Once a year, for example, I accompanied Robin on an official visit to the newsroom, where he would discuss with the staff the company's annual accounts. It was an admirable attempt at openness not fully appreciated by most of the journalists, especially those who had never worked on other newspapers where such a thing would have been unthinkable, but it usually only succeeded in making him look vaguely foolish (which by then, I confess, I rather enjoyed).

My function was to stand beside him, giving him moral support by nodding sagely at appropriate intervals and chuckling at anything that might have been a joke.

On one occasion Dave Gudgeon, the father of the chapel (or chairman of the office branch of the NUJ) and a man who could cut to the heart of any argument in a deceptively genial and apparently innocent way, asked him to explain exactly what Joe Harris, the chairman of the main board, did to justify the many thousands of pounds he earned in a year.

'He chairs the board meetings,' Robin replied.

'And tell me, Robin, how many board meetings are there?'

'Six a year.'

'And how long does a typical board meeting last?'

'Oooh . . . a couple of hours maybe. And sometimes they might run into lunch.' Robin looked puzzled and, unlike almost everyone else in the room, seemed unable to see where the conversation was going.

'So Joe does, say, 12 hours work a year . . . for which I calculate he is paid something like £1,000 an hour if I've got the maths right. Nice work if you can get it!'

Robin at last grasped the point of Dave's line of questioning, and I struggled to keep a straight face as he cast around for a defence. 'But he does a lot of other valuable work for the company too, of course,' he said.

'Like what?'

'Well . . . he's chairman of Penrith magistrates for a start. That's very important.'

'But he's not working for the company then, is he? Unless, of course, he sits on the magistrates' bench wearing a *Cumberland News* T-shirt!'

Joe Harris was a thoroughly decent man, probably the last one who deserved to be the butt of Dave Gudgeon's political point-scoring. He was a gentleman farmer from a family which had made its wealth from mining in West Cumbria, and, though being of a class and generation whose menfolk still expected their women to leave them while they knocked back the port after dinner, had an easy charm that enabled him to get on with all who met him, no matter where they stood on the social scale. He had a privileged position in the community, and knew it, and felt obliged to put something back into the society that had given him so much. As such he served not just as chairman of the local magistrates' court (though never, as far as I know, while wearing a T-shirt) but in a host of other unpaid positions in which he fought for the good of all who lived in the rural community, both locally and nationally. I never met anyone who did not both like and respect him.

The same could not be said of some of those who, as chairman of

Cumbrian Newspapers, he had to invite to the company's annual meeting. This was an occasion attended by all the company's directors and shareholders, after which I and other members of the senior management team were invited into the boardroom to be reminded of who it was we were working for, just as, generations ago, the cooks and chambermaids might have been allowed to go upstairs in the big house once a year to have a glass of sherry with the Lord and Lady who had been good enough to employ them.

Some of the senior shareholders I already knew and liked – Lord Inglewood, the local Tory Euro MP with a stately pile on the fringes of the Lake District, for example, was another thoroughly decent man, in the mould of Joe Harris; and David Trimble, a local businessman was another with whom I always got on well despite (or maybe even because of) his bizarre belief in the flying saucers in which, he said, beings from other worlds would one day arrive to save Earth from the mess we were making of it.

These were the men, good company both, who, after arming myself with an impressive plateful of chicken legs, sausage rolls and vol-au-vents, I sought out at the firm's post AGM lunches. Talking to them meant that at least I didn't have to spend much time with the rest – an odd bunch who included an array of elderly ladies (mostly distant members of the Burgess family, it appeared) who were keen to tell me how I should be doing my job.

They, like so many people who have no idea how the industry works, were always happy to let me in on the secret of how to cope with the problem of making our newspapers more successful: Print the paper with ink that doesn't come off on your hands, pack it with good news, ignore all those nasty murders and car crashes and publish lots of nice pictures of local beauty spots. Do that, they would tell me, and all would be well.

20

SOMETIMES I HAD TO PINCH MYSELF when I remembered that I was being paid to live and work in such a spectacularly beautiful part of the country. My frequent trips to talk things over with my fellow editors in Whitehaven and Workington, or to meet contacts in the northern Lake District, took me through magnificent countryside – especially if, as I usually did, I made the time to take a detour over the Caldbeck fells, or through the winding country lanes that provided an alternative to the main road to west Cumbria.

I felt that Cumbria was a place I had been waiting all my life to discover.

In May 1993, with the children old enough to look after themselves when we went on holiday, Tricia and I decided to take our new interest in fellwalking to new extremes – by tackling Alfred Wainwright's Coast to Coast walk, 190 miles from St Bees in Cumbria to Robin Hood's Bay in Yorkshire. Neither of us had attempted anything like it before, and, despite many weeks' hard training (broken only when I fell down a drain outside our front door and twisted my ankle) we had no idea whether we would succeed.

I left the office to a cheerful 'Have a good holiday!' from Robin, with whom I'd spent the afternoon discussing what I planned to do with the *Cumberland News* and *News & Star* when I got back. The next day Antony drove us to St Bees to begin our adventure. It was a challenge both Tricia and I were ready for – and, somehow, what living in Cumbria was all about.

It took us 12 days to cross the country. Twelve unforgettable days in which we walked through some of the world's best scenery, drank some of its most welcome beer and nursed some of its most aching muscles. Only once did we wonder whether we would make it – at the end of the third day when, after coming down from the last Lake District fell, we were so tired Tricia entered the pub at Shap on her knees. Literally.

Nobody who saw us then would have foreseen that little more than a week later we would be striding down the hill into the little village of Robin Hood's Bay, with great grins on our faces, to dip our feet into the sea on the other side of England. The healing powers of a couple of pints of beer, a decent meal and a good night's sleep truly are astonishing!

I returned to work feeling on top of the world. I was 44 years old and for the first time in my life had just successfully accomplished a major feat of physical and mental endurance. As I walked into the office on that Monday morning I felt fit to face whatever problems being an editor could throw at me. 'Robin wants to see you,' my secretary Alison told me, and I raised an eyebrow, surprised that the managing director had arrived for work before me.

He was sitting at his desk and motioned me in and I imagined he wanted to talk more about the plans we had been discussing the last time we had met, on the day before I went on holiday.

'Had a good holiday?' he asked.

'Yes, thanks,' I said cheerily. 'We did it. Fantastic!'

'Well, I'm sorry to spoil it.'

I said nothing, assuming he had something more to add.

'I'm afraid I have decided it's time for us to go our separate ways,' he told me, and for a glorious moment I thought he was telling me he was leaving.

But then the truth began to dawn: It wasn't he who would be going, it was I. I was being sacked! Until then I had hardly noticed the A4 pad lying on the desk in front of him, but now I paid it more attention, and using the skills acquired over 25 years as a journalist (one of the first things a reporter picks up is the ability to read upside down – very useful when interviewing people careless enough to leave supposedly confidential documents strewn around their desks) saw that my worst fears were confirmed.

His scrawly upside-down handwriting told me all I needed to know:
Had a good holiday?
Sorry to spoil it.
Separate ways . . .

And, right at the bottom, *£23,000* – the year's salary, less tax, that he was going to offer me as a pay-off.

Christ, I thought, the man can't even sack me without notes!

He told me – rather unnecessarily, I thought – that I had not turned out to be the sort of editor he had hoped for, that I didn't give the leadership he required, that I was arrogant, that I was autocratic . . .

I sat there, stunned by an almost physical shock that hit me in the stomach and forced an unwanted wetness to my eyes. I knew there was no point arguing with him, or demeaning myself by begging, because once the relationship between a managing director and an editor has reached such a low point there is no hope of rescuing it well enough for it to continue.

A million thoughts passed through my mind and the seconds passed almost in slow motion. I had time to wonder if, with hindsight, I would have done anything differently; to feel for the friends I had left in Nottingham, who I knew would be sad that my adventure up north had met with such an end; and, most of all, I had time to wonder why, while I was shocked and angry and disappointed, I was, strangely, not hurt. The explanation was fairly obvious: If I had been sacked by Eric Price or Barrie Williams, or even Christopher Pole-Carew, I would have been mortified, but it does not hurt so much being dismissed by someone whose opinions have long since ceased to matter very much to you.

He passed to me a typed Press statement, with which the company planned to announce my departure: 'Richard Harris, Editor of the *Evening News & Star* and *Cumberland News*, is relinquishing his job forthwith. This follows a disagreement with the Company on future policy. Richard Harris joined the Company as Editor of the *Evening News & Star* and *Cumberland News* in January 1990.'

A slightly longer statement prepared for the staff added, rather dishonestly: 'Richard and the company have disagreed on the overall policy and direction of the Editorial Department and it has been agreed that he can best further his career elsewhere.'

I foolishly agreed to the statements being distributed. Only later did I wish that as a last symbol of defiance I had insisted that, if he wanted to sack me, Robin should at least have had the courage to admit to the world that that was what he was doing.

'You'll have to leave straightaway,' he told me.

'There are people I'll have to say goodbye to first,' I told him firmly.

'Really?' he said, looking genuinely surprised.

'Of course,' I snapped

As I left his office I was glad that he had given me that last reminder of how far apart our thinking was. Did he really think that I would walk away without saying goodbye to the people with whom I had worked so closely for more than three years? Did he really think I didn't want to thank them for their hard work and, in many cases, their friendship? Did he really think I didn't want to wish them luck in the future – and to give them the chance to do the same to me?

Sadly, he did, and I'm glad he did because it served better than anything to underline our differences.

I walked back to my office in shock. Alison and Bill were at their desks, busy with their usual early morning chores. 'I've just been sacked,' I told them quietly.

I wanted to speak to the whole department – all the journalists, the photographers, the copytakers and the editorial assistants – but suspected I wouldn't have the self control to do that. I didn't want to be remembered as the editor who broke down in tears while saying his goodbyes, so I asked Alison to call just the heads of department into my office.

'As of five minutes ago I've not been your editor,' I told them. 'I've been sacked.' Nobody knew quite what to say – neither I nor they – but I did, I think, manage to thank them for their efforts and to wish them good luck in whatever their futures held. 'Now you'd better go – you've got a paper to get out.'

One by one they shook me by the hand, and a couple even hugged me around the shoulder, just as those men at the mushroom farm had hugged me as I had left them all those years before, and then, three years, four months and 24 days after I'd first sat in the editor's chair, it was over.

As I drove away from the office to break the news to Tricia at the family centre where she was working that day, I allowed myself a wry smile. 'Never mind,' I told myself, 'you never really wanted to be a journalist in the first place.'

EPILOGUE

HE WAS RIGHT, OF COURSE. Although I still despise the way he did it, waiting until I was away on holiday after making me go through the charade of planning for a future he knew I would not have, I have to accept that I was never going to become the type of editor Robin Burgess needed to take his newspapers into the 21st century. And I have to accept that I would never have taken the newspapers on, regularly to win awards as the best of their type in the country, as other editors have done since I left. And he was never going to be the type of managing director I wanted to work for either.

I had given it my best shot, and failed, but at least had the comfort of having failed while doing it my way and remaining true to my principles. I had done it, as my dad would have said, without shitting on the people I had passed on my way up and I was fairly confident that few of them would now feel the need to shit on me on my way down. It was a great comfort when some of those people took the trouble to tell me that they were almost as stunned by what had happened as I was.

The first of many letters I received was from NUJ officials Dave Gudgeon and Sue Crawford. 'Everyone was stunned and angered at the abrupt method employed by the company,' they said. 'The feelings of all editorial staff are with you and your family.'

Irene Shearer, a long-serving sub, told me: 'I hope you don't have to leave an area you have grown to love.' And Alan Air, a reporter whom I had promoted to a position from which he had won an award for a series of stories on the environment, wrote: 'I have worked for Cumbrian Newspapers for ten years and can honestly say that I gained more professional satisfaction during your reign than at any time in the previous seven years. I was brought up to despise bullying, egotistical-style management and found your open-door attitude refreshing.'

Graphic artist David 'Shep' Kirkbride wrote: 'You cannot always guarantee that you are going to get on with everyone new that comes into your life, either socially or through your workplace, but occasionally someone will come along who you immediately think of as a friend. I have always felt that we had a very professional working relationship but more importantly a good friendship.'

John Penman, a reporter whom I considered one of our brightest young talents and who has since proved it by filling several senior positions on major Scottish newspapers, wrote from the *Northern Echo* in Darlington, to which he had moved despite my best efforts to persuade him to stay: 'I want to express my thanks for your support and encouragement. Your faith in me gave me the confidence to seek out new challenges. It seems such a short time since you started at Carlisle – a very short period in which to achieve laudable aims.'

Carlisle's MP Eric Martlew wrote wishing me well, BBC Radio Cumbria's manager wrote to thank me for my 'much more open attitude to this station' and the local bishop, Ian Harland (who, early on, had taken great delight in giving me and Tricia a guided tour of the ramparts of the castle in which he lived) assured me: 'I was never convinced by the use of the word "relinquished".'

Janet wrote from Nottingham: 'Bolts from the blue don't come much bigger. I really fail to understand how anyone could not appreciate the value of somebody like yourself, who is easily the best journalist I know' – which I knew was absurdly extravagant praise (as she herself admitted later) but at the time was comforting nonetheless.

And, after the report of my sacking appeared in the next week's *UK Press Gazette*, I received the most unexpected message of them all – a fax from Rosie Staal, from whom I had not heard for more than 20 years: 'Don't let the buggers get you down!'

Tricia was much more angry about the situation than I was and – even though he has since told me that, while he still believes (as I do!) that sacking me was necessary, he regrets the 'brutal' way in which he did it, which he puts down to his 'youth and inexperience' – it is probably just as well that she has never met Robin since. I though I bear him no great ill will and am in fact rather grateful to him for the way he brought me to a part of the country I love and then set me free in it by dispensing with my services.

Even so, I took great delight when, a short time after my sacking, the *News & Star* launched a fantasy football league – a competition in which readers were invited to 'manage' imaginary football teams, made up of real players who scored points based on how well they performed for their clubs in the proper football league. The pleasure I obtained from entering my team – and, more particularly, naming it Boring Dossers United – was immense. But it was as nothing compared with the joy I felt when, after reaching ninth in the competition's league table, my team's name was published in the paper for all to see. Only a very few people would have realised that in Boring Dossers United I had managed to get 'Sod Robin Burgess', or a fairly accurate anagram of it anyway, printed as my team's name in one of his own papers.

No number of silly jokes at Robin's expense could disguise one fact, though: For the first time in my life I was unemployed. I had most of the things I had always wanted – a wife I still loved; three growing children of whom I was, and always have been, enormously proud; a lovely home in a beautiful part of the country; many friends; my health; and, for now anyway, a goodly amount of money in the bank. But the £23,000 pay-off I had banked after my sacking would not last long. I simply had to get a job.

Our first decision was that, while Robin Burgess had taken away my job, we were not going to allow him to take away the way of life we had come to enjoy so much. We would stay in Cumbria – and, more than that, go on living at Woody Glen – even though that meant almost inevitably that I could no longer be a journalist (Cumbrian Newspapers had a virtual monopoly in the area and there was no way I was going to work for them, in some lesser role than editor, even if they would have had me).

It's true that, like most journalists, I was not qualified to do anything else, but that did not stop me considering all options, no matter how apparently absurd, and there were few ideas that we rejected as unfeasible. Perhaps I could buy a tea shop or small café, run a pub, become a full-time writer, turn to teaching or (the job I really fancied) try my hand at long distance coach driving. Or – and this came to me strangely and suddenly, just a couple of months after what I had come to call my 'demise' – perhaps I should simply listen to my heart and do the one thing that I realised was the only thing I really wanted to do. It had been many years since, as a reporter, I had gone out looking for news. Management had got in the way of the part of the job I most enjoyed, and was probably best at, and as I had moved up the career ladder I had become more of an administrator and less of a journalist. Now, after spending a few weeks of a glorious early summer working in the garden and taking long country walks, I had a craving to turn the clock back, to pick up a pencil and a notebook and to start living on my wits again.

I became a freelance reporter.

Having been an editor at least meant that the organisations I approached offering my services – all the papers and radio and TV stations in Cumbria as well as most of the national newspapers – took me seriously and came to a loose understanding that they would both consider any contributions I sent them and call on me if jobs needed to be done for which they did not have their own staff.

I learned very quickly though that this was going to be no way to make a living. Although I enjoyed living the life of a reporter again, and seeking out stories which appeared to have been missed by everyone else (a man brought out of a coma by his dog licking his face as he lay in his hospital bed, for example, or a group of servicemen who left their RAF base to help out on a farm whose owner had broken his leg just at the time when the harvesting was due) it was obvious that in Cumbria there was simply not enough going on for me to make anything like sufficient money to survive; the stories I got published in local papers paid no more than a few pounds each, and the payment I received for those that found their way into the nationals (several features in the *Daily Express*, for example) did not begin to justify the time I had spent working on them.

I was beginning to wonder what more I could do . . . when my career was saved by an American gangster called Michael Austin.

Austin had set up the coldblooded execution of a Lancashire businessman who had dared to interfere in an extraordinary multi million pound scam in which ships were scuttled in mid-Atlantic to disguise the fact that cargoes of contraband cigarettes supposedly bought and paid for by criminals in Europe had in fact never existed.

The British police had not found the killers, nor even Austin himself, but they had arrested the intermediary between the two, a petty criminal called Stephen Schepke, and charged him with conspiracy to murder. His trial was to be held at the newly-built Crown Court in Carlisle, which, with the help of armed policemen patrolling the streets and keeping watch from the top of nearby church towers, was reckoned to be much more secure than Manchester, Preston or Liverpool and therefore less likely to be a target for those of Austin's henchmen thought to be keen either to spring Schepke from jail or, more likely, to kill him.

It was a great story but the national newspaper reporters, typically, did not want to waste their time sitting through the whole six-week trial. So they decided to attend just the first day and the last . . . and leave the rest to me.

Tricia and I had a holiday in the Greek Islands on the proceeds but, more importantly for me, it alerted me to the fact that a potential living could be made covering events at Carlisle Crown Court. For, while covering the Schepke trial for the nationals, I discovered that much more was going on in other courtrooms there – the routine cases of drug dealing, fraud, rape and grievous bodily harm that occupy any provincial court – and most of it was going unreported by any newspaper or radio or television station, who by then simply did not have enough staff to be there.

It was an opportunity too good to turn my back on; the chance to make a living doing something I had, many years before, enjoyed almost more than any other aspect of journalism. I had found my niche. Or rather, in another of the happy accidents that have punctuated my career, my niche had found me. And, more than 20 years after sitting beside a giggling Clive Jackson and listening to the sad saga of One-Ball Hancock on the press benches at Wells Assizes, I became a freelance court reporter. My career had turned almost full circle. And I was just as happy as I had been a quarter of a century before.

THE END